S0-AUU-449

Create Your Own Graphics Workstation

Horace W. LaBadie, Jr.

McGraw-Hill, Inc.

New York   San Francisco   Washington, D.C.   Auckland   Bogotá
Caracas   Lisbon   London   Madrid   Mexico City   Milan
Montreal   New Delhi   San Juan   Singapore
Sydney   Tokyo   Toronto

©1995 by **Horace W. LaBadie, Jr.**
Published by McGraw-Hill, Inc.

pbk   1 2 3 4 5 6 7 8 9 DOC/DOC 9 9 8 7 6 5

Library of Congress Cataloging-in-Publication Data
LaBadie, Horace W.
    Create your own graphics workstation / by Horace LaBadie.
        p.   cm.
    Includes index.
    ISBN 0-07-035955-5
    1. Computer graphics.   2. Windows (Computer programs)   I. Title.
    T385.L33   1994
    006.6\2—dc20   94-31175
                                                                       CIP

Acquisitions editor: Roland S. Phelps
Editorial team: Robert E. Ostrander, Executive Editor
            Aaron G. Bittner, Book Editor
Production team: Katherine G. Brown, Director
            Rhonda E. Baker, Layout
            Linda L. King, Proofreading
            Jodi L. Tyler, Indexer
Design team: Jaclyn J. Boone, Designer   WK2
            Katherine Stefanski, Associate Designer   0359555

Create Your Own Graphics Workstation

Other books in the Create Your Own Series

Configuring a Customized Engineering Workstation
by *Harley Bjelland*

Create Your Own Virtual Reality System by *Joseph R. Levy and
Harley Bjelland*

Create Your Own Multimedia System by *John A. McCormick*

Contents

Introduction

 ## The purpose of this book

This book has been designed to provide the end user a little help in sorting through the hype and hyperbole that advertisements and magazine columnists are prone to use when touting the latest and greatest products unveiled at the latest and greatest trade show for advertising executives and columnists.

There is a never-ending flood of new products, each of which makes obsolete the product that was, only last week, the ultimate in that particular line. If you look for a bit of temperate advice on just what a product will actually do, then things become a lot quieter. The reviewers seldom answer the question that you would ask if you had the chance: Do I need this software/hardware? What problems will it solve? What problems will it create? Is it worth the price? Will something else do the same thing? For less money?

Windows has taken over the desktop computer industry, but it is mostly uncharted territory. There are things about Windows software that never had to be considered about DOS software, things like adherence to the common user interface, execution of the interface, and speed in a completely graphical environment. There are capabilities that did not exist before Windows; these must be

evaluated. This book attempts to form judgements about hardware and software in the light of these new realities and to make sensible, reasonable recommendations. Not every product is really a necessity. Sometimes the small program will do very nicely. Not every computer has to be the fastest, nor every program the largest.

Systems should be assembled based on fulfilling a need. Simply buying the computer that everyone is talking about is not the way to go. While I have great respect for most trade magazine columnists, they do tend to have a narrow vision of the computer market, focusing on the future trends rather than on actual machines and programs that are being used today. It always amuses me when a columnist will confess that the machine he or she uses on a day-to-day basis to produce his or her work is really a 286 running DOS 3.3.

What do you want the computer to do for you? That is the first question to ask. To answer that question, you must first determine what tasks the computer will be expected to perform, and what software will be capable of performing those tasks. When you know the software that you need, you will know the hardware that you need to run the software.

Reading through this book should help to assess the software and to bring the hardware into focus. The computer you use is not a status symbol, anymore than a carpenter's claw hammer is a status symbol. Both are tools, and you want the right tools for the job.

What is a graphics workstation

T HE term "graphics workstation" is subject to redefinition as we progress, but for the purpose at hand we may consider it to be a terminal or microcomputer capable of displaying high-resolution graphics and existing on a network. An example of the traditional graphics workstation that would fit the definition is a Sun Microsystems minicomputer, or a Tektronix graphics terminal as a link to a mainframe. To help create a comparable Windows microcomputer-based system is the goal of this book.

In the past, the workstation was a peripheral to a larger computer, but as microcomputer technology grew more powerful, the minicomputers and mainframes were replaced by stand-alone workstations connected in networks. Where the workstation was once only an entry point into the mainframe (on which all the computing was done) and a display device (upon which the results of the mainframe's work was displayed) the new workstation increasingly became the actual site of much of the computing itself, while only the more complex and time-consuming processes were handed off to the mainframe. Eventually the mainframe was replaced entirely, and the workstations became autonomous work sites, each handling some particular task contributing to the completion of some larger job that was assembled from the pieces.

Whereas the migration of graphics applications to the PC previously had been at best spotty in both quality and quantity, the success of Windows has brought a steadily increasing tide of graphics software and display hardware to the desktop computer. Programs like AutoCAD, the massive and indispensable standard of high-end CAD, and Adobe Photoshop, the all-purpose photoimage manipulation

program, can now be found running under Windows on the PC. The successful revisions and enhancements of the Windows interface must be given most of the credit for the sudden and rapid growth in the number of the programs available for high-end graphic work, because the basic CPU hardware has been available for some time.

Depending on its uses, a graphics workstation display will be capable of resolutions of VGA (640 pixels horizontally and 480 pixels vertically) to 1280 pixels by 1024 pixels. (Higher resolutions can be found in very specialized systems.) Diagonal viewing area will range from a minimum of 15 inches on a flat, square monitor to about 21 inches on a conventionally curved monitor. The vertical refresh rate is in the neighborhood of 60 Hz at the low end and exceeding 70 Hz at the high end to reduce flicker. Rates up to 90 Hz are not uncommon. Horizontal scanning falls within the 30 kHz to 80 kHz range. A wide bandwidth, perhaps 130 MHz, is found in high-performance monitors. The dot pitch (the size of the pixel) falls between 0.31mm and 0.25mm; the smaller the pitch, the sharper the image.

Display adapters for the traditional graphics workstation are generally of the TARGA or TIGA type, so called because of the Texas Instruments Graphics controller around which the boards are built. TIGA boards are generally full-length and heavily populated. The common upper limit for their resolution is usually 1280 × 1024 pixels. Resolutions beyond that are still fairly exotic, although 1600 × 1280 is not all that rare. At the high end, 65,000 (16-bit) colors is usually the maximum, with 16.7 million colors in the lower resolutions. The TIGA boards are not especially speedy in normal VGA work, and are often paired with a VGA or SVGA board, although some TIGA boards do have their own VGA controller. The great strength of the TIGA board is in the hardware panning and zooming that they provide, both of which are instantaneous.

Input pointing devices found at the graphics station are usually more sophisticated than the mouse, like a trackball or graphic tablet coupled with a stylus or puck for finer control. The puck is more closely related to hockey than to the demon of A Midsummer Night's Dream, being a small, rounded object, usually with inset cross-hairs, and capable of greater precision of movement than the mouse. The graphic tablet and stylus offer a more comfortable analogue to the

drawing board and pen than do the mouse and mouse pad, allowing pressure-sensitive software to be used in imitation of natural media.

Scanners are used to input photographs or slides for manipulation. Color flat-bed scanners normally exceed 600 dpi in resolution, although 300 dpi can be sufficient. Even at low resolutions of 72 dpi, a 24-bit color image can approach photographic quality. Naturally, the higher the resolution, the longer the scan time and the more memory and storage space that will be needed for the digital image.

Printed output from the graphic station will normally be sent to a high definition device, either for proofing before final printing by a professional printing house or for the final product. CAD drawings normally are printed on plotters. Color illustrations or photographic images are printed on dye sublimation or thermal wax transfer printers. Black-and-white or gray-scale illustrations are normally handled by laser printers with resolutions beyond 300 dots per inch. Animations are recorded to tape.

An adapter for the display should be able to drive the monitor at its highest synchronization rates and at its best resolution. While 256 colors (8 bit) will be acceptable for most applications, the adapter should have the capability of displaying 16 million colors (24 bit/ 32 bit) in at least the 640 × 480 pixels resolution, and 65,000 colors (16 bit or High Color) in at least one higher resolution for real color photographic and video image editing. Speed will be important in the higher resolutions and in the higher bit-per-pixel color depths, because screen redraws can consume inordinate amounts of time as both parameters increase. Options like panning and zooming can be helpful in eliminating speed bottlenecks. Software implementations of those features are workable, and are found in some of the better accelerated SVGA (Super VGA) adapters, but they can also degrade performance. Hardware panning and zooming can usually be found only in the TIGA-type boards, with acceleration in normal VGA and SVGA resolutions. More than one display adapter may be required, therefore; one for accelerated VGA and SVGA, and a TIGA or TARGA board for its hardware capabilities.

The Windows graphics workstation

A graphics workstation is as much a function of its software as of its hardware. While the hardware for a PC-based graphics workstation has existed in some form for years, the software has been DOS-dependent, with no common user interface among applications and the operating system. Windows has changed all of that.

Windows put a common user interface and the components of that interface at the disposal of the hardware and software developers. The importance of this common nature of the interface cannot be overemphasized. The Windows interface, as dictated by Microsoft (for all of its failings), has brought a kind of regularity to Windows-dependent products. This has relieved the developers from having to reinvent the wheel, and has made the users more comfortable. Users no longer have to learn hundreds of obscure keyboard-driven commands for one program and hundreds more different commands for another. Programs adhere (more or less) to the common menu and command structure, using the mouse to make their programs fit the Windows environment. Users can move from one program to another (in theory), with little time devoted to relearning what they have already learned in Windows itself. That ease of use and transportability of experience is the theoretical basis for a Windows workstation. Yet, there is no free lunch, of course.

The early releases of Windows were designed to allow the gradual migration of user and developers to new environments. The 80286 was the machine of choice, and most users could, if they so desired,

move to Windows without significant hardship. But the performance of Windows has always been laggardly on the existing hardware, whatever that contemporaneous system might be, and it has driven the development of new hardware.

The Windows graphics workstation would consist of the hardware as outlined in the previous chapter combined with the refined Windows software, both environmental and application software. The interdependence of hardware and software has become an unavoidable issue of the spread of Windows. Windows programs must have a certain level of hardware, and hardware can determine the level of software that you use. The rule that required software determines the required hardware has never been more true. There are, then, different needs for different types of software. The type of software that you need to perform the work you will be doing will make the choice of hardware fairly straightforward.

The software that you purchase must be, then, the first consideration. Software for a Windows workstation should be judged on two basic criteria: one, its ability to perform and produce the results that you require, and two, its successful use of the Windows environment. Software reviews in this book will use those two criteria. The fidelity of the product to the Windows guidelines is as important as its power; many otherwise-useful programs will be found wanting when the question of fidelity to Windows is raised.

This book will consider three levels of Windows workstation: an entry-level system, a more capable general-purpose system, and the high-level, high-performance system for heavy-duty applications. The entry-level system, based on an 80486 DX2 50 MHz ISA bus computer, would be suitable for common graphics tasks, occasional photo editing, general object drawing and drafting, simple CAD, and some multimedia work. The midlevel system, based on an 80486 DX2 66 MHz VL bus computer, would be suitable for most graphics tasks, extensive photo editing, high-level CAD, simple 3D shading, multimedia, and simple 2D animations. The high-level system, based on a Pentium or RISC computer with PCI bus, would be suitable for 3D surface rendering, full-motion video editing, and 3D animations.

Input hardware

THERE are basically two types of input devices to the workstation, apart from the keyboard: the digitizer and the scanner. A digitizer is a manipulative device, used to move the cursor around the display in response to manual analogue motions. The digitizer measures the movement of the hand in two variables, speed and direction. These measurements can be made in a number of ways.

The simplest way is to move a device containing variable resistors that register a change in resistance as they are rotated. A ball fitted into a socket will make contact with small bearings or wheels situated at right angles to each other around a diameter of the ball. The ball will rotate in the socket as the hand moves, and the bearings or wheels are rotated in turn. As the bearings spin, they move the potentiometers. The potential is measured by the computer a set number of times per second. As the resistance changes, the computer interprets the readings into measurements of motion. The increase and decrease of resistance are translated into positive and negative motion on the horizontal and vertical axes.

Mouse and mouse alternatives

By now you should have guessed that I have been describing the typical mouse. Some mice use optical varistors to measure the movement of the mouse, a light sensor counting the interruptions of a light source to detect increments or decrements in the X and Y axes. Some optical mice use an etched mouse pad and no ball. These mice count the etched lines in the pad to measure motion. This type of mouse is very accurate and has no moving parts to wear out or to become dirty.

The best mouse replacement, in the opinion of many users, is the trackball. The trackball has the advantage of inertia to aid it. The mass and size of the ball make possible very precise movements and the trackball takes up little room on the desk, unlike a mouse, which requires a fair stretch of clear surface on which to maneuver.

MicroTouch markets a product called the Felix mouse replacement. Basically, it is a miniature joystick. The movement of the small joystick is restricted to an area about an inch square. Surprisingly, it is possible to make accurate movements within such a tiny area. One of the most important features of such a device is that, like the trackball, it takes up only a very small space on the desktop.

Light pens

At one time, light pens were predicted to become the most popular pointing device for computers. This has not occurred. Light pens have been touted by their advocates, mostly manufacturers and vendors, as the most natural means of drawing on a computer. However, only a brief usage of a light pen will demonstrate that the attitude that must be assumed in order to use the pen is very uncomfortable, a consequence of the vertical position of the monitor screen. If the monitor is lowered and tilted back with respect to the user, so that the screen is at waist level and points upward at an angle toward the user, then the attitude becomes natural, and the pen becomes useful. However, this arrangement is seldom possible. Light pens are much less appealing than other pointing devices.

Digitizing tablets

For drawing, however, the graphic tablet is probably the best choice. The digitizing tablet can be used as a replacement for the mouse. It can be used with a puck or a stylus. The puck is like a mouse but with more buttons, and it has no moving parts in the tracking system. The puck has a small, circular wire encased in clear plastic on a tab at the front. The tab has a cross-hair inscribed in the transparent plastic. The tablet senses the position of the puck through the electromagnetic properties of the circular wire.

The stylus works in generally the same way. The tablet sends out pulses that are returned by the stylus. Either puck or stylus can be cordless or corded, although cordless pucks are not all that common. The use of a pressure-sensitive stylus is especially desirable when using software that can react to changes in pressure, such as Fractal Design Painter, Adobe Photoshop, or Aldus PhotoStyler. Kurta, Summagraphics, Calcomp, AceCad, and Wacom all make digitizing tablets. The sizes of the tablets range from 6 × 9 inches from Wacom and Summagraphics to 12 × 12 and 12 × 18 inches. AceCad makes a very small (5 × 5 inches) tablet with a cordless stylus that can be used almost anywhere. The larger tablets usually have templates for applications such as AutoCAD, on which certain areas are set aside for program specific commands. The Wacom ArtZ tablet and pressure-sensitive stylus are reviewed with Fractal Design Painter.

 # Scanners

Scanning is a form of automatic digitizing. It converts continuous tone images into pixels, and the source can be either static or dynamic. That definition includes both conventional scanners and video digitizers. A video digitizer might be called a three-dimensional scanner.

Conventional two-dimensional scanners come in three forms: hand-held, sheet-fed, and flat-bed. Hand-held scanners are small, portable, and can scan an image that's about 4 inches wide and of variable length. A hand-held scanner may scan monochrome, grayscale, or color, depending on its construction. With the proper software and some additional hardware, it can be almost as useful as a full-page scanner. Sheet-fed scanners are capable of scanning a full letter or legal-size page. They cannot scan bound matter or pages composed of heavy paper, because the original is moved through the scanner by a system of rollers in much the same fashion as paper through a dot-matrix printer. Sheet-fed scanners can also be capable of monochrome, grayscale, and color scanning. Flat-bed scanners can scan legal or larger pages, usually up to 17 inches, and the original can be bound or of any thickness. Like a common office copier, a flat-bed scanner can scan anything that can be placed on its scanning bed. Line art, black-and-white, and continuous-tone art (grayscale and color) can be scanned.

Hand scanners were introduced as a cheaper alternative to the more expensive sheet-fed and flat-bed scanners. Now that the prices of the full page scanners have been reduced, you might expect that hand scanners would disappear, but that has not happened. Hand scanners do have uses: they are small and can be used right at the computer, scanning without requiring the user to get up from the keyboard; they can capture text from a book or magazine for inclusion in a word processor document by way of OCR software without interrupting the flow of work; and they are, simply put, convenient.

The resolution of hand scanners is usually adjustable from 72 to 800 dpi, but the most common resolutions are found in the range between 100 and 400 dpi. Resolutions above 400 dpi are almost always interpolated: the scanner actually scans at four hundred dots-per-inch, and the scanning software adds pixels by averaging. Thus, if one pixel has a grayscale value of 200 and the next pixel has a value of 210, the software might reasonably create a pixel between them with a value of 205. The created information is derived from the actual data, but it does not represent a true higher-resolution scan.

There are problems with hand scanners. Some are problems inherent to the format, while others are the result of necessary compromises. Inherently, hand scanners cannot scan an area larger than their optics without some compensatory software magic. If you want to scan a document larger than the scanner, you obviously must make more than one scan and piece them together. That hurdle has been cleared by adding a stitching module to software. This takes overlapping areas of scans and matches them to combine scans into a single image.

It is virtually impossible to maintain a constant speed while hand scanning, which leads to a difference in the sampling rate and a stretching or compressing of areas can result. Software must compensate for that. It is almost impossible to scan in a straight line and to keep the scanner perpendicular to the line of scan. Skewing of the scanner and side-slipping can only be corrected by using a scanning guide of some sort. The simplest scanning guide is a ruler, but there are inexpensive scanning trays that do a better job of keeping the scanner straight and correctly aligned. Color scanning with a hand scanner also produces results that are not always as good

as one would like. Because the light sources of hand scanners are LEDs, they have a definite color bias, and they are rather weak.

Sheet-fed scanners are an improvement over hand scanners. You can scan an entire page at once, and there is no worry about the image being scanned at an inconstant rate. The optics are generally better than in a hand scanner. Because the optics are fixed and the page moves, however, there can be problems with skewing of a misfed page, and, occasionally, as in a printer, a page can be mangled by the scanner's paper feed mechanism. And there might be photographs that you do not want to risk pushing through the scanner, which will, at the least, apply a curl to the paper.

Flat-bed scanners have more to offer than other types of document scanners. You don't have to worry about mangling a priceless photo of great-great-grandfather in his Civil War uniform. You can scan from a folio-sized book. But the flat-bed scanners do have the drawback of requiring a large area of the desktop. There is a bit more maintenance for a flat-bed scanner than for a hand-held model. The fluorescent tube that provides the illumination of the document will not last forever, or even as long as an LED, so you may have to replace it at some time. Basically, however, the flat-bed scanner is the best choice for serious scanning.

Resolution is one subject that will be of primary interest in considering a scanner. It is also one of the subjects about which very little is written that is sensible. If you consider that the average 35mm photograph contains several magnitudes (powers of 10) more information than can be scanned by even the best scanner, you will realize that the importance of resolution is extremely overstated by scanner manufacturers. You should scan a photograph with one thing in mind: how it will be printed.

Scanning resolution is a function of the printer that you plan to use as the ultimate destination for the scanned image. The general rule-of-thumb is that you should scan at a resolution about twice the line screen to be used by the target printer. Thus, if the printer will print its best at 103 lines per inch, then the best resolution at which to scan images for that printer will be 206 dpi. The file size of an image increases dramatically as resolution increases, especially when

scanning in 24-bit color. A 24-bit color scan at 72 dpi is probably as good as you will need for most purposes.

The human eye cannot discern the difference between all of the shades possible at a color depth of 24 bits. In grayscale images, 256 shades of gray will almost always be the upper limit supported by editing programs. Grayscale scans should not be made at more than 256 shades, and most monochrome printers will struggle to deliver more than 64 shades of gray.

Flat-bed scanners are available from many companies, and many of them are based on Canon scanning engines. UMAX, Hewlett-Packard, Epson, Sharp, and Microtek are among the better brand-name scanner companies.

Slide scanning can be a consideration in purchasing a flat-bed scanner. Some scanners can be fitted with an accessory that accepts 35mm color slides. If you need the capability, then that potential must be a factor in the choice of scanners. Dedicated slide scanners will probably do a better job than the flat-bed with its accessory, but the improvement in quality must be weighed against the frequency of use, because a good slide scanner from, say, Nikon can cost about twice the purchase price of the flat-bed scanner.

Scanners with a slide attachment option:

> - Advanced Network Systems, ArtiScan series, 800–1200 dpi, $1,000–1,400, SCSI

> - AGFA, Horizon Plus, 1200 dpi, $20,000, SCSI

> - Computer Aided Technology, CAT BluePrint Scanners, 400 dpi, $1,900 (24 × 36 in)–2,500 (36 × 44 in), parallel

> - DPI Electronic Imaging, resolutions up to 9600 dpi, $800–2,500, SCSI

> - Logitech, ScanMan series, hand-held, 400 dpi, $400–500

> - Logitech PowerPage, desktop, 400 dpi, $800, parallel

> - Relisys RELI 2400T, 600 dpi, $1,600, SCSI

> - Relisys RELI 9624DPI, 9600 dpi, $4,000, SCSI

Nikon CoolScan dedicated slide scanners have resolutions of 2700 dpi. There is an internal model, with SCSI interface, that sells for $2,300, and an external version that sells for $2,600. Polaroid also makes a 2700 dpi slide scanner, priced about $2,500. Microtek sells its own slide scanner, the ScanMaker 35t, with a software-interpolated resolution of 3600 dpi. It sells for $1,400.

 # Scanning mechanics

While Siskel and Ebert already may have passed final sentence on the practice of colorization of black-and-white motion pictures, colorization in computer artwork has another form, of which even those severe critics might approve. The fact of the matter is this: almost all color scanners are really nothing more than black-and-white or grayscale impostors wearing rose-colored glasses (not to mention sky blue and grass green).

Perceived color is a result of reflectance of certain wavelengths of the visible electromagnetic spectrum. The amounts of particular wavelengths present in the reflected light determine the color perceived. White is a mixture of all wavelengths, while black is the absence of color resulting from the absorption of the incident wavelengths. Everything else is the result of selective absorption and reflectance. When the longer wavelengths are reflected, the color red is perceived. Shortening of the reflected wavelengths shifts the color toward the violet.

Because light is a composite, it is possible to disassemble the light into its components (with a prism or spectrograph) and to assign to each component its relative value in the mixture, values that can then be used to reconstruct the color at a later time. That disassembly can be accomplished quite nicely with a grayscale scanner with the proper driver software, and three acetate filters. Scanning through each of the three filters results in three separate measurements of light intensity for each given spot on the image.

If we were to add the results of those three measurements together, we would have a complete picture of what the original light contained

in color information. With a grayscale scanner, these values can be accurately determined, and a nearly perfect color image interpolated from the combined results of the scans. This method, the three-pass color scan, is used by most color scanners.

This method works with all grayscale sources, including video. A black-and-white video camera can easily be made into a color digitizer by purchasing three glass filters at a camera supply store. Using a product such as ComputerEyes from Digital Vision, you make three versions of the image to be colored: one each using the red, green, and blue filters. You save them as RED.TIF, BLUE.TIF, and GREEN.TIF, and then combine them in the appropriate software.

KaliedoScan

KaliedoScan is a stand-alone utility that is available in versions for both the Macintosh and for Windows 3.x. KaliedoScan, from Impact Research, is packaged with a set of matched acetate filters for use with flat-bed scanners, but the program works equally well with digitized images from other sources. If one of the supported flat-bed scanners is being used, then the whole process is reasonably quick and automatic. Hewlett-Packard ScanJets are supported in both versions, and HP-driver compatible scanners should work as well. In the Mac version, Abaton, UMAX, and Microtek grayscale scanners are also directly supported.

If one is working from saved imported images, then the program recognizes families of images and will open all three members of a family when one member is selected. This simplifies file selection, but complicates filenaming. Some scanning programs balk at saving in the filename extensions recognized by KaliedoScan, and it can be necessary to use the RENAME command to change the filenames for KaliedoScan's importation. Also, some TIFF graphics may not work with KaliedoScan. BMP files can be used if TIFF will not work.

The program is designed to require as little user intervention as possible, and construction of the final color image is commenced by selection of the appropriate command from a menu. KaliedoScan can

create either 8-bit or 24-bit (32-bit Macintosh) images from the source files. Although user intercession is not required in most instances, KaliedoScan does provide the tools by which the user can affect the created image. Because each brand of scanner exhibits its own peculiar biases with regard to the detection of certain wavelengths of the spectrum, there are inevitable deviations from the perfect representation of the original colors.

Directly supported scanners using the supplied filters (those listed under the scanner sub-menu) are precalibrated within the software, and, barring any individual bias in the scanner, no further correction should be necessary. Unsupported scanners can be calibrated by the user through the No Scanner (Macintosh "Other") selection in the sub-menu. A calibration card is provided with KaliedoScan, to fine-tune the process.

The operation of KaliedoScan is rapid, and a snapshot-sized picture can be rendered in less than a minute in the 8-bit mode and in slightly more time in 32-bit color. (Rendering ran more quickly on my Mac SE/30 than on a 386DX, due, no doubt, to the Mac's FPU.) If calibration does not reproduce a particular picture's coloring correctly, KaliedoScan has separate Enhancement (Macintosh "Merge") settings that can be used to adjust the brightness of one or more of the three primaries to change the balance of the merged image.

On the whole, the program accomplishes its single purpose with alacrity and competence, and there is enough margin for variation built into its levels of control to allow the user to compensate for almost any situation.

CAT Color Converter

Hand-held scanners present special problems for the conversion of grayscale scans into color images. One, they tend to have light sources that provide insufficient illumination for use with a filter. The image resulting from a filtered scan often lacks detail and is too dark to be of use. Two, the LEDs in hand scanners are often either green or red, causing a severe bias in certain areas of the color spectrum

that can be difficult to overcome. Three, the hand-held scanner is notoriously erratic in even the steadiest hand, and achieving consistent scans to assure proper registration of three scans is nearly impossible. Using a grayscale hand-held scanner for color scanning is usually impractical.

The CAT Color Converter from Computer Aided Technology of Dallas, TX, is an ingenious solution to the aforementioned problems. It can convert almost any of the popular hand-held scanners into color-capable scanners, equal in quality to the newer, more expensive dedicated color hand-held scanners. The Converter is a package of software and a hardware accessory for DOS-based systems.

**CAT Color Converter
bottom view**

Figure 3-1

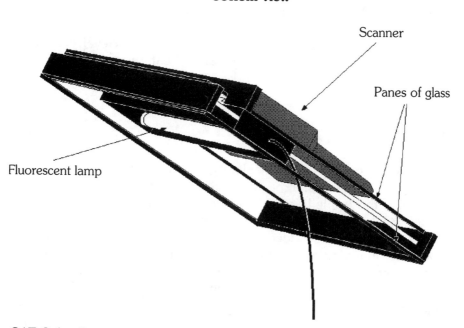

Scanner

Panes of glass

Fluorescent lamp

CAT Color Converter is a combination light table and scanning tray, with software support for color scanning with a grayscale hand-held scanner.

The software guides the user through the process of three-pass filtered scanning and color image derivation in the same general manner as KaliedoScan. Importation of saved scans is not supported. The

ingenuity of the product is invested in the accessory, a combination of a scan alignment guide and light table that solves the hand-held scanner's two biggest problems: consistency and light intensity.

The scanning takes place in the normal fashion, with the CCC software signalling when to begin a scan and which filter is to be used. When all three scans have been made, the software can then be directed to combine the images and to create a color picture. Color correction can be made after the scans have been combined, or bias in the filtration can be compensated for during scanning through menu-selected items.

There is a calibrated linear registration template affixed to the bottom of the base pane. The lines are scanned each time with the color graphic, allowing precise alignment of the scans during combination. This reduces the width of the available scan area, but it helps to assure that no color halo is created in the final image due to misalignment of the three scans. In all, this is a very clever piece of work, and it integrates nicely the necessary features to make hand-held scanners usable for color work.

Video digitizers

Video digitizing has been available for personal computers for ten or more years. Digital Vision has made its ComputerEyes digitizer since the days of the Apple II, and the current PC and Mac versions can capture single frames and motion sequences in color or black-and-white from all common video sources. Video capture boards usually have other functions added. Genlock capability is the one most useful added function. Genlocking allows the overlaying of text and images on the video signal and the combining of the sources into a single output frame.

Video still cameras are the current "hot" topic. Canon has marketed the ZapShot for several years. There were other digital cameras before the ZapShot. Apple Computer markets one, the QuickTake. While the video still camera may, indeed, be the coming thing, it is a little too early to be run over by it. Kodak's creation of the Photo CD

is one sign that the time is near for the arrival of video still cameras. The problem is one of resolution.

No video camera can equal, let alone rival, the film camera. Television resolution, even high-definition television resolution, is illusory. It is certainly easier to use the video still camera than it is to use a video digitizer to capture single images; however, don't expect photographic quality from any video source, hype notwithstanding.

Display hardware

T HE topic "display hardware" covers a variety of subtopics, including display adapters, screen capture devices, display accelerators, and monitors.

Display adapters

Display adapters have suffered and benefited from the Windows environment more than any other PC components. The display adapter is the most visible bottleneck in the Windows data flow channels; it has attracted the most complaints and, consequently, the most attention from developers. Windows relies on the rapid movement of large numbers of pixels around the display area. Simply redrawing the screen can be an arduous task when the resolution and color depth are both high. When you add to the job of maintaining the image, the task of moving elements about the screen, the burden can slow Windows to a crawl.

The task can be made easier when it is understood that the whole screen seldom changes, and that the most common actions are those that affect regions or areas of the screen. Moving groups of pixels from one area of the display to another becomes easier if the pixels are treated as groups. By storing a region of the screen in a memory buffer and then moving the whole image, the computer can speed up Windows.

The graphics load of Windows falls by default on the host CPU, and the best way to improve the CPU's performance is to lighten its load by shunting the graphics gruntwork to a processor on the graphics adapter itself. The coprocessor is designed to move large numbers of pixels about in memory very quickly. Because it is concerned only with graphics, the coprocessor can be streamlined to improve both

the internal data flow and the input/output of data between the display and the coprocessor. The main CPU, then, is free to tend to the other chores imposed by Windows.

The best graphics adapters have a processor capable of handling large numbers. Generally, the larger the numbers that can be handled, the better the performance of the processor. This applies to graphics processors in particular, because they are almost entirely concerned with locating large numbers of pixels in the display. The more points that can be addressed at one time, the faster the display will be redrawn; this has led to processors that are better at addressing than the host CPUs themselves.

Whole companies have been founded to produce video processing chips. Companies such as Cirrus Logic, Oak, S3, Tseng Labs, Western Digital, and Boca produce families of graphics processors for use in their own adapters and others. Other companies, such as Matrox and ATI, have developed their own chips for more restricted distribution.

Memory is the second most important factor in the improvement of graphics speed. If the graphics processor must use the computer's memory to form and manipulate the display image, then both the display adapter's and the computer's operations will suffer. The display adapter will have to move the bits from the computer memory through the motherboard, through the motherboard slot, and into its own board. Then it must move the new bits back to the motherboard RAM while the rest of the display is calculated. Meanwhile, the computer must carry on its other operations with a reduced amount of useable memory, thereby reducing its efficiency.

This bottleneck is removed when memory is placed directly on the adapter board and on the processor's own bus path. The more RAM that the adapter's processor has available to it, the faster it can work. But one last RAM bottleneck is located in the RAM itself; normal Dynamic RAM (DRAM) can be read from or written to, but not both at the same time. Faster DRAM can reduce the time that the data path is occupied by either input or output. The speed and power of a very fast processor can be wasted if it is forced to wait for the RAM to be ready for transferring data.

One way to remove this bottleneck is to make RAM that can be written to and read from simultaneously. This type of RAM is called Video RAM or VRAM. It can allow a fast graphics processor to operate at its best speed. Naturally, it is more expensive than normal DRAM. The amount and type of RAM have a large influence on the price of the adapter. Some adapters use a mixture of RAM to moderate cost.

The last consideration in the speed of graphics processing is the actual bus width of the computer slot into which the graphic adapter is fitted. While the main part of the graphic work may now be done on the adapter rather than in the computer, there are still large arrays of information concerning the changes in the display that must be moved from the computer to the display adapter. After all, the computer is actually keeping track of where items are on the display and how those items are interacting. If the mouse moves, the cursor must be moved to follow, and the computer and the adapter need to communicate information about the cursor's activity. This requires the movement of data bits between the CPU and display adapter, which is done via data bus.

The most common data bus is the Industry Standard Architecture (ISA), which is up to sixteen bits wide and runs as fast as 12 MHz. When the need for a 32-bit bus became obvious, IBM proposed and adopted the ISA-incompatible Micro Channel Architecture for its proprietary machines. In response to this licensing ploy, a consortium of IBM's competitors updated the ISA bus to thirty-two bits as the EISA (E for Expanded) bus. A separate 32-bit scheme was created for video by a committee of engineers and called the VESA (Video Engineers) Local Bus. Then came the PCI bus, another IBM creation, that makes use of a 64-bit-wide bus structure for the newer 64 bit-computers such as the Pentium. Additionally, as the bus width was expanded, the bus speed was increased from about 8 MHz to 33 MHz in VESA and EISA buses, and then to 60 MHz and above in PCI. Backward compatibility of the buses is usually assured so that older components can be used in the wider slots. If your computer has a wide bus structure, you can improve graphics performance by making use of the full bus width. Graphic adapters are now usually marketed in three bus forms: ISA, VESA, and PCI. It makes little sense to use an ISA bus adapter in a VL or PCI bus computer, because you are losing the advantage of the faster bus.

I have elected to test the boards in a manner that reflects actual work. I have measured the time that it takes a board to perform a task with a particular software product. As nearly as possible, I have used the same test on each of the boards in several programs with similar functions. I have not combined or weighted results to reflect any preconceived idea of what test is more important. Regard the tests with suspicion, and take the results with a grain of salt.

Lastly, in what may appear to be a heretical statement in a book touting the latest and greatest, I suggest that you run Windows in a 256-color (8-bit) mode for all but a few programs. Excepting painting and image-enhancement programs, in which 24-bit color is necessary, most Windows programs demonstrate their best performance in 256-color mode. Indeed, some programs such as AutoCAD and Virtus WalkThrough are designed specifically to be run in the 8-bit color mode.

The obvious advantages of 8-bit over 24-bit color are a reduction in cost and an increase of speed. If you do not have to purchase the RAM that supports the greater color bit-depths, you save money. While not all graphics adapters run faster in the 8-bit mode than in the 16- or 24-bit modes, most do, and the drivers for the 8-bit modes are generally more stable. Having the option for 24-bit color is certainly worthwhile, but the trade-offs in cost and speed generally favor 8-bit color in the minimum RAM configuration.

Matrox MGA

Matrox, a company based in Quebec, has taken a leading role in the development of high-capacity, moderately priced graphic adapters. The Matrox MGA video adapters are based on the PC industry's first internal 64-bit graphic coprocessor chips, MGA-I and MGA-II. Matrox has enjoyed an early advantage in producing the next generation of graphic adapters for the PCI bus.

The MGA-I chip offers hardware acceleration for 8-bit, 16-bit, and 24-bit color, for 2D and 3D wire-frame and shaded CAD, and for video motion. The MGA-II offers the same characteristics, with the exception of 3D support. Twenty-four-bit color is available at

Figure 4-1

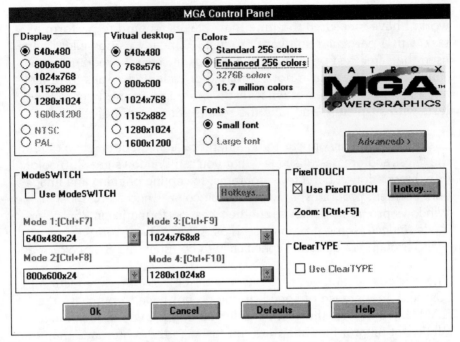

Matrox uses custom dithering in 8-bit mode to select best colors for rendering of Hi-Color and True Color images.

800 × 600 resolution for all memory configurations, and up to 1280 × 1024 resolution with 4.5 MB of VRAM.

The installation of the Matrox boards is simple and foolproof. The installation creates the MGA control panel in Windows, from which the features of the software and board can be set. Resolutions and color depths are complementary or interactive; choosing resolutions determines which color depths are available. There is a similar relationship with the virtual desktop (a screen area larger than the actual display) that can be activated. Certain resolutions can have virtual desktops and others cannot, depending on the amount of memory installed on the board. The virtual desktop extends beyond the edges of the display, so that the area actually viewed on the screen is a port or window within the desktop window.

This arrangement allows you to have the equivalent of a dual-page display or larger monitor without the expense or loss of space on the

real desktop. When you wish to gain access to some element that is beyond the edge of the screen, you simply move the cursor to the edge of the screen beyond which is the portion you wish to see. The desktop automatically and smoothly scrolls beneath the cursor until you reach the edge of the virtual desktop, which stops the cursor. This feature is common in most high-level TIGA boards; Matrox uses the same approach at about half the price. Zooming is also provided in hardware.

The MGA control panel has the very handy ModeSwitch option that allows you to assign function keys to various combinations of pixel depths and resolutions. With this feature enabled, you can switch instantly from one resolution and color depth to another without leaving Windows and restarting. This is an option that all board manufacturers ought to provide.

In 8-bit color, Matrox has created a proprietary dithering scheme that allows you to simulate 24-bit color by creating custom palettes. Because this is a proprietary feature, it is useful mainly for viewing images imported from other computers rather than for preparing images to be seen on other computers. Additionally, there is a software module, WinSqueeze, that can automatically provide JPEG compression for 24-bit color images. Because JPEG is becoming standard in graphics programs, you may not find this feature of much use.

In tests, the Matrox boards performed flawlessly, and they provided the greatest acceleration for many tasks, equalled only by the Number Nine boards. Regardless of the software being run, the MGA was equal to the task. The real-world tests were to load and manipulate a large bitmap image in a bitmap editor, and to load and manipulate a vector drawing in drawing programs.

Number Nine GXE

Number Nine Computer Corporation of Lexington, MA, makes the GXE line of graphics accelerators. The Level 12 local bus version that I tested performed almost perfectly. Both the hardware and the software drivers were easy to install and a pleasure to use. In most instances the GXE was the equal of the Matrox MGA; quite an impressive feat, given the price comparison. The GXE had 2 MB of

VRAM and 1 MB of DRAM, a compromise in design that offers sufficient VRAM for speed and enough DRAM to support extra features like virtual desktops and Hi-Color in the higher resolutions. Like the MGA, the GXE could support 24-bit color in the 800 × 600 resolution and still deliver a virtual desktop.

Figure 4-2

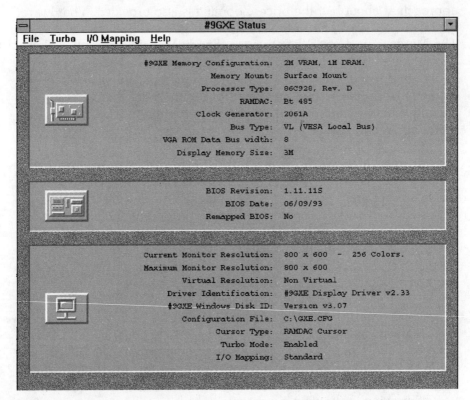

#9 Status Report utility gives information on board configuration.

Software for the GXE includes the HawkEye utilities, a control panel in which you can change resolutions, color bit depths, virtual desktop size, instantaneous hotkey zooming that is variable with resolution, and a "Chameleon" cursor that will change the color of the cursor when it passes over a background that might otherwise tend to make the cursor difficult to see. The virtual desktop of the GXE is every bit as snappy and responsive as the normal display

Figure 4-3

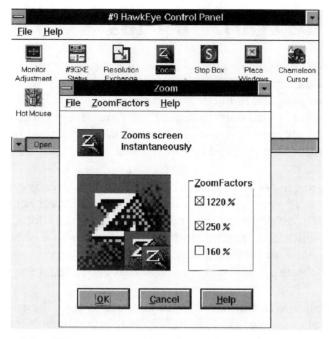

*#9 hardware zooming is configured in Zoom utility.
Degree of zooming varies with resolution and color
depth.*

desktop. The GXE comes with a package of useful display utilities
for custom configuration.

The board worked well with all the monitors I tried, and auto synching
between monitor and board was truly automatic. The single caution
that should be issued concerns the use of the COM 4 input/output
address. This address is usually vacant on most computers, and video
drivers sometimes require that you map the video board's I/O to that
address. This is the case with the Local Bus version of the GXE.

The board supports horizontal scan rates of 100 Hz, although you
are unlikely as yet to find a monitor that is capable of such
performance. In the meantime, it will drive your monitor at its
highest scan rate. The newer GXE64 boards are less expensive
because they use DRAM; in most other respects they are the same as
the earlier GXE models.

 # Volante Warp 10 Plus

The Warp 10 boards are middle-of-the-road accelerators. They are better than the ordinary Windows graphic cards, but they do not come close to matching the Number Nine and Matrox boards. This is the only graphic adapter board that gave me hardware problems. The first unit that was shipped to me quit after about five hours of use. The replacement, however, finished out the test period with no problems.

The software drivers were also a bit troublesome. This is a common occurrence with video graphic adapter software. Drivers cannot be tested in all possible hardware and software configurations, and some incompatibilities can crop up. In this case, there was a ghosting effect that extended from vertical lines outward to the right, sometimes enough to obscure the display. An updated driver fixed the problem.

The installation was simple, with no jumpers to set. The software installer is also simple. Besides the drivers, it creates a Windows program group for the Volante utilities that regulate board resolution and color depth. The Volante board gave good speed and clear displays. With 1 MB DRAM, it supports resolutions up to 1280 × 1024 at 16 colors. The software drivers provide for a software implementation of zooming and panning, rather than the hardware method used by Matrox and Number Nine. It seemed to work just as well as the hardware version.

Figure 4-4

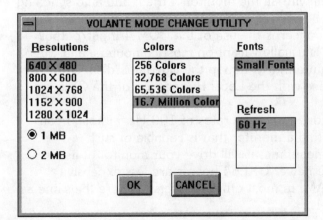

Volante control panel integrates resolution, color depth, font sizes, and refresh rates settings.

The more recently released Volante WarpVL boards are based on the Tseng Labs W32i version of the ET4000 chip that has been used for years.

Hercules Dynamite Pro

The Hercules Dynamite Pro is the low-end member of the Hercules Windows accelerator family. It uses the Tseng Labs ET4000 W32i chip and supports 2 MB of fast 40ns DRAM. The board is half-length. There are jumpers to disable IRQ 2, which is necessary to ensure backward compatibility with some DOS software that requires CGA resolutions. If you are not using such software, then the jumpers can be ignored in most other cases.

The board supports all resolutions from 640 × 480 up to and including 1280 × 1024. Twenty-four-bit color is limited to 640 × 480, but 16-bit color is supported in the 800 × 600 SVGA mode, with 256 colors supported at higher resolutions. It supports vertical refresh rates in excess of 100 Hz.

Aside from some minor software compatibility issues, the Hercules Dynamite Pro ran beautifully in all resolutions and color depths. The speed is not up to the standards set by Matrox and Number Nine, but it is superior to that of most other Windows accelerators, including the Volante board. The displays were sharp and showed no untoward tendencies toward smearing or the propagation of artifacts.

The Hercules installer creates the Hercules program group, the main constituent of which is the Picture Window utility, with which resolution and color bit depth are set. Display fonts can be selected from any installed fonts. One important utility, PowerHz, is necessary for using the board for what the manual terms SuperStable displays, i.e., those with refresh rates over 90 Hz. The software does not support panning and zooming, although virtual displays can be used when 2 MB of RAM are present.

This board permits user installation of the second bank of DRAM when the one-megabyte version has been purchased. Fast DRAM is

Figure 4-5

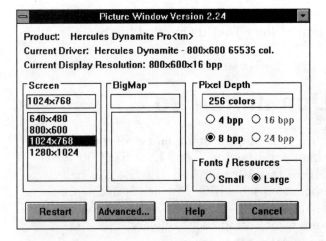

1024 × 768 resolution has maximum 8-bit color with 1 MB, and 16-bit color with 2 MB.

needed, with speeds between 60 ns and 40 ns recommended. When all the RAM sockets are populated, the board can address 32-bits of RAM across the banks, improving display speed dramatically in most resolutions. The extra RAM increases the vertical refresh rates at certain resolutions: 72 Hz for 640 × 480 in 24-bit mode, and 72 Hz for 800 × 600 in 16-bit mode. Also, the installation of 2 MB of memory makes 256 colors possible at the 1280 × 1024 resolution and 64K colors at 1024 × 768. Use of 2 MB is highly desirable. In the 16- and 256-color modes, the highest vertical rates are 120 Hz at 640 × 480, 110 Hz at 800 × 600, 76 Hz at 1024 × 768, and 87 Hz at 1280 × 1024 interlaced.

During software installation, you must select a monitor type to be used with the Dynamite Pro. The selection will determine what combination of sync rates and resolutions will be used by the board. Given its capabilities, and despite the rare software incompatibilities and the lack of some amenities, the Hercules Dynamite Pro is a fine product and a great value.

Video input adapters

Video input has become an important function of the graphic workstation as the microcomputer has taken over the production of "multimedia" works. The acquisition and modification of a television

signal (which might seem a trivial matter, due to the superficial similarities of the television and the computer monitor) is really quite complex. The television signal is a composite bearing the actual video and the information that tells the receiver how the video is to be displayed, and it is very different from the video signal used by the computer display.

The standard US television displays 30 frames of video per second, a number chosen because it is half the 60 Hz of common alternating current (ac) available at the wall outlet, making timing easier for the engineers. The actual picture is composed of 525 interlaced scan lines. Despite that there are some 150,000 individual dots on the television screen, the smallest package of information which can be manipulated on the TV screen is the line, which is composed of analog voltages describing the gradations of intensity of the phosphor excitement on the face of the picture tube.

The television receiver must acquire the signal, amplify and decode it, and then display the video according to the information embedded in the signal. The tuner is the portion of the receiver responsible for the acquisition of the signal. The remainder of the TV set is concerned with breaking down the signal into its parts and then using those parts to form the picture.

The first thing that must be done to make the computer and the television compatible is to add the tuner to the computer. This is not absolutely necessary, as it is possible to use another video source such as a VCR or video camera to supply the video input signal to be displayed. But the addition of a tuner makes the computer more versatile, and it adds very little to the cost of the system. Further, with the addition of the tuner, VCR and video camera compatibility are assured.

At first, putting a TV receiver inside your computer might seem difficult; but when you consider that a complete TV can be made small enough to fit in the palm of a child's hand, the task is really only that of adapting the existing components to the computer. There are a number of such adaptations available.

Video capture is the added feature of television boards that most users need. The capture of full-motion video is the precursor to .AVI

and QuickTime movies. The interdependency of computers and video is well-established already, and the border between video and the computer-generated display has disappeared. The art of the impossible is now on the desktop; but there are still some physical limitations.

First, the quality of the output depends on the quality of the input. The absolute quality of the signal is fixed by the NTSC broadcast standard, and although the television picture might appear to the human eye to be detailed and natural, it contains very few actual pixels. The natural appearance of the television picture is the effect of the analog color that smooths over the jagged edges of the low-resolution display. The imminent introduction of a standard for common broadcast High Definition Television (HDTV) will change that, but the current situation will persist for some years.

Second, there is the conversion of the analog television picture into a digital equivalent for the computer display. A television picture will always appear to be better than a computer rendition of the same picture at comparable sizes, because the computer can't efficiently handle the high number of digital bits that a converted analog signal generates. Typically, the computer display of a television picture will be at a reduced size, and the frame rate will fall below the normal 30 per second. Therefore, you cannot expect to capture true full-motion video in a computer format.

To capture video, then, you must use complementary factors of resolution, picture size, and color bit depth. You can capture 24-bit color video, but the resolution must be low, picture size must be small, and the number of frames captured must be few and far between. Or, if you are willing to sacrifice color fidelity, you can increase the resolution, picture size, and number of frames captured. In practical terms, you can expect to be able to capture a video sequence at a rate of 10–15 frames per second with a palette of 256 colors at a resolution of 320 × 240 pixels for 15–20 seconds before exhausting the resources of your computer. You might be able to capture a single VGA resolution image per second in 24-bit color for a few seconds at best. It is likely, however, that the best results in terms of natural motion will be found at resolutions of 240 × 180 in 256 colors.

Of course, capture is only the beginning. You must be able to work with and display the captured sequences. Editing a video sequence can put your CPU into shock, and playback can be as trying as recording and editing. If you need to record and play back broadcast-quality video, then you must use videotape. You can edit the video sequences using the computer, and simply assemble from actual video segments a finished presentation that is recorded directly to tape. It does not make much sense right now to try to turn the computer into a VCR; but it does make sense to use the computer to drive the VCR or LaserDisc player.

PC TeleVISION

PC TeleVISION from 50/50 Micro Electronics, which places a 119-channel cable-ready television tuner and VGA/SVGA monitor controls on a full length 8-bit board, lets you view video input from any NTSC-compatible source. The board uses a pass-through connection to allow the display of computer-generated graphics or text.

The card is cable-ready, and there are backplane connectors for the input from the computer's VGA board and another of the same type for the monitor cable. The computer display is routed through the same port as the TV picture, the user toggling between them via keyboard or mouse. Sound is delivered to Labtec's amplified speaker supplied with the board. Stereo is not supported. Sound quality of the speaker is excellent, considering its size. The speaker is shielded to prevent magnetic interference with the computer or its display.

The fitting of the board into the computer is the most difficult part of the installation process. The connector for the antenna cable extends beyond the backplane, which makes installation difficult. The board requires a full length slot, and the geometry and the population of the nearby boards can limit the room in which you have to work. Also, the slot chosen should allow free circulation of air once the board has been installed; the board generates considerable heat. With the larger, hotter CPUs now being used in many PCs, additional heat should be viewed with some concern. In use, however, the board gave no trouble whatsoever.

The setup program establishes the basic parameters of operation. The picture can be centered horizontally, the brightness and contrast adjusted, tint and color corrected, and the input source selected (cable, antenna, or video player). Cable options are standard, IRC, and HRC. Video players can be VCR or laser disc. Settings are saved as the basic configuration that will be used whenever the PC TeleVISION software is run. Perhaps most importantly, the Sync Polarity can be altered. The Sync Polarity affects the proportions of the TV picture. Thus, if the picture is elongated or compressed, either horizontally or vertically, the defect can be corrected by running the setup program's Modify Configuration option and choosing Sync Polarity. There are four adjustments for aspect ratio.

The software supplied with the board installs more easily than the board itself. The Windows application for PC TeleVISION consists of a small panel that permits most features of the board to be customized. The parameters from the base configuration can be changed permanently from within the application. The Input Source, Video display parameters, and Channel functions can be selected from menus. The Input and Video parameters are the same as those in the setup program. Input source is always shown in a small windoid or box on the left of the panel, just above the 50/50 logo.

Figure 4-6

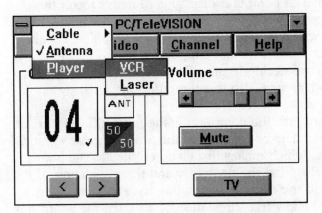

Video signal input source for PCTV is selected from a menu. Sensitivity of the receiver depends on the source chosen.

The Channel functions resemble those found in common remote controls for normal televisions. The user can select channels by typing on the keyboard's keypad or by using the mouse on the graphic simulation. After reaching a preferred channel, you then click on the

"F" key of the keypad graphic and the channel becomes locked in as a favorite. Thereafter, a stroke on the left or right arrow keys moves to the next favorite channel. The channel count can be incremented or decremented singly by use of the up or down arrow keys.

Other features in the small PC TeleVISION control panel include the sliders for Brightness, Contrast, Tint, and Color. Each of the controls can be changed by mouse or from the keyboard. Typing the initial of each control will increase the degree of that element, while the use of the control key in addition to the initial will result in the decrease of that element. Keyboard movement of the sliders is incremented; mouse control is continuous.

The video image from the PC TeleVISION is better than that of any but the most expensive television receivers. This is a result of the general superiority of computer monitors to televisions. The specifications for monitors are uniformly better than those of televisions. Thus, for instance, the better convergence of the color guns renders the picture more sharply, and higher sync rates reduce flicker.

The PC TeleVISION Plus is the current model. It uses a slightly different arrangement of display routing than its predecessor. The Plus version integrates output with that of the graphic adapter of the computer, using the chromakey method that is standard in video applications. With this ability, it is possible to overlay one electronic picture with another so that they appear to be one. It then is possible to display both the television and Windows desktop simultaneously. The television picture can be placed in a window in the desktop, resized, moved, and captured by the normal Windows screen-capture software.

This arrangement also makes possible the capture of sequences from the incoming signal and the total integration of video and Windows. The only fault is that the quality of the picture displayed is determined by the graphics adapter. If the graphics adapter cannot display the full range of television analog color, then there is a degradation of the television picture, and the chromakey will eliminate an entire color from the television display. The difference between the television and multimedia becomes less noticeable, but that is a backhanded compliment.

PC TeleVISION can be used as a source of full-motion video, or it can be used with a VCR or videodisc player to acquire still-frame images. It can be valuable for training videos because there is no need for a separate TV, and the user can toggle between software and videotape.

ProMovie Studio from Media Vision

The ProMovie Studio card is a video capture device on a half-length ISA-bus computer board. Refreshingly, it has a simple design and a simple function. The board is easy enough to install, fitting in any ISA slot available. There are two external input connectors, one RCA socket for common composite video, and one DIN connector for S-Video. You supply your own input cables. The board requires no internal cabling.

There are software drivers and applications for either DOS or Windows installation, but the program will automatically install the Windows version if Windows is present. The DOS software is installed in a default directory called PROMOVIE, which can be relocated and renamed, but the Windows software must be installed in the Windows directory. The slim installation manual provides basic information on installation.

Sound is supported when a SoundBlaster or compatible board has been installed in the computer. The ProMovie board itself does not have audio capabilities. While the DOS software allows the board to be used immediately, for Windows you must install the provided Video for Windows software. Video for Windows is the Microsoft package of applications to capture, edit, and play .AVI files. Video for Windows is a general-purpose software suite that has numerous features, not all of which are useable with every capture board. The ProMovie board uses only the essential features of the software.

There is a fair amount of control over the capture of video. The Video Source menu item allows you to make adjustments to the incoming signal and to process it in various ways prior to recording.

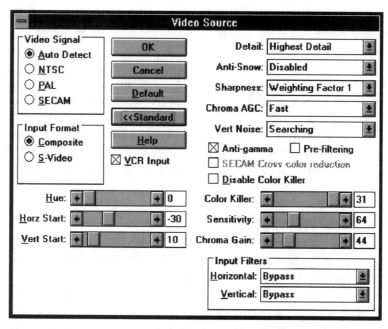

Video Source options dialogue permits fine tuning of the input.

The software supplied with the board is not extraordinary. (AuthorWare Star is also included for creation of multimedia projects.) Video for Windows 1.0 permits the capture of single or still frames, the editing of sequences or still frames, and the export of .AVI files. The capture program, VidCap, is where you begin.

The incoming video is displayed in a window at the resolution, quality, and size designated for capture. You can choose to have the video preview displayed as continuous motion or with periodic updates of still frames. Continuous motion is not actually continuous, even when the highest frame rate is selected; the motion is stiff and jerky.

The capture sampling rate varies with the resolution, the color depth, and the rate setting. In the higher resolutions and greater color depths, the rate that you set will seldom be reflected in the real capture rate. The rate of capture is merely a suggestion to the program, which will dance as fast as it can. Frames will be dropped when the program cannot keep up with the flow of incoming data,

and the percentage of frames dropped to frames captured will be displayed. In the higher resolutions or color depths, the drop ratio will be more than 4 to 1.

When the sequence has been captured, you can edit the captured video by starting the VidEdit program of VFW. This will load the sequence and display it. You have the usual controls for playing, rewinding, and single-stepping the sequence. You can move through the sequence frame by frame, or you can play it in real time. The timeline can reference either frame numbers or elapsed seconds.

Display monitors

The monitor is (to make no pun) the most visible element in the computer system. It dominates setup, and choosing a monitor can be the most important decision you make when assembling your system. The wrong monitor can make a session at the computer as unpleasant as a visit to the dentist, and, because monitors can be very expensive, the wrong monitor can be a financial headache as well as a real one.

Choosing a display

The choice of a display is based on many factors, but the one that you will probably consider most is the price. A good monitor will cost a goodly price, but don't be too eager to buy a high-priced monitor. You might do better for less. The specifications are where you begin looking for a monitor. Specifications can be deceiving, but if you know what to look for, you can get a lot of information from specs. The usual specifications will list the diagonal measurement of the monitor, the dot pitch, resolutions supported, color capability, the horizontal scan rate, the vertical refresh rate, and whether the display is interlaced or noninterlaced.

The monitor should support all resolutions up to 1280 × 1024 in noninterlaced mode. Interlacing most often occurs at the higher resolutions (allowing the manufacturer to save money) but it also

makes the display flicker, and the actual resolution is diminished by interlacing.

The diagonal size of the monitor is fundamental. You will see many attractive prices for 14-inch monitors with excellent resolutions, dot pitches, refresh rates, and scan rates. Ignore them. The smallest acceptable diagonal measurement is fifteen inches. Almost all 15-inch displays have flat, square screens. Fourteen-inch displays have, almost universally, the ordinary rounded CRTs. The monitors compensate for the round CRT by restricting the actual display area, creating the familiar black border. The centering of the display tends to keep straight lines straight when they approach the edges of the display, but it results in the display area being reduced to maybe 12 inches or less. The flat, square CRT of the 15-inch monitor nearly eliminates distortion; the monitor does not have to shrink the display to compensate for induced curvature, and the display can be edge-to-edge. The 15-inch monitor serves at resolutions of 640×480 and 800×600. Higher resolutions require a larger monitor. Even though the 15-inch monitor may have excellent specs even at 1280×1024, it will not be of any use because the individual elements of the Windows display, icons, and text in particular, will be too small for extended use.

The next common monitor size is 17 inches. You will see some 16-inch monitors advertised, but these are older models with rounded CRTs. The 17-inch monitor is probably the best choice among monitors at this time. At the lower resolutions, it presents you with a magnified display that is comfortable for extended sessions. It offers a large viewing area, legible text, and comfortable icon sizes at higher resolutions. The flat, square design makes the 17-inch monitor the practical equivalent of a rounded 19-inch monitor.

Above 17 inches are the monster monitors, from 19 to 30 inches. In general, these monitors are still being made with the rounded CRT, but with other design changes to compensate for the roundness. The 19- and 21-inch monitors are meant to be used only at the higher resolutions; in VGA and SVGA, the enlarged items of the Windows display are gross and jagged.

Dot pitch, normally expressed as a decimal millimeter fraction, is a measure of fineness of the dots on the CRT. The smaller the number, the finer the pitch and the crisper the image that the monitor will produce. The color image is formed of converging dots from the three color guns; the smaller the dots that they can make, the closer that those dots can be to one another, and the sharper the perceived image that is made. Monitors in the 15- and 17-inch sizes will have a 0.28mm or smaller dot pitch. A 0.28mm pitch is as fine as you need for normal purposes. Larger monitors will have slightly coarser dot pitches, and 0.31mm in a 19-inch monitor is acceptable.

Sync rates can have a bearing on monitor selection. The horizontal and vertical sync rates must match the rates of the graphics adapter, or the picture will be scrambled or out of phase. Typically, the higher the resolution, the lower the sync rates. A good monitor will have a wide range of horizontal and vertical sync rates over a range of resolutions, although at the very highest resolution it is acceptable for a monitor to sync only at one rate. The greater the range of rates, the easier it is for the graphics adapter to provide its best possible display.

Other matters may influence your choice of a monitor, like the type and location of controls, an antiglare screen, compliance with MPRII electromagnetic emissions ratings, whether it conserves energy, or even its weight. You must take note of the input connectors. Most monitors use the standard DB-15 connector, but others accept BNC or RCA connections as well. TIGA boards usually need BNC connections, although there are cables that mate BNC to DB-15.

The monitors bundled with computer systems are usually in the package because the vendor can get a good deal on them, not because they are the best. If you are buying a computer and monitor at the same time, insist on the monitor of your choice, not the dealer's.

Panasonic PanaSync/Pro C1795E

The PanaSync/Pro C1795E is a 17-inch flat, square-screen, multiscanning monitor. It has automatic sensing and adjustment to horizontal frequencies between 30 kHz and 79 kHz, and vertical refresh rates between 50 Hz and 90 Hz. It has a bandwidth of 130

MHz. The dot pitch is 0.28mm. Its maximum resolution is 1280 × 1024 noninterlaced. It consumes 140 watts, is Energy Star compliant, and complies with the Swedish MPR radiation standards.

There are two D-SUB connectors, one for Macintosh and one for VGA cables, and the normal five BNC connectors (one each for red, green, blue, horizontal sync, and vertical sync). The green BNC input can also be used for those adapters that use sync on green, and the horizontal BNC input can be used for computers that produce a composite plus horizontal signal. You can select the method of connection or allow the monitor to sense and select the active connection.

Thus, you can use the monitor for a Macintosh and a PC-compatible, and when the monitor has been properly adjusted on each, it will adjust itself to the incoming video signals without user intervention. It would be nice if you could store different settings and could cycle through them manually, but there isn't really much reason for multiple settings for a particular computer system.

The real test of a monitor, of course, is in the using, and this monitor worked well. After about three months, it did develop a single pixel void, a failure of one screen phosphor. This is practically invisible. In the course of daily use, you would tend to forget that it is there. In every other respect, the monitor was flawless. It handled all the adapters that I used in three different computers without a single instance of asynchronization. When used with the PC TeleVISION board it became the best possible 17-inch television, with a better clarity than a normal television.

If you intend to buy a new 15-inch monitor, consider spending a few hundred dollars more to purchase a 17-inch monitor instead. The PanaSync/Pro C1795E would be a better-than-average choice.

Panasonic PanaSync/Pro C1991

This is a 19-inch monitor. It has a traditional curved CRT. The C1991 is a physically imposing monitor, weighing more than 68 pounds. It is twenty inches deep front-to-back, and 18.5 inches wide;

you will need a sturdy desk to support it. The tilt-and-swivel base is put to the test by the sheer bulk of the monitor.

This monitor is not as bright and sharp as the 17-inch Panasonic. The image was clear at all resolutions, but the display lacks the "snap" of the smaller monitor at the highest resolution. Contrast and brightness were only acceptable at 1280×1024. At 640×480 the display was very good, although the grossness of Windows at that resolution is unattractive. There was no flicker at any resolution or refresh rate. Despite the curvature of the CRT, there's room for a very large Windows workspace in 1280×1024 mode, with good edge definition.

The C1991 has the same two D-SUB connectors for VGA and Macintosh cabling and the standard five BNC connectors. There is also a switch that is used to select input voltage. This is used primarily when the monitor is being used concurrently with another display. The effect is to brighten the display (don't use it to artificially brighten the display when only the C1991 is in use).

I would recommend this monitor if the price were right; shop around. It is a reliable and well-behaved monitor, and generates surprisingly little heat. While it does not equal the C1795E, it holds its own.

LCD flat-panel displays

An alternative to the CRT display is the Color Liquid Crystal Display. LCDs have obvious advantages over CRTs: LCDs are lighter, take up less space, produce no distortion, consume less power, generate little heat, and emit no harmful EM radiation. Their disadvantages are equally numerous: LCDs cost more to manufacture than CRTs and are thus smaller, they are harder to see in bright light, their color is not as vibrant or subtle, and their response is slower than that of a CRT.

Color LCDs come in two varieties, passive-matrix and active-matrix. The active-matrix LCD is closer in display quality to the CRT than is the passive-matrix, but the passive-matrix display is about half as costly as the active-matrix. Passive-matrix LCDs also exhibit slower response times, fainter and fewer colors, and a pronounced tendency

toward ghosting. The slower response time shows up most frequently in the disappearance of the mouse pointer during rapid movement, a failing called submarining. Faint colors are caused by filters used to make the display, which absorb much of the light and have a narrow color capability. The ghosting is evident in vertical and horizontal lines, which tend to extend beyond the ends of the line across or up and down the screen.

Despite some problems, the color quality of active-matrix color LCDs approaches that of the CRT, making them highly desirable. It has been predicted that, eventually, all computer displays will be flat-panel technology of some type.

Printed output

PRINTING from Windows has never been simple, but it has been getting less arduous. You can now attach almost any printer to a Windows computer and achieve good results, both on the actual printed pages and in the ease of use.

Black-and-white printing

The standard high-resolution printer will print at 300 dots per inch. There are two broad types of such printers, laserprinters (page printers) and inkjet printers. While inkjet printers now can print at 600 × 300 dpi in black-and-white, laserprinter prices are now low enough to make the page printer preferable. Price aside, there are good reasons to prefer a page printer.

Although an inkjet is excellent for correspondence, it cannot equal the laserprinter's effective resolution and graphics capability. In large dark areas, the inkjet may start banding (laying down horizontal stripes, often separated by fine white lines). Also, the inkjet will saturate the paper with ink, and wet paper tends to buckle or pucker when it dries, leaving a rumpled page. The page printer is less likely to produce banding, and it does not rumple the paper. Blacker blacks and a wider range of grays are the two great advantages that a page printer has over inkjets.

The inkjet's resolution is fixed forever, while page printers can be modified for higher resolutions. The modification may be to add memory to accommodate the greater number of points to be calculated, or to add a controller board that uses dithering to simulate higher resolutions. You can even modify some laser engines by changing the crystals that control the line and dot frequency to increase the real resolution of the engine.

Another reason to prefer the page printer is PostScript. You need a PostScript printer, preferably one containing PostScript Level 2, which is faster and more efficient than Level 1. Hewlett-Packard compatibility is a given, but PostScript is a practical necessity for any high-level printing. Even if the final pages won't be printed by a print shop, you should have a PostScript printer to make use of its special characteristics. PostScript is not an option in inkjets unless you use an interpreter (such as Freedom of Press, from ColorAge) to preprocess the PostScript file. The result will not equal the page printer's, and is not recommended.

Speed is another factor. Look for eight pages per minute. There are many printers rated at four pages per minute, but they are generally so small that the paper gets curled as it passes through their print engines. An eight-page-per-minute printer will generally be larger and heavier, the pages it produces will be flat, and it will usually be able to handle heavier stock.

The PostScript printers that are consistently rated best are Apple LaserWriters. Apple is always introducing new models of LaserWriters; the benefit of Apple's planned obsolescence is that you can usually get a discontinued model for about half-price by waiting a few minutes. The 600-dpi models are especially good.

The other real alternative is the HP LaserJet. PostScript is now an option, and Hewlett-Packard makes uniformly excellent products.

Color printing

Although black-and-white choices are, well, black-and-white, color printing is a different matter. The color printer that you choose can come from any of four different types.

At the low end, suitable for proofing pages, are inkjet printers; Hewlett-Packards are the popular choice. They print excellent primary colors, and approximate tints and process color. While they can print at up to 600 × 300 dpi in black-and-white, the color resolution will be in the range of 70–120 dpi at best. Dithering

(placing color dots close together to simulate other colors) reduces resolution and slows down a printer; it must place dots at random to prevent banding. Patterned color will speed things up, but it will degrade color quality and make banding almost certain.

When printing text, inkjets switch to black ink. There is still the problem of puckering of the page due to wet ink; four inks can only worsen things. Because color printing does not use each color evenly, you may have to discard a cartridge when a single color is exhausted. The cost-per-page increases with the amount of color coverage, making the ultimate cost (purchase price and per-page cost) exceed that of a more expensive printer.

Inkjets work well with plain paper. Printing transparencies on an inkjet will take time, because the printer will use extra ink to ensure saturation. Transparencies from lower-cost printers like the DeskJets are uneven in quality, but transparencies printed on the more expensive HP inkjets are uniformly excellent. If your normal work is mostly text with small amounts of color, choose the inkjet.

Thermal color transfer is the next step up from inkjets. The thermal-transfer printer uses wax-coated ribbons, each as wide as the page, and a heating element to melt the wax and affix it to the page. The cost per page is constant regardless of coverage, as a ribbon can't be rewound; a page with little color uses as much ribbon as one with a lot of color. Therefore, while small color jobs may cost more when printed on a thermal-transfer machine as compared to an inkjet, large color jobs can cost less on the thermal printer.

The thermal-transfer printer's output beats an inkjet's in almost every instance. An exception is the poster-size output that some giant inkjets can produce; but usually the thermal printer will do a better job. As with inkjets, colors other than the primaries are simulated with dithering, and the resolution will not be the claimed 300 dpi.

Thermal printers are generally faster than inkjets. The available print area of most thermal printers is usually smaller than that for other types of printers; the necessary registration requires wide margins to grip. One bonus of thermal-wax printers is the ability to print iron-on T-shirt transfers.

The next step up is to the color laser printer. Color lasers use four toner cartridges, one for each primary and one for black. Colors are dithered. Speed is not impressive in most cases, due to the complexity of the printing process, but the output quality is excellent and the printers use plain paper. The colors are fixed and won't smudge. As you might expect, the cost per page will be higher than for thermal printers or inkjets

Dye-sublimation printers are the top of the line. They resemble thermal-transfer printers, using similar wax ribbons; but the thermal-transfer printer melts the color and deposits it on the paper, while the dye-sublimation printer vaporizes the color, then prints it almost like an inkjet. It prints true 300 dpi, laying down the color dots precisely to mix colors on the page. The result is photographic-quality printing on the desktop. While the quality is of the highest, the price is too.

Having mentioned resolution, and having noted the superiority of the dye-sublimation process, I need to point out that no graphic is ever printed at the actual maximum dpi of the printer. Graphics are printed as halftones composed of variable-sized dots at particular angles. Printing many colors accurately requires coarser screens than the maximum dpi or lpi that the printer can generate.

Dye-sublimation evades this limitation by calculating exact shades. All other printers are effectively limited to about 100 lpi at best. Remember, higher resolution translates into more possible screens, but not necessarily more or better colors.

Among the inkjet printers, the HP DeskJet 550C-560C series is fine for limited use and rough proofing. They are non-PostScript printers that start below $500, in either parallel/serial or LocalTalk versions. The HP DeskJet 1200C/PS is a PostScript Level 2 printer that dries the ink on the page. The graphics resolution is 300 dpi. It is fast (about 2 minutes per page), and the price is about $2,100 ($1,500 without PostScript) with LocalTalk and parallel interfaces. It uses four single color cartridges, so that there is no waste when one color has been expended. The HP PaintJet 300XL is a PostScript Level 2 printer that also dries its ink. It is slow and costs over $2,300, making it the least desirable of the inkjets. It does offer serial, parallel, and LocalTalk interfaces. All of the HP printers work with plain paper.

Canon Bubblejet 800 series print at 360 dpi, and prices have been reduced to about $1,500. They don't do PostScript, but their print quality is generally good. (An OEM version briefly produced by Apple, the Apple Color Printer, has all the same specifications and sells for about $500.) Bubblejets have SCSI and parallel interfaces, and use plain paper.

The IBM LexMark 4079 PS Jetprinter is a PostScript inkjet printer. Its resolution is 360 dpi. It uses the PhoenixPage PostScript emulation, a reliable Level 1-compatible interpreter. Its price is around $2,500, including serial, parallel, and LocalTalk interfaces. LexMark gets high marks from most reviewers, although this printer is fairly slow in its highest quality dithering mode.

The most interesting member of the thermal wax clan is certainly the Fargo Primera. Its price is extremely low for a printer in this category ($700), one of the reasons that it is so interesting. Another reason is the upgrade option that sells for $220, that converts the unit into a dye-sublimation printer, a total of less than $1,000 for technology usually costing about six times that price. The catch is that the resolution is 203 dpi (rather low for many purposes, especially text). The color is excellent, although the dithering tends to break down because of the lower resolution. It is a non-PostScript printer, requires special paper, and it has no control panel: all changes to the setup have to be made with jumper settings or software drivers. It has only a parallel interface.

The Seiko Personal ColorPoint PSE is a 300-dpi thermal-transfer, PostScript Level 1-compatible printer that uses PhoenixPage emulation and is HP compatible. Special paper is required, but it does print to a variety of sizes, such as postcard. You have the option of using a black ribbon, a four-color ribbon (CYMK), or a three-color ribbon (CYM). Both text and color graphics are considered excellent. The price is about $2,600, including serial, parallel, and LocalTalk interfaces. Ethernet and SCSI interfaces are optional.

The Calcomp ColorMaster Plus 6603 PS is a 300 dpi thermal-transfer printer. It uses the PhoenixPage emulation for Level 1 PostScript compatibility. Like the Seiko printer, you can install a black, 3-color, or 4-color ribbon. Unlike the Seiko, it offers no HP emulation. Print

quality of both text and graphics is good. The price is about $3,900, including parallel, serial, SCSI, and LocalTalk interfaces.

The Tektronix Phaser 200e is a 300 dpi-thermal wax transfer printer with Adobe PostScript Level 2 interpreter and HP emulation. It uses a three-color ribbon. It is the fastest printer in this category, printing at about 2 pages per minute. The output in both text and graphics is excellent. It includes parallel, serial, and LocalTalk interfaces. Perhaps the most important feature of this printer is the optional ColorCoat upgrade that makes the use of plain paper possible. The ColorCoat process adds a sealant to the paper before dispensing the finished page. The use of plain paper can pay for the upgrade, which costs about $200. The price of the printer is about $3,500. A faster version, the Phaser 200i, is also available. Cost per page is estimated at a not-unreasonable $0.60.

The QMS ColorScript 1000 is the first desktop color laser printer. It prints at about 2 pages per minute in color and 8 pages per minute in black-and-white. The printer uses plain paper and prints at 300 dpi. It is PostScript Level 2 compatible. This printer is meant to be used for high-volume color printing, where price and speed must be considered. It is a substitute for the print shop or service bureau. The price is under $13,000, about half the cost of other color lasers. The color and the text are both outstanding.

The ProofPositive dye-sublimation printer from SuperMatch (SuperMac) is the high end of color printers. This continuous-tone printer prints at 300 dpi and sells for about $10,500. The printer has no intelligence built in, relying on the computer to do all the work of creating the raster. The cost per page is high, about $5.00, but it replaces a fifty-dollar trip to the print shop for color proofs. Obviously, it is not to be used for high-volume printing, but it can be used to create one-of-a-kind projects.

You can, if you desire, use a color laser copier as your color printer. The ColorQ 2000 from ColorAge is a server that connects a PC network to a color copier, turning the copier into a network color printer. Xerox and Canon color copiers are supported. The system includes 64 MB of RAM, a PostScript Level 2-compatible interpreter, color calibration software, color correction software, and lists for about $30,000. This is

a corporate network item, supporting Novell, AppleTalk, Windows for Workgroups, and Windows NT network managers.

 # Plotters

Plotters are a fairly static technology. Typically the pen plotter is slow and clattering. The most innovative product for plotting is the PostScript inkjet plotter, ProTracer, from Pacific Data. It accepts "A," "B," and "C" size paper and contains the PhoenixPage emulator that has been used for several years in the Pacific Data PacificPage PostScript cartridges. The ProTracer is based on the 360 dpi Canon Bubblejet engine and is basically the wide-carriage model of that printer with PostScript compatibility. The advantage of this printer/plotter is that it can do double-duty, serving both the plotting and text output needs of a network or small office. Prices for the ProTracer range between $1,350 and $1,850, depending on memory configuration and optional HP plotter language compatibility.

Windowing environments

YOU should already be familiar with Windows. What you will find here is not a tutorial, but some information on the usage and limitations of Windows and competing systems.

⇨ Windows

Windows began as a response by Microsoft to the success of the Macintosh. While most computers were running 4–8 MHz 8-bit Intel 8088 or 8/16-bit 8086 CPU chips and 64K of RAM with the antiquated operating systems MS-DOS or PC-DOS, the Macintosh debuted with something completely different. The Macintosh was based on a true 16-bit microprocessor, the Motorola 68000. It used a revolutionary filing system that replaced typed commands with icons and menus activated by a mouse. The original Macs were not powerhouses, but they could do things that were impossible on fully loaded MS-DOS machines, and they quickly got bigger and faster.

Microsoft had already begun writing programs for the Macintosh before the Macs had shipped to dealers. Apple had absolute control of the Macintosh operating system. Microsoft, however, obtained a license from Apple to use certain elements of the operating system in Macintosh software. These became the core of Windows.

While Windows 3.1 has been almost universally accepted as the replacement for the character-driven OS, it is still only a shell to DOS. Windows 3.1 uses 16 bits while the 486 is a 32-bit CPU, and it doesn't account for networking. Microsoft has remedied some of those faults with Windows for Workgroups.

 # Windows for Workgroups

Windows 3.1.1 (Windows for Workgroups) incorporates all of Windows 3.1, plus enhancements like 32-bit file and disk access, and network management tools. The 32-bit access perceptibly increases hard drive operations. Unfortunately, the 32-bit modes are severely restricted by Microsoft's decision to support only some hardware and later OS versions. Only the Western Digital family of disk controllers is supported for 32-bit disk access. This eliminates all SCSI drive controllers, which would be much faster if 32-bit disk access were enabled. This is inexcusable. And, even worse, if you have MS-DOS 6.0 and are using DoubleSpace, you can't use 32-bit file access. You must install MS-DOS 6.2 to use both DoubleSpace and 32-bit file access.

Which points up the real problem that Windows has always had: the division between Windows and the underlying operating system. Windows is still a facade between the user and the real OS, and it can do nothing alone. Try erasing MS-DOS from your hard drive and leaving just Windows, and you will see how much of an operating system Windows 3.1 or 3.1.1 is: none at all. Windows for Workgroups 3.1.1 paves the way for integrating the user interface and operating system.

Windows 3.1.1, therefore, might also be viewed as a transitional product: it links the 16-bit single-user Windows with the 32-bit multiuser network Windows NT (New Technology). WFW makes the network active in Windows, allows limited 32-bit file access, allows sharing of network peripherals, and facilitates e-mail. If you are using Windows 3.1, you should upgrade to Windows for Workgroups. You don't have to be on a network to benefit from the upgrade; the 32-bit file access is reason enough to upgrade. The fax manager is another. Also, upgrade to the latest version of DOS while you're at it.

 # Windows NT

Windows NT is the future of Windows. It is a recognition that Windows cannot grow unless it becomes a full-fledged operating system supporting the 32-bit and 64-bit CPUs to come. It discards the concept of Windows as a mere user interface.

Windows NT is an operating system; it is also a monster, taking over 70 megabytes of disk space for installation. The installer will likely recommend a swap file of about 40 MB, for a total of over 110 MB of hard drive space just for the operating system. This amount of drive space seems disproportionately large. Apple's System 7, by comparison, requires about 2 megabytes for a robust installation and is fully 32 bits wide.

You had better have about 16 MB of RAM installed, although the system will run with 8 MB of memory. And that Windows accelerator you had been considering had better be from Matrox or Number Nine, because anything less will be a waste of money. An ordinary accelerator will not do. Windows NT is slow, a magnitude slower than any other version of Windows.

Why? One reason is that 32-bit apps do not exist. With the exception of a few programs like MicroStation, there is no 32-bit software in the marketplace. Ordinary 16-bit programs will run, but they will run like thoroughbreds in water, because they will be in the equivalent of a Windows emulation. To see the difference that native 32-bit programs have over 16-bit applications in the NT environment, you need only run some of the applets that are included in the NT package.

Windows NT is a true multitasking, multiprocessor operating system. You can regulate the degree to which resources are used by a program, giving priority to tasks as needed. You can also run more than one CPU at the same time through the same Windows environment, not in a network but in parallel. If software were available that could use the extra processing capacity, such a feature would be invaluable; but none exists.

Windows NT offers options during the process of installation that help to illustrate its split personality. It offers you the option of installing an OS Loader, in case that you desire to use other operating systems. This is an option you should exercise, since the Windows NT will not be your operating system of preference unless under compulsion. You will want this option if you decide to trash NT, as you cannot rid yourself of NT's modifications of the boot sequence of your system without totally erasing your hard drive.

NT's file format is the same way. The future, in Windows as in life, is a one way ticket. Once you have decided to convert to NT's native format, if you decide to remove NT from your drive, you will not be able to access those converted files from MS-DOS. That much is understandable. However, it is incomprehensible that you cannot, as part of some sort of rescue procedure, convert NT's filing system into a form compatible with MS-DOS. The lack of a de-installation procedure is unforgivable. Microsoft might want everyone to stay with NT, but they should not impose a penalty on those who don't. You can decide to change the filing system after installation—if you erase the hard disk.

Windows NT doesn't support DoubleSpace or any other compression scheme, making your computer's hard drive capacity especially important. You must have space to store your programs and files, not to mention space for virtual memory. The 540 MB limit on disk size with current IDE drive controllers runs up against the demands of NT very quickly. Fortunately, NT supports SCSI controllers, which have no limitations on drive size. SCSI is definitely a prerequisite for Windows NT.

Hardware support is rather uneven under NT. In the list of approved items that are compatible, some items (like motherboards) are well represented, while others (like SCSI CD-ROM drives) are not. All SCSI devices must support SCSI parity to be supported by NT. Many devices do not, and you must install a proprietary driver if a device is not supported by NT. The catch to that is that there are very few devices for which Windows NT drivers have been written. Corel SCSI, the SCSI user's *de facto* standard, does not support NT. The hardware compatibility list is being updated constantly, so it would be futile to make such a list available here. Check with Microsoft and the hardware vendor or manufacturer before plunging into the NT sea.

If you install Windows NT on a drive on which Windows is already resident, the installer will preserve your Windows settings and transport them into Windows NT. Your Windows installation will not be altered or deleted by installing NT. During installation you will be required to initialize the security functions of NT. The System Administrator (presumably you, in a single-computer setup) must establish passwords and users for granting system access. Don't forget the passwords, or you will be locked out of your own computer.

Considering the current lack of 32-bit software and the abysmally sluggish performance of 16-bit software under the Windows NT environment, you would be wise to wait until the Chicago revision has been released before committing yourself and your computer to Windows NT. If you must run Windows NT, then an advanced computer system with a PCI-based graphics accelerator is a necessity.

⇨ OS/2 and OS/2 for Windows

OS/2 is IBM's alternative to Microsoft's future of computing. It was originally jointly supported by Microsoft and IBM, but Microsoft, seeing that it was backing a product competitive to its own, chose to abandon the parallel track and concentrate on Windows NT. IBM, which had been licensing Windows code, was left with the basis of a good operating system but with only a small piece of the marketplace. OS/2 comes in two forms: The full version, which (like Windows NT) is an icon- and menu-based graphical operating system, and OS/2 for Windows, a shell for the Windows shell.

The full version of OS/2 is an advanced 32-bit environment. It supports preemptive multitasking and makes full use of the iconic graphical interface. It offers all of the features of Windows NT with more polish. It supports Adobe Type Manager and long filenames. It runs Windows applications by using Windows elements licensed from Microsoft; you need not own a copy of Windows to run Windows software in OS/2. In addition, there are OS/2 (fully 32-bit) versions of some important software. Because this license has not been extended, newer Windows features might not be supported.

OS/2 for Windows eliminates the necessity of IBM licensing Windows software technology. You must have previously installed Windows on your computer to be able to use OS/2 for Windows. OS/2 for Windows then uses the installed Windows software as the basis for running any Windows applications. In this way, IBM can graft Windows onto OS/2. You get the benefit of OS/2's memory management and superior iconic interface without having to buy entirely into the rather massive OS/2 environment.

Vector or object-oriented drawing programs

D RAWING and painting programs differ in the way the computer handles the image. Drawing programs use mathematical descriptors of the image: a square is an object, and its mathematical properties are the same wherever it may appear. Painting programs deal with individual pixels; a square does not exist for the program, only the pixels of which it is composed. This is a useful division, but it can be ambiguous. The two kinds of software have merged and mingled their features, each taking on characteristics of the other. The differences are becoming increasingly blurred.

Drawing programs offer varying degrees of fidelity to the mechanical drawing model, depending on their tool sets and their precision. At one end of the spectrum, adjacent to the painting programs, are the general illustration programs such as IntelliDraw from Aldus and GraphicWorks from Micrografx. At the other end of the spectrum are the design programs such as Deneba's Canvas for Windows, IDS MacDraft for Windows, CorelDraw 4.0, and Micrografx Designer 4.0.

Aldus IntelliDraw

IntelliDraw is an innovative, advanced program from Aldus Corporation that sets the standard in its class. It allows drawing, presentation, simple animation, and pseudo-3D object creation along with highly useful "smart" linkages that remove some of the tedium

from repetitive drawing. IntelliDraw supplies tools for the usual primitives and commands, but adds new tools like the Symmetrigon, Connectigon, and Distribution Frame. Even some of the old favorites, like Groups, are given new flexibility.

The intelligence in IntelliDraw is in the programmer's attention to the typical uses made of drawing programs in the average business office. As a result, charts are given much attention. Floor plans and space assignment are another area of concern in business, and their preparation is simplified. The program places great stress on the relationships of objects. Relations are assumed to have certain properties that will be maintained. The basic term used in the program is that of Connections.

Connections are considered elastic, and a whole set of elastic tools have been devised. Connectors, the simplest connection tool, are lines that attach objects that are physically removed from one another and define the relationship between those objects (as of hierarchy or precedence). The Connectors tool is versatile, its function depending

Figure 7-1

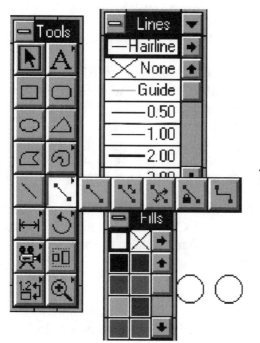

The Connectors tool's variants.

on the nature of the relationship it is supposed to represent. It is useful for flowcharts, in which the positions of objects may alter but the relations of those objects remain unaffected. In addition to being affected by their objects, Connectors can also affect the objects to which they are attached.

The concept of Connectors is based on the principle of "stickiness." Connectors adhere to certain points of other objects, usually the centers or corners. When deployed, they automatically attach to those points and stick to them singlemindedly: that singlemindedness is the limit of their intelligence. But there are other sticky objects with more "smarts."

Connectigons are polygons with "sticky" vertices. Their corners adhere to the corners of other objects below them. This property can be used to create simple pseudo-three-dimensional objects, for the sticky objects will alter their original shapes as the objects to which they are stuck are moved. This permits perspective in two-dimensional drawings and frees the user to arrange the elements of a drawing at the beginning, without wasting time making later changes. The individual components "know" their relative positions in the drawing and maintain them. Connectivity adds proportion to objects drawn with the Connectigon.

Connectigons stick to other objects at their vertices. A vertex is a point created by a mouse click at which two lines meet. Some objects, therefore, are not candidates for adherence by a Connectigon. Symmetrigons constitute one such class of objects.

Symmetrigons are special objects created by reflection of mouse motions and clicks across axes. One axis creates an object with bilateral symmetry. The Symmetrigon creates objects in which the only real vertices are defined by mouse clicks; the reflected part is made of virtual points extrapolated from the real ones. A Connectigon will stick only to the real points of the Symmetrigon; it will not adhere to the phantom points derived by the Symmetrigon tool.

The reduction of objects to virtual points occurs in the Symbol function of the program. Any object in an IntelliDraw document can become a Symbol. A Symbol is stored in a special area of the

Figure 7-2

Connectigons

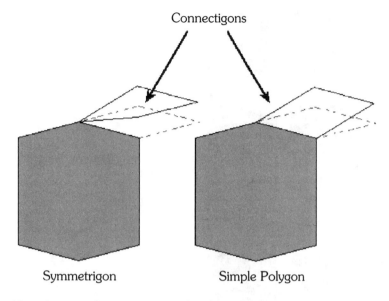

Symmetrigon   Simple Polygon

After changing Symmetrigon and Polygon in same manner.

Symmetrigon's cannot be changed proportionally.

document, where it acts as a master object that can be cloned. The clones have all of the properties of the master object but are actually virtual objects, mere images of the original. All of the clones can be changed at once by making the change to the Symbol.

Figure 7-3

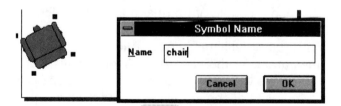

Any selected object can be made into a Symbol.

Another use of virtual objects occurs in the Tile feature of the program. Tiles have the property of filling any area with duplicates of themselves. This is intended for the creation of bar graphs, in which the bars are composed of units of the commodity being represented. As a bar is resized to reflect changes in number, the tiles are repeated

Figure 7-4

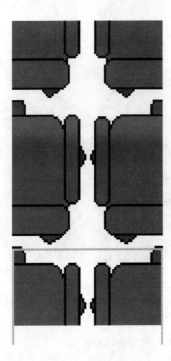

A Clipping Tile arrangement fills areas with partial tiles as needed.

or deleted as necessary to fill the area of the bar. Conversely, by using the dialogue box associated with a tiled bar, you can change the length of the bar by simply typing in a new numerical value.

Alignment is a major preoccupation in drawing, and IntelliDraw has all of the usual and a couple of unusual means by which objects can be aligned. The on-the-fly method of auto-alignment has existed in other programs, but IntelliDraw's Auto Align is rather better than most implementations of the idea. Auto Align signals that the aspect by which an object is being dragged, or the aspect that is being currently created, is in alignment with corresponding aspects of background objects by displaying vertical and/or horizontal lines that radiate from the mouse pointer.

There are several manners of alignment in IntelliDraw, some of them scattered across different menus or tools. Choosing the precise mode of alignment suitable to your particular purpose can be daunting and can have radical effects on subsequent actions.

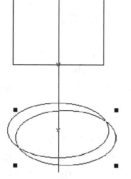

Figure 7-5

On-the-fly alignment of objects using the Auto Align feature of cursor.

While on the subject of invisible objects, IntelliDraw provides visible but nonprinting points that can be used as anchors for ordinary objects. These "nondimensional" points can be used to modify the behavior of objects by restricting or constraining the operation of actions on objects attached to them. They can also be used as registration marks.

A major feature unique to IntelliDraw is the ability to create so-called "smart" objects. The prime example of this form of intelligence is the

3902

Figure 7-6

Fixed Spacing tiles maintains spacing and changes tile numbers as needed to fill area.

combination of duplication with the Attach to Shape command. Attach to Shape forces a foreground object to adhere to the outline of a background object. The foreground object can then be moved only around the perimeter of that particular background object. While this is novel, it would have little practical effect except that the object also retains its directional and spatial relationships to the background object. Thus, if you wish to add duplicates of the foreground object arranged about the edge of the background object, the duplicates can be forced to place themselves equidistant from each other and with exact amounts of rotation about their own individual axes to preserve the aspect of the original object relative to the background object. The program's documentation uses a conference table and chairs as an example.

Figure 7-7

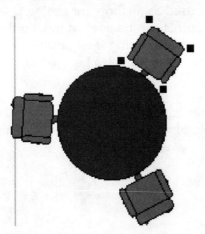

The chair is reduplicated, and copies are placed around the table in same relationship as original, spaced equidistant from other chairs.

Complex shapes in drawing programs are generally made by using one of the polygon tools. IntelliDraw offers another set of options for the easy construction of complex, irregular objects: the combination of primitives through addition, subtraction, or intersection of multiple objects. Thus, to create a given shape you could use either the traditional method, painstakingly editing the figure until the curves and angles were approximately correct, or you could combine by addition the objects shown to instantly create the finished object. Subtraction of objects removes from the background object that portion covered by the overlapping foreground figure. Intersection leaves only that portion of the background figure that had been overlapped. In each case, the resultant object takes on the fill and line attributes of the background object.

Figure 7-8

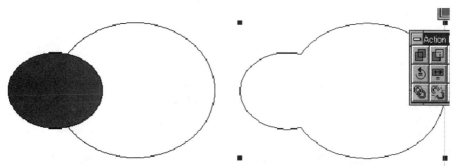

A complex object can be constructed quickly by Adding objects together to form a single object with a compound shape.

Figure 7-9

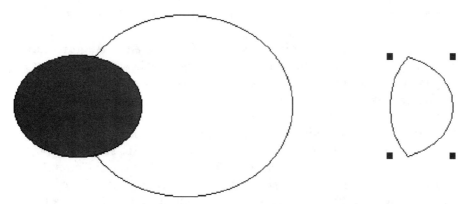

Intersection creates a new object from a shared area.

The Inset command might be mistaken as identical to Subtraction, for some drawing programs have a command of that name that will subtract the area of an overlaying object from the interior of a second object. IntelliDraw's Inset command is not a combinative form of subtraction. Instead, Inset creates in the interior of an object a smaller copy that has a shape identical to that of the object itself. The thickness of the wall that is created is set by the user in a dialogue box. It is possible to make a figure larger than the original by specifying a negative value. The amount of curve or angularity of the inset can also be varied.

IntelliDraw has some problems. Faced with a choice of using familiar terminology or inventing an entirely new nomenclature, the

Figure 7-10

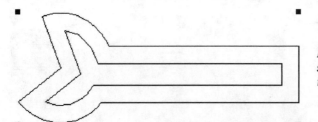

Inset duplicates the shape of an object inside the object itself.

programmers have decided to do a little of both, not always without confusion. The manuals generally make the differences clear, and Aldus has taken the additional step of including a training videotape as part of the documentation, but there is an unavoidable interval during which the user must acclimate to the new environment.

The program does not provide a visible grid. The Auto Align feature makes up for this to some extent, since objects will snap to the auto alignment guides during movement or creation of an object, but the visible grid would make some movements easier to calculate.

The program has autodimensioning, with three types of dimension lines available, but there is no way to know the exact size of an object as you are drawing it, nor is it possible to duplicate an object and move the copy an exact distance from the original. This lack of precision means that subsequent copies cannot be exactly placed. They can only be distributed after all duplicates have been created.

For those who care about such things, almost any command, feature, or tool can be selected by keyboard equivalents to mouse actions. There is also a floating palette of iconic Action Buttons that duplicates some of the program's commands such as those used to create Additive, Subtractive, or Intersecting groups. Other features are flip books, animation, and slide show capabilities.

Flip books are special forms of groups, in which all of the objects in the group are stacked sequentially in a pile, like a deck of cards. The top card only is visible, but there are handles on the sides of the piles that act as forward and reverse buttons, allowing the user to step through the pile one card at a time. Each of the objects in the pile can be modified separately from the others. Thus, the user can

accumulate different models of an item and then flip through them to create variations within a standardized drawing.

Animation is simplistic, provided as a means of showing some important actions of an object, such as in a cutaway drawing of a piston in a cylinder. The animation instructions are kept in a button object inserted into the drawing. Animation is accomplished by making changes to the drawing, recording the new state of the drawing with the animation command, making further changes, recording those, etc. Apple QuickTime animation support has been added to version 2.0.

Slide shows are IntelliDraw's presentation mode. It makes use of the program's ability to produce documents with more than one page. Slide shows step through the pages of a document. The program is well-suited to presentations; it can economically store a common background as a Symbol. With its limited animation, linkage of data to graphics, and flip books, very few users will need more than IntelliDraw provides for presentations.

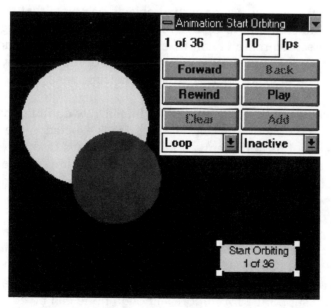

Figure 7-11

Animation is created in an Animation Button, which is controlled by settings in a panel.

Figure 7-12

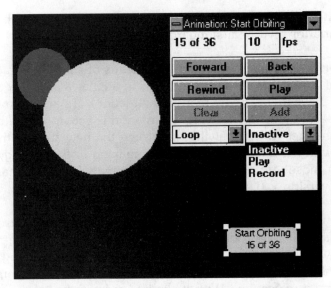

Animations are recorded and edited from the Edit Animation panel, accessed from the Object menu.

The principal shortcoming of the program is its slowness. So many of the program's actions are on virtual objects or points that they place an inordinate load on the CPU. Moving about in the drawing and waiting for screen redraws can be an ordeal. The program does have an Outline Only mode that speeds execution of redrawing by eliminating all fills, but speed is still a handicap.

As with all things, the best features of IntelliDraw do not come without a price. In the case of IntelliDraw, the price is exacted in the file compatibility of its documents. IntelliDraw can save or open documents only in its native format (.IDW). It can Import a fair number of file formats by placing the foreign file in an already open IntelliDraw document. Files saved by other vector-oriented programs in these formats can be imported and be separated into their component objects: AutoCAD .ADI and .DFX, Adobe Illustrator 88 and 1.1, Eikon Systems .ART, .CGM (Computer Graphics Metafile), Microsoft Excel Chart, Hewlett-Packard HPGL, Lotus .PIC, Micrografx (Draw, Designer, Charisma), and Macintosh PICT. Bit-mapped file formats are supported for import, although none can be edited at the pixel level: .TIF (or TIFF—Tagged Image File Format), .BMP (Windows

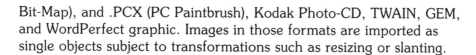
Bit-Map), and .PCX (PC Paintbrush), Kodak Photo-CD, TWAIN, GEM, and WordPerfect graphic. Images in those formats are imported as single objects subject to transformations such as resizing or slanting.

Text files in ASCII format can also be imported. Files can be exported in .EPS (Encapsulated PostScript), Windows Metafile, Illustrator, .DXF, CGM, and TIFF. Limited file compatibility had been the greatest handicap to the program's acceptance. That problem has been addressed. In addition to the formats already mentioned, all PageMaker 5.0 import/export filters can be used in IntelliDraw.

IntelliDraw is not perfect, but it is a major revision of the entire concept of a drawing program. Aldus aims it at the casual user rather than the power user, but it has enough precision to merit close examination for some of the more demanding tasks of the office.

Deneba's Canvas

Canvas, while new to Windows, is a seasoned product imported from the Macintosh environment. Its development history on that platform is extensive, and many of the features now common in drawing programs were innovations of previous Canvas releases.

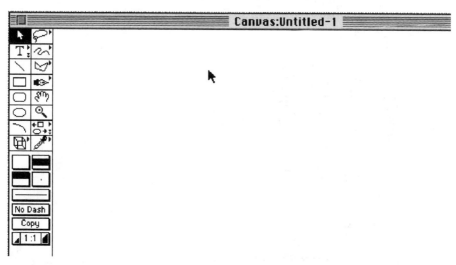

Figure 7-13

Deneba's Canvas presents a clean interface.

Canvas is a no-nonsense drawing program. It handles two-dimensional vector drawing and bitmap editing as well. Bitmaps can be placed in any layer of a Canvas document. They are treated as objects and can be scaled, rotated, cropped, and transformed in the same manner as other objects. But they can also be edited as bitmaps from within the program. Canvas has all of the requisite tools for precision two-dimensional drafting and professional level illustration, both for vector and for bitmap creation and editing.

Canvas's painting tools include the selection Marquee and the Lasso, both of which have multiple functions when used with modifier keys. The Lasso can select an entire contiguous color block by double-clicking its pointer within the color. You can expand a selection by depressing the control key as you drag the pointer, and you can subtract from the selection by using the control and option keys as you drag. Normally, the Lasso will exclude the background color from a selection, but the background can be included by using the option key alone as you drag the pointer.

Figure 7-14

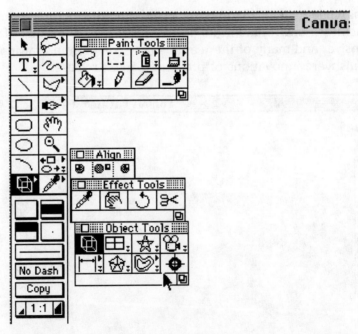

Simplicity of interface hides multiplicity of tools in tear-off menus or floating palettes.

The Paintbrush has preset shapes that vary from the simple square or dot to the fanciful. Any of the shapes can be changed by the user, or new brush heads can be created and saved. Likewise, the airbrush or Spray Can can have a number of different size and pattern sprays, some fading according to direction. The Spray Can responds to the speed of the mouse movement, laying down a lighter spray the faster the mouse tracks across the screen.

The area fill or Paint Bucket will fill an area, bounded or unbounded (it can leak through a pixel-wide gap) with either a solid or a pattern made of the current foreground color. Patterns can be chosen from the standard ones provided with the program or from those designed by the user. User-designed patterns can be saved and retrieved later for use in other drawings. Hatching is available for standard Canvas draw objects.

The Pencil tool is the simplest of the painting tools, a single-pixel freehand instrument. It draws a line in the current foreground color. It also can erase the current foreground color a pixel at a time.

Painting occurs in Paint Objects, rectangular Canvas Objects that float above the Canvas drawing surface. You create a Paint Object by simply selecting one of the paint tools and beginning to draw. Paint Objects can have differing resolutions, in standard resolutions ranging from 72 dpi to 300 dpi, with 72 dpi being the default.

The Eraser can be used to replace the foreground color with the background color, Erase, in the currently active Paint panel either in the whole panel, by double-clicking the Eraser tool, or selectively.

The drawing tool box in Canvas include all of the standard tools, squares/rectangles, circles/ovals (ellipses), irregular polygons, and regular polygons (Multigons), and some more unusual tools. There is a tool for parallel lines that can draw not only parallel straight lines, as for double walls in architectural drawings, but also polygonal figures with double walls and smooth polygons with double walls.

Of interest is the regular polygon tool. Besides the standard pentagons, hexagons, etc., you can draw skeletal polygons that consist only of radii, or the radii can be drawn within a regular

Figure 7-15

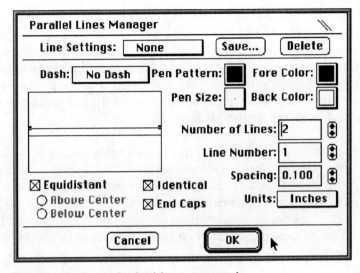

Parallel lines can be highly customized.

polygon, creating a spoked object. With the correct modifier key, you can also round the points of the spoked polygon to produce florettes, such as might be found in decorative millwork.

There is also a Star tool that will create stars of up to 100 points, either with or without radii. Smoothed stars have the look of orbital models of atoms. Rounded stars composed only of spikes or spokes can be combined with rounded multigons to produce flowerlike objects.

Among the other object tools is a cube tool, which can produce 2D cubes. With a modifier, it can draw perspective cubes, the front face of which is larger than its rear face.

Figure 7-16

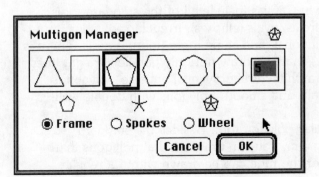

Multigons (regular polygons) can be designed with unusual options.

There is also a Grid tool, which creates a tabular or meshlike grid of boxes with a user specified number of rows and columns. And there is a Point tool, which is used to make nonprinting registration marks or invisible points that can be used to anchor other objects.

Most objects can be modified by selecting them and choosing Object Specs... from the Object menu. This command produces a dialogue box that contains information about the object. The dialogue allows you to alter most of the defining properties of the object, even its object class. This is one of the most useful features in any program.

Canvas has some tools that are missing from much more expensive programs. You can Join lines that are not in proximity to one another simply by selecting the lines and choosing Join from the Curves command submenu in the Object menu.

There is a Blend command that takes two objects, which can be of dissimilar type, shape, and color, and creates an intermediate series of objects that bear differing degrees of the properties of the two parent objects, in other words, morphing the candidate objects. The

Figure 7-17

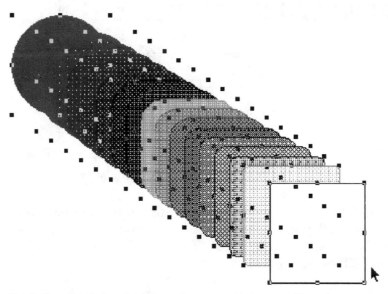

Both the shapes and colors of terminal objects affect the formation of intermediate objects in blend.

program produces steps of transformation according to the number you enter in the Blend dialogue. You can also set the type of color model to use for the color range.

Canvas has a Combine command with a submenu of variations. Using the Outline variation, you can combine two objects so that their perimeters are merged and they form a single solid object. The merged objects take on the color of the object that had been topmost. With the Add subcommand, two objects are effectively glued together where they overlap.

Canvas objects can be filled with color, patterns, crosshatching, or gradient fills. Crosshatching is available from the Object menu. Standard ANSI hatch patterns are supplied, and you can create and save your own patterns. Hatching can be applied over a color or gradient fill, or hatchings can be edited to a color.

Figure 7-18

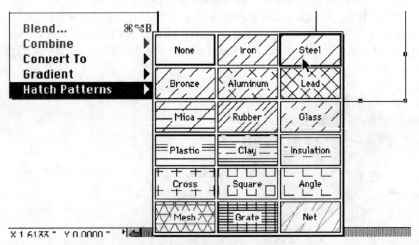

Standard and user defined Hatchings can be applied to objects.

Gradient fills, called fountains, can be applied to any draw object. Some prepared gradients are supplied, but you can create or alter gradients to suit your own needs. You can select the way that a gradient fill will be applied.

You can also specify starting and ending colors of the fountain, the rate of change between the end colors (constant or accelerating), and

Figure 7-19

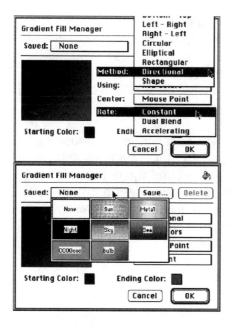

Some of the options for Fountains (graduated fills) are shown in this composite illustration.

whether the fountain is uni- or bidirectional. When choosing the color range, you can specify if the range will be from the color palette, from the RGB color mix, or by dithered pattern.

Text in Canvas is handled in the normal Windows manner, but with a few embellishments. Text can be entered simply by selecting the Text tool from the tool box, clicking on the drawing surface, and beginning to type, or you can outline a text object with the text tool

Figure 7-20

or you can outline a text object with the text tool, and then begin typing when the cursor appears at the top left corner of the box you outlined....The second method produces a text box within which text will behave as though being entered in a word processor, with words wrapping to the next line when the cursor reaches the edge of the bounding box.

Text can be made to flow around objects.

and then begin typing when the cursor appears at the top left corner of the box you outlined. The first method, click and type, creates unbounded and separate text lines that do not wrap. You must enter a carriage return to make the cursor begin a new line. The second method produces a text box within which text will behave as though being entered in a word processor, with wrapping.

The second method also permits text flow within the bounding box, allowing you to place the text object so that it overlaps another object in the drawing, and the text will flow around the object or the object's outline, as in a good word processor or page-design program. Text can also be made to fill an object's outline, and any overflow will spill out of the object and assume a normal appearance in the text object.

Figure 7-21

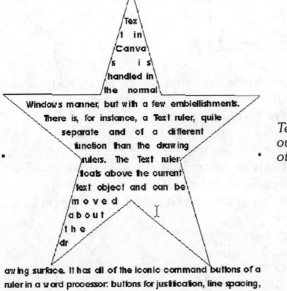

Text can also fill an object's outline and overflow into other objects.

There is a Spelling Check dictionary that can function interactively as you type (use only if you are a good typist who makes few typing errors) or to check text blocks or all text contained in a Canvas document. Text can be imported in common word processor formats.

Text can also be manipulated in other ways. Text can be automatically converted into grouped Bezier curves, which can then be ungrouped

and edited in the same ways that any other curves can be. Once converted, text becomes a draw object and can no longer be edited as text by the text tool. Text can also be bound to any arbitrary path. These are functions not found in many high-end drafting or CAD programs.

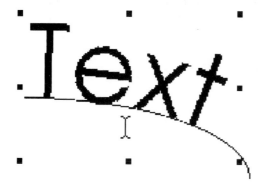

Figure 7-22

Text can also be bound to an arbitrary path and still be edited as text.

Dimensions in Canvas are invoked from the Object Tools multiplex icon. The dimension type can be selected from the Dimension tool's subpalette: radial, angular, and linear dimension modes are available. You can select the placement of arrows, the placement of the dimension text, the precision, tolerance, units, and scale, among other things. Dimensions can be chained, perpendicular, horizontal or vertical, aligned automatically to an object's sides, oblique, or with a center mark for curved objects.

Dimensions do not move with the objects, and they do not change if the object for which they were made changes in size. Dimensions are separate draw objects and are treated as such. A peculiarity arises from this fact: dimension objects are actually larger than the dimensions they display.

Besides Dimensions, Canvas also has a Show Size function that will display the dimensions of any object clicked on with the cursor or of any object as you draw it. When the Editing tool (pointer) is active, the Show Size function will measure distances as you drag the mouse or show the size of a selection area as you make a drag selection. The Show Size and Dimension measurements may not always agree when the object is very small, despite that their precisions are the same.

Figure 7-23

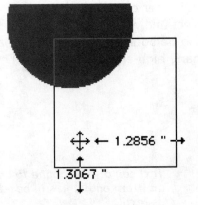

The Smart Mouse can Show Size of an object being dragged or drawn.

Figure 7-24

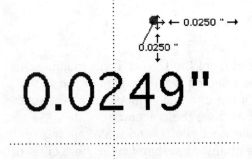

Dimension objects are separate from the objects they measure and are not themselves the size that they represent.

Rulers in Canvas are not static along the edges of the drawing surface: they can be torn off and placed anywhere on the drawing to allow direct measurement of objects. As in any good drawing program, the origin or zero point can be reset.

Canvas was one of the first programs to invest the cursor with "smart" functions, the ability to detect and display contextual information. The cursor, called Smart Mouse, changes as it nears objects to exhibit what properties are available to act as guides to drawing new objects or to position dragged objects. It also generates dotted lines to show the relationship of the cursor to more distant objects, such as its alignment to edges or vertices.

Constraints are set in the Smart Mouse Manager, a dialogue that is called from the Managers menu command. In the Smart Mouse

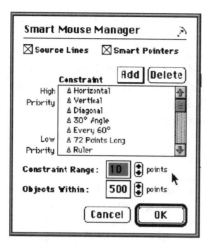

Figure 7-25

Smart Mouse features are enabled/disabled in panel.

Manager, the user can add or delete constraints, and set the parameters that will activate a constraint. Some constraints, such as Length and Object Fraction, can have more than one value active at one time. Therefore, you can set the Smart Mouse to look for both quarter fractions and tenth fractions of an object's side.

Among other conveniences offered by Canvas are a magnification pop-up in the tool box that allows you to zoom up and down, up to a 32:1 factor in either direction. There is also a magnifying glass that can become a reducing glass with a modifier key.

There is an eyedropper tool to pick up color. There is a free rotation tool, as well as Rotation commands that will rotate an object in 15° increments or to a user-specified degree. There is an Auto Trace tool that can be used to create draw objects from bitmaps. Objects can be skewed, can have 1- or 2-point perspective applied, can be stretched or distorted, and can be flipped horizontally, vertically, or both. You can also scale objects and crop images.

There is an align command, available either from a menu or the tool box that simply and logically permits you to align objects by their left or right sides, top or bottom edges, centers, either vertically or horizontally to each other or to the page. In contrast to the alignment command in other programs, Canvas's alignment functions excellently. Canvas can create and save color prepress

separations, with complete control given to the user to set up the separation specifications.

Canvas supports CGM (Computer Graphics Metafile), DXF (Drawing Exchange Format), IGES (Initial Graphics Exchange Standard), EPSF (Encapsulated PostScript Format), Illustrator (PostScript), TIFF (Tagged Image File Format), PICT (Apple Macintosh), and Deneba's own Canvas and UltraPaint formats. Canvas supports the PANTONE color matching system.

Canvas is an exceptionally versatile and yet precise illustrating and drafting program. It can take the place of both a bitmap editor and a drawing program, and can double as a page layout program. Canvas is an excellent value, but more importantly, it is an excellent performer.

CorelDRAW

CorelDRAW is a package of programs that work interactively. The CorelDRAW package consists of CorelDRAW, CorelChart, CorelShow, CorelPhoto-Paint, CorelMove (an animation program), CorelTrace, and CorelMOSAIC (an album application to manage libraries of images).

CorelDRAW resembles Canvas or Windows Draw in the simplicity of its user interface. CorelDRAW surely has the simplest user interface going. There are no tools for multigons, none for parallel lines, and none for any primitives except the curve, the oval, and the rectangle. So how do you draw a triangle or a pentagon or even a straight line? You draw everything the old-fashioned way: from scratch. It is basic, but it is the most natural and most responsive way to draw. CorelDRAW is an illustrator's, rather than a draftsman's, drawing program.

How do you draw a straight line in a program that supports only curves? Quite well, actually. You do not, as in other programs, click and hold the mouse button as you draw out the line. Instead, you click the mouse button on the point where you want the line to begin, point to the place where you want the line to end, and click again.

Figure 7-26

Managers provide access to settings and controls of many of Canvas' tools and functions.

There is no arc tool. Every serious drawing program must have an arc tool, mustn't it? Well, a circle is one big arc, and if you cut a circle you have smaller arcs. And that is what you do in CorelDRAW to make arcs, cut a circle or ellipse. Using the Ctrl Key constrains the angle to 15° increments. (Using the Ctrl Key

Figure 7-27

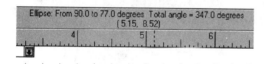

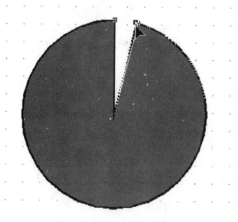

CorelDRAW's uncluttered user interface is refreshing.

with any of the drawing tools imposes a constraint on the action. Using the Shift Key draws the object from its center.) The default can be changed in Preferences.

There is a Grid, and the Snap to Grid feature can be active even if the Grid is not visible, which is as it should be. Snap also has a setting for Objects. Objects have snap points to which you can Snap a dragged object. When the Snap to Objects option has been selected, it takes priority over the Grid and Guidelines options if they are also active.

CorelDRAW documents can have up to 999 pages and the number of layers is limited only by memory. Objects can be brought to Front, pushed to Back, shifted one order up or down, and the order of selected objects can be Reversed. Undo is configured in the Preferences. The number of levels of Undo is limited by memory.

Zooming is accomplished by means of the magnifying glasses or with F Keys. There is a zoom to All Objects command that allows you to find stray objects, even if they are away from the drawing area, and there is a zoom to page.

All of the popular Transformations for objects are available at the top of the Effects menu: Rotate, Skew, Stretch, Mirror, and Perspective are there. All transformations can be cleared at once with the bottom command in the menu.

All of these things are more or less standard across all drawing programs. Some programs have improved user interfaces by which these processes can be used, but the processes themselves are almost always the same in their results. It is at this point of conventionality that CorelDRAW takes a sudden departure and goes off on its own.

CorelDRAW has a unique addition to the graphical user interface, the Roll-Up. The Roll-Up is a control panel, dialogue box, or palette that pops up to set the operating parameters for and to activate some or other feature in CorelDRAW. The uniqueness is in their design. While other dialogue boxes can be made to drop down or pop-up or fly-out, Roll-Ups are like venetian blinds or window shades that can be pulled down for use and then rolled up into their title bars and placed discreetly out of the way on the screen.

Figure 7-28

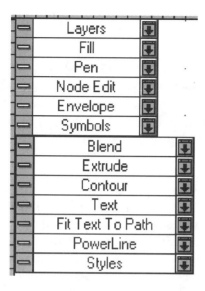

Roll-Ups are CorelDRAW's contribution to interface design.

There are three kinds of text in CorelDRAW: Artistic text, Paragraph text, and Symbols. Artistic text is entered in lines of 250 characters or less, without word wrap. Artistic text can be extruded, converted to curves, warped, and have contours or PowerLines applied. It is still

Figure 7-29

Some of the effects that can be wrought on Artistic Text, top to bottom, Extruded, Warped, and Fitted to a Path.

text, even after any of these changes have been made, and can be edited and changed by the Text Roll-Up.

Symbols are graphical objects that have TrueType attributes. CorelDRAW provides several thousand of these symbols that can be used as ready-made draw objects. You can also create your own symbols and add them to the libraries. Within the capabilities of the display or printer, Symbols can be scaled to any size without loss of detail or smoothness.

CorelDRAW has a warping feature. Warping is based on the concept of Envelopes, special containers that are applied to objects. They can be reshaped, and thus provide a new shape for the objects they contain. The advantage to this system is that, if the envelope is removed, the object it contained emerges in its original condition. There are some preset envelope forms, or you can use a generic rectangular envelope on any object. You can derive envelopes from many, although not all, types of objects in CorelDRAW. Symbols are the only types of objects that can serve as templates for custom envelopes for paragraph text.

Blending is another familiar concept from other drawing programs. Two objects are designated as beginning and ending points for the creation of a series of intermediate objects. The object is to create the appearance of a time-lapse metamorphosis of one object into another; some of the hybrids produced can be interesting in and of themselves. You can control every aspect of the Blending process via Roll-Up.

Figure 7-30

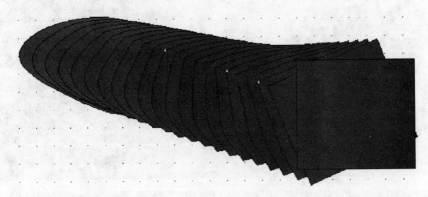

A CorelDRAW blend operation's result, oval to square with rotation.

Another form of blend, Contour, uses one object and creates from it a series of concentric replicas, each with the same outline as the original but at a different size. The new objects can be created inward or outward. You can specify the outline color and the fill of the last object formed, and the transitional objects will blend the outline and fill colors from the original to the last object. The effect is similar to that seen in contour mapping, and can also be used to create a 3D appearance.

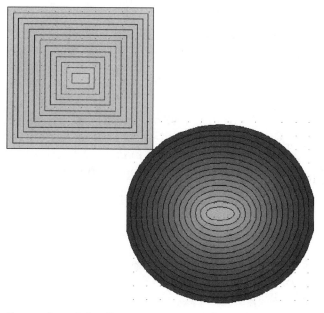

Figure 7-31

Examples of the Contour command.

While on the subject of three dimensions, CorelDRAW offers one type of 3D object creation, Extrusion. Artistic text is a prime subject for extrusion. You can make the rear and front faces the same size, or vary the sizes and create perspective. There is no rotational 3D object view creation.

The most interesting and only unique Roll-Up is the one that controls the PowerLines. With PowerLines, CorelDRAW can continuously vary the width of lines as they are drawn. This is a feature so unusual that it alone makes CorelDRAW worth the price. PowerLines can be made to react to a pressure-sensitive stylus and graphic tablet.

Figure 7-32

PowerLines Roll-Up contains preset PowerLine styles and PowerLine options to make new styles.

The PowerLines Roll-Up displays the list of currently programmed lines, and enables the user to create new custom variants that can be saved and reused. You can adjust the maximum width or thickness of the line, the shape of the nib and its angle, and the flow rate of the "ink." With the pressure-sensitive nib, you can modify the response of the point to speed or pressure of the stroke.

Figure 7-33

Calligraphic script, as in a signature, is easy to produce using PowerLines and a graphic tablet with pressure-sensitive stylus.

The basic concept of the PowerLine is that it will change over its length. The speed of the stroke and the sharpness of any curves in the stroke can affect the look of the line. With the pressure-sensitive stylus, you can turn off all the defining attributes and allow the stylus to do all of the work, making the line wider or thinner, introducing skips, and showing the effects of speed and pressure on the digitizing tablet. Any PowerLine can be edited after being drawn.

PowerLines are, at bottom, not lines at all, but rather draw objects that have been created with a single stroke. They are a series of draw objects that have been grouped and bound to a path. The default PowerLine has no fill. PowerLines, unlike those that emit ELF, should be in great demand everywhere. Of course, there is a down side.

The down side with PowerLines is the number of nodes that they produce when drawn. If you use the Separate command on PowerLines, they can be Ungrouped and edited with the Node Editor. Node editing of PowerLines can be a sobering experience, since even a short section of a PowerLine can have a hundred or more nodes. The Node Editor's Auto-Reduce command has some effect in simplifying the curves, but there will still be a lot of manual labor involved in deleting nodes.

CorelDRAW can fit text to a path; the process is painless. Text can be placed on either side of the path, the distance from the path adjusted, the baseline adjusted, justification arranged, and (once the transformation has been accomplished) the path can be deleted, leaving the bound text behind. There are things that can be done with bound text in CorelDRAW that cannot be done in other programs. You can move the text along the path, character by character, word by word, or all at once. You can move the text away from the path. All of this can happen while the text is still bound.

Figure 7-34

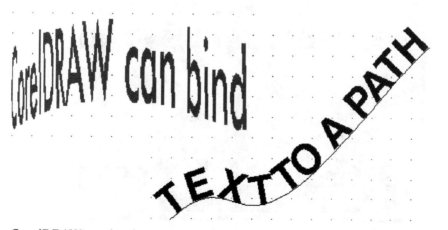

CorelDRAW can bind text to an arbitrary path with ease and with many options to adjust the final result.

Fills in CorelDRAW have their own Roll-Up. Besides the usual solid and pattern fills, there are gradients (linear, radial, and conical) and fractal bitmaps. Conical gradients are unusual in that they combine elements of radial and linear fountains to produce a pronounced 3D effect, either of a prominence or of a depression, depending on their coloring and their orientation. There are color and monochrome bitmap patterns. CorelDRAW has a fair number of fractal fills built-in and ready to apply. The names are the most enigmatic thing about fractal fills, with some tending to the simply off-the-wall. You have access to PostScript patterns in addition to the monochrome and color bitmaps in the Roll-Up. CorelDRAW supports PANTONE and Trumatch color calibrations.

Figure 7-35

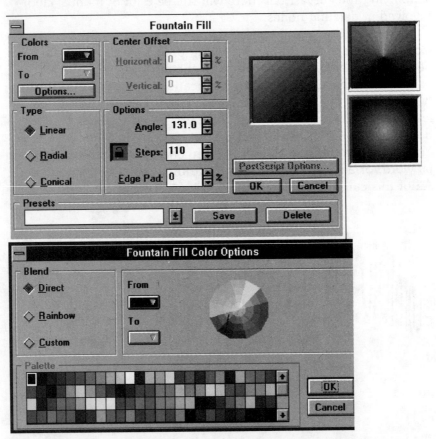

Fountains can be linear, conical, or radial. Angle, Steps, Color, and Color range direction in gradient can be controlled.

Figure 7-36

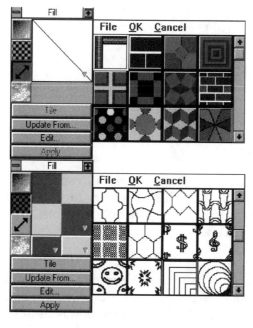

Both color (top) and monochrome (bottom) patterns are available.

An unexpected feature of CorelDRAW is the ability to compile object data into a database format for export. Object data can be used to assemble price lists or component lists, complete with attached specifications. This is the sort of feature that one might expect to find in only a precision drafting program, not one with its emphasis on illustrative creativity.

An idea that has caught on in Aldus's IntelliDraw is that of the Clone. A clone is a kind of duplicate of an object, but it retains a link to the master object from which it was cloned. If you change the fill of the original, all of its clones will take on that same fill. If you delete the master object, the clones vanish as well. You can break the connection of a clone to its creator object by altering the clone's attributes.

CorelDRAW supports Combinations and Welded Objects. Combinations are used to create objects that must have vacant and transparent areas within their perimeters. This allows background objects to show through the apertures. Welds are another kind of group. Welded objects assume a single outline path, and space between objects becomes filled. Welds can extend to objects across layers.

Figure 7-37

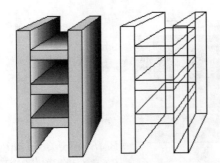

CorelDRAW's weld function.

Printing from CorelDRAW has needed improvement, especially with PostScript devices. The limits of most PostScript printers seem to be easily exceeded by very little text and very few object points. Corel has included hundreds of TrueType fonts, but that seems a poor attempt at a fix, and the fonts take up space (22 MB).

Corel has declared its corporate intention to issue new versions of its major products annually in May. Version 5.0 of CorelDRAW will have been on the market for several months by the time you read this review of Version 4. Because of this ambitious schedule and the large number of bugs discovered in Version 4.0, there are fewer new features in Version 5.0 than in 4.0. This will give the programmers the chance to make the code that ships much more reliable. CorelDRAW 5.0 is expected to include transparent colors, a Paste Inside function such as found in FreeHand, and better text and font management, making a good product even better.

Micrografx Designer

Designer is the name of a suite of programs from Micrografx, including the eponymous Designer drawing/illustration program, PhotoMagic, a bitmap image editing program, and SmartSep, a color separation pre-press utility. They make an integrated group that can be invoked from within their constituent members.

Designer is a high-end product. It has a versatile and very ambitious toolset. The program is attractively constructed and uses the Windows iconic command structure. The user interface is obviously the product of considerable thought. The tools and commands, unfortunately, are rather taxing to master.

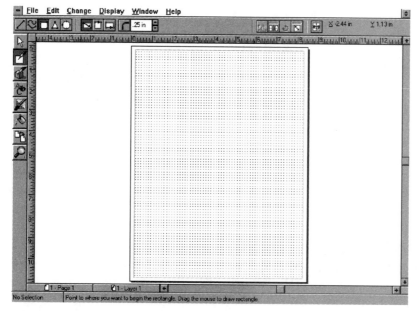

Micrografx Designer default workspace.

Figure 7-38

While Designer lives up to its billing on the box cover as "Powerful" and "Precise," it is definitely not "Easy." It is not the sort of program that one can use straight out of the box. Unlike many Windows programs, the manual is an absolute necessity with Designer. There does not appear to be a summary of all the tools and their functions; one must rely on the Hint line and Help for that, but neither is particularly lucid. The uses of most options and the order in which they must be invoked are what can only be called counter-intuitive.

The pointer, the topmost tool in the toolset, is called the editing tool. In most drawing programs, the function of the pointer is simple: it is used to make an object active and to manipulate the object in various ways. In Designer, it has a similar set of functions assigned to it, but, unlike other programs where the function is determined from a menu choice, the Editing tool must be toggled through its functions by clicking on the appropriate buttons in the ribbon above the drawing area. Thus, depending on the latest use of the options in the ribbon, the pointer may not be a pointer at all. The pointer as pointer is selected only when the redundant pointer button in the ribbon has also been clicked.

Figure 7-39

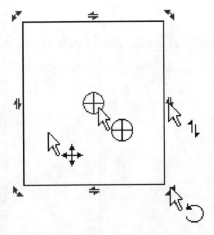

Cursor signifies its changing powers with small icons, clockwise from center, Shift Center of Rotation, Skew, Rotate, Move.

When the pointer is only a pointer, it can resize or move. When the second button in the ribbon has been clicked, the pointer can rotate or skew an object (symbol), depending on where the pointer attacks a symbol. The pointer signals these changes in function as it moves across the symbol's active points by acquiring supplementary iconic characteristics. Passing over the symbol's corners, the pointer adds a circular arrow to itself, indicating the potential to rotate the object. At the center points of the sides, it takes on the skew icon of opposed half-arrows.

Figure 7-40

Warp Button of Editing Pointer tool enables yet other buttons (right of center).

Clicking on a button can enable other buttons in the ribbon. The third button in the ribbon is the Warp button. When it has been clicked on, other tool buttons replace the property/name slot that normally occupies the right-hand area of the ribbon. The user can then select the method of warping. A Warp envelope is placed around the selected object when the warp method is selected.

The line warp causes an object to be distorted in a linear fashion, with straight lines remaining straight. The curved warp allows you to bend the symbol. Bezier warping places control points and handles at the user's disposal to finely control the warping of the symbol. If you

desire, the envelope can be replaced with a new one that has not been warped. The symbol within the envelope retains the impression of the first envelope.

Bezier warping permits the changing of a line to a curve, or of an angle to a cusp. By making such changes, you can further alter the shape of the envelope by dragging anchor points and control points. It is another annoying fact that warping cannot be undone until the editing tool pointer has been selected again from the ribbon. In order to undo a warping, and then continue with other warp effects, one has to proceed through the effect, return to the edit mode, undo the warp effect, then start over again by clicking the warp button.

This brings us to the main complaint against the program's execution, which is that too many effects are compound operations involving too many buttons in too precise an order. For example, a very desirable effect in a drawing program is the ability to bind text to a curve or arbitrary path. Designer provides this capability, but with needless complexity. In most programs where this feature exists, the procedure is simple: select the text to be operated on and shift-click to select the path to which it is to be bound, and then choose Bind To Path from a menu. There is a simple logical progression to the effect that anyone, even someone unfamiliar with the program, can execute.

To bind text to a path in Designer, however, one must first select the path or the text (one or the other, not both), then chose Align

Figure 7-41

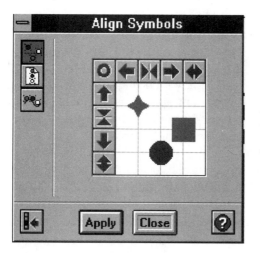

Binding text to a path is not straightforward. Select path. Use of Align command is not obvious, but select anyway.

89

(NOT Bind Text to Path) from the Change menu. This produces a dialogue box. There are no prompts. After one chooses the correct button, the third on the left, (which, by the way, does not show text being aligned to a path but rather objects), the display in the dialogue changes. There is nothing to indicate what should be done next, but it turns out to be a long and complex string of operations conducted without the help of prompts, informative icons, or helpful command names.

Sadly, this is typical of too much of the program: power, but at a price exacted in the form of a long learning curve. Virtually every function must be complicated by a plethora of options that are only available through a seemingly bottomless valise of panels, menus, and unexplicit icons that would confound even Mary Poppins. Surely most of these options could be combined into one panel for each tool?

Figure 7-42

Result. Simplify! cried Henry David Thoreau.

Moving down the tool set, the second icon is the drawing tool. Clicking the button changes the ribbon above the drawing area. You are presented with a line, two wavy lines (compound line), three simple polygons (rectangle, polygon, ellipse), and then a subset of the currently selected drawing mode. The selected tool, which ought to have a default action, is inoperative until one of these sub-options is also selected. (With many tools, the most recently used option is the default.) The line tool will not draw a line until another line tool is chosen.

The Simple Line tool (an oxymoron, surely) allows you, to quote the manual, to draw "single, parallel, and perpendicular lines, as well as arcs and parabolic lines." Another useful, indeed necessary, feature for a high-end drawing program is the Dimension line, which provides

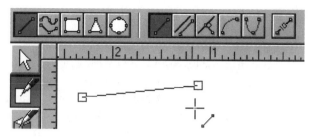

Figure 7-43

First option is "Simple Line" (Hah!) Its options are shown at top right. First is line. Cursor acquires new icon.

an easy-to-use way of adding measurements to figures. This feature is not as easy to use as in IntelliDraw, but it is rather more simple to activate than most other options.

Compound lines are multijointed. They can consist of curves, angled segments, B-splines, Beziers, and freehand lines. Some of the features of compound lines and simple lines appear to be redundant, such as the ability to make line segments continuous. One can achieve similar, if not identical, results with several methods, which makes one wonder if the same subroutines are being used.

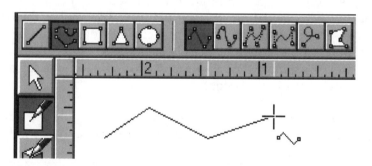

Figure 7-44

Compound Line's first option is straight line with angular joints.

The Bezier method is the most flexible mode of controlled drawing. The manual warns that you must let the program catch up to you when drawing Beziers. A quick mouse click can prematurely terminate the Bezier curve being drawn, resulting in a straight line. Freehand drawing and irregular polygons are the last of the

compound line options. Again, too rapid drawing will result in incomplete figures.

The rectangular drawing tool would more properly be called the parallelogram tool; one of its options is not constrained to creating figures with perpendicular edges. It has four options: drawing by specifying height and width, drawing on a diagonal, drawing squares by drawing one side, and drawing with rounded corners.

The Polygon tool draws regular polygons with 3 or more sides (99 is the upper limit). The tool can create all the ordinary multisided figures and, with the number of sides set to the larger numbers and the mode to stars, can be used to draw toothed gears. Polygons can be drawn from the center out.

The Elliptical tool is used to draw circles, ellipses, arcs, or pie segments. Circles can be drawn by dragging for the diameter or by dragging and clicking at three points. Ellipses can be drawn by dragging a diagonal or by dragging the height and width. Ellipses can thus be rotated from the horizontal or vertical axes.

Ellipses can be changed into pie sections. This is a useful but flawed function, since the ellipse selected to be turned into pie sections disappears when clicked on with the pie tool. This makes the drawing of precise sections difficult. An existing circle or ellipse can be converted into a pie wedge by double-clicking on it with the mouse, then moving the handle that appears of its circumference to form the wedge. This creates one wedge.

The Text tool, which was mentioned earlier, is probably the most flexible and useful to be found in drawing programs. Text can be

Figure 7-45

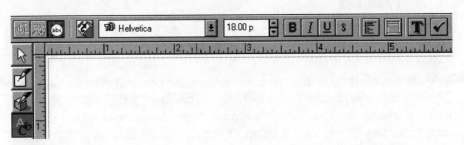

Skipping, for the moment, the 3D tool, the Text tool comes next.

entered either freeform or in blocks. Block text can be placed in symbols and will fill them, conforming to their shapes. Block text can also be made to flow around symbols, as in any page makeup program or most WYSIWYG word processors.

All the familiar text formatting options from word processors are available. Recently used type fonts can be recalled from a special menu activated by a button in the ribbon, next to the font window. There is a spelling correction function, which may or may not be useful in a drawing program. Text need not consist entirely of alphanumeric characters. Designer allows you to embed graphic symbols in a text block, and thereafter the application of formatting commands will affect the text and the graphic alike.

Designer supports special text effects, such as drop caps, as well as the application of graphic effects to text. Text can be converted into curves and the individual characters reshaped as might any other symbols. The number of points created can be too large to be comfortably managed except in high magnification.

Text can be made to flow from one container to another on the same page, but text cannot flow from one page to the next, a serious

Figure 7-46

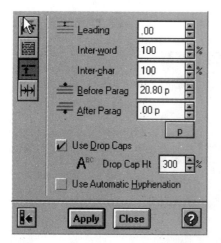

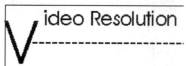

Drop Caps are built into Designer's text capabilities.

shortcoming in a program with Designer's pretensions to page makeup status. Text containers can be subjected to the same warping and reshaping as can other symbols. The text will adjust automatically to fill the new shape of its container.

It must also be mentioned that the handling of text in Designer is unduly slow. Importing a text file into a container or as freeform text can be a tedious business. Additionally, text paragraphs imported as freeform text are entered as single lines with infinite margins, a throwback to the old manner of DOS text editors. After importing, of course, the text margins can be set. Still, a preset should be available for margins, even in freeform.

The bitmap tool is really a gateway to whatever bitmap (i.e., Paint) program you have designated to be linked with Designer. The default is the PhotoMagic program supplied with Designer. Another function of the bitmap tool is to automatically trace bitmaps that have been imported into a document, thereby converting them to vector graphics.

The amount of detail and the number of points created in the vector trace are determined by the tightness of the trace to the bitmap. A finer

Figure 7-47

Paint Tool Button

Paint objects must be made or modified in a linked image editor. Designer has no bitmap editing capabilities, unlike Canvas.

quality will increase the amount of detail traced, but it will also increase the number of points, which can lead to the creation of an object with points so numerous that they cannot be discriminated. A fine trace can also take an inordinately long time to complete. A coarse setting will yield a more manageable trace. The favoring of lines or curves in the trace segments also influences how manageable the final object will be. If there were controls that allowed the user to set the tightness of the trace more precisely, the trace function of Designer would be more useful. In many instances, it is easier to trace a bitmap manually than to rely on the autotrace function and to edit the result.

The Paint Bucket icon is called, for some unfathomable reason, the Style Tool. Clicking on it changes the ribbon's contents to include those attributes of a symbol that are most basic: color and thickness of lines, solid or broken lines, line ends, and type of interior fill.

Figure 7-48

As expected, Style tool affects object fills, but also controls line types, line weights, line ends, line fills, etc.

The line ends can be virtually any shape or size. Designer provides a panel of installed options, but the user can add to them at will. Any graphic element can be pasted into the panel to form a new end type. Thus, besides the typical square ends, lines can have rounded ends, arrow ends, bracket ends, dotted ends, triangular ends, etc. And one end can be different from the other. There is an equally varied choice for line styles, from solid through dashed to invisible.

The line weight has more than just thickness to distinguish it. Lines can be hairline, weighted, and/or calligraphic. Calligraphic lines can be drawn with an angular nib, which is set in the Weight panel. Specifying a different width and height and a pen angle allows you to create lines that vary their thickness according to the direction in which they are drawn. Applying calligraphic settings to a polygon produces exotic symbols, the sides and corners of which have distinct thicknesses and angles.

Lines can have numerous "fills" besides the ordinary solid. They can have gradients, hatchings, images, or symbols. The last two are

Figure 7-49

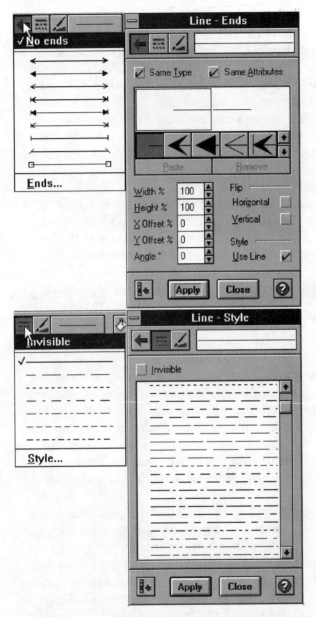

Line ends menu (top) contains programmed and user-defined line terminations. Line styles menu (bottom) contains a variety of dashed lines in addition to solid and invisible.

interesting in that the image is selected from a group of "textures," bitmaps that resemble the surfaces of such natural substances as brick, stone, rattan, or mosaic tiles. There are also ordinary paint program patterns available. Symbol fills consist of bitmap shapes

(squares, circles, triangles, stars, etc.) arranged in patterns. Both types of fills can be edited, and new fills created. Objects or symbols have available the same fill options as do lines, and they can be more extensively edited.

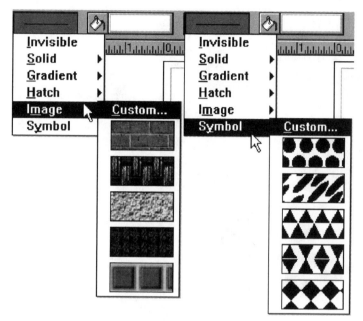

Figure 7-50

Image and Symbol fills are excellent for textures.

Undoubtedly, the greatest strength of Designer resides in its ability to create and manipulate three-dimensional objects. In this it is unsurpassed by other programs in its class. Three-dimensional objects can be created in three ways: by selection of primitives from a gallery, by extrusion of a drawn symbol, or by rotation around an axis of a drawn symbol, a process called sweeping. By drawing crossing sections in two dimensions, an almost infinite number of three-dimensional shapes can be created.

The gallery of primitives includes cubes or boxes, spheres or spheroids, cylinders, cones, and pyramids. Drawing any of these preset figures is accomplished merely by choosing the appropriate icon from the ribbon of the 3D tool and dragging the mouse the requisite distance horizontally and vertically. The 3D primitive will be drawn by the program to fit a box defined by those movements.

Figure 7-51

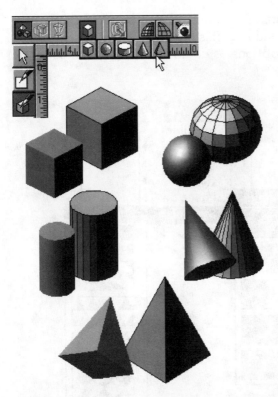

First option is to draw 3D primitives, Cube, Sphere, Cylinder, Cone, and Pyramid.

In Extrusion, a two-dimensional shape forms an outline through which a three-dimensional object is drawn. The process is simple, although a number of variations are provided. In the main, the variations really add up to nil; you end up with the same shape however the extrusion is made.

Oblique extrusions are made by simply extending the face of the two-dimensional object into the third-dimensional plane. The back and front faces of the new object are, therefore, exactly the same. An isometric extrusion produces a figure that, when rotated, does not possess exactly the same aspect as an object projected diagonally. When rotated, its aspects do not remain the same, and its shape is altered to simulate a changing viewpoint. Extruded objects can be changed, also, by dragging the corner handles to make one face larger than the other.

The third method of creating three-dimensional objects is by sweeping. The object to be used as the sweeping template is selected

Figure 7-52

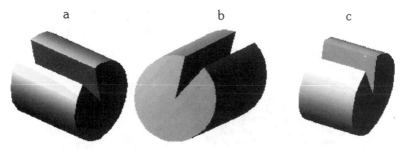

a   b   c

Extrusion a is obligue. Extrusion b is isometric. Extrusion c is a copy of b rotated to match a. The difference is evident.

and then the sweep button in the ribbon is chosen. An axis of rotation is produced, which can be moved away from the symbol, or moved to sweep vertically or horizontally.

The lighting for the 3D object can be changed. The position of the light source in all three spatial dimensions, its intensity, and the strength of the ambient light can all be set in a panel.

Figure 7-53

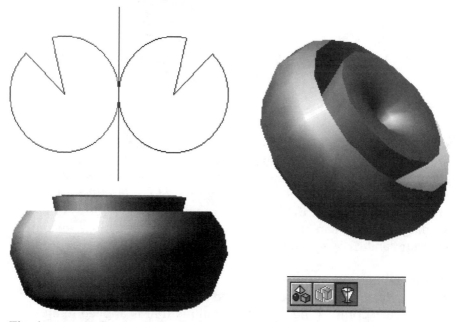

Third option is Sweep tool, which rotates a 2D object around an axis to form a 3D object.

Figure 7-54

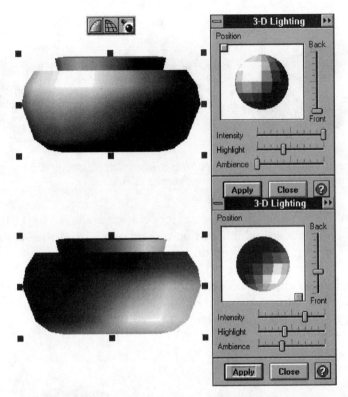

Lighting is controlled from panel, accessed by clicking on iconic button in ribbon. (Third button in ribbon section at top.)

Shading can be varied from a menu. Three types of shading can be selected: Unshaded, which produces a faceted object in which there are no shadow effects generated, representing the absence of a simulated natural light source; Shaded, in which a faceted object is created but with allowance for the presence of a natural light source; and Smooth, in which the facets are replaced by a smoothly graded shading. Shading can also be affected by the other settings for Fine, Average, and Coarse, which affect the size of the facets produced.

All three-dimensional objects can be rotated on all three spatial axes, X, Y, Z. Perspective can be simulated by moving the perspective slider, which controls the degree of slanting that is applied to an object's Z-dimensional face.

Figure 7-55

Text can be extruded. Also, 3D objects can be filled.

Text can be converted into a three-dimensional symbol by extrusion. This can produce some excellent results, especially when the final symbol is rotated.

Fills can be applied to three-dimensional objects, although a symbol that has had a fill applied may not produce a three-dimensional object with the same fill. Fills are best applied to 3D objects after the object has been created. Pattern fills are not applied conformally or in perspective. Patterns, images, and symbols are all applied in a two-dimensional or flat manner, and there is no continuity along edges. Pattern, image, or symbol fills do not rotate with the object, but remain fixed in two dimensions relative to the object.

There are other limitations to the creation of three-dimensional objects. The original object cannot be a grouped object. Therefore, you cannot assemble symbols into a compound object and then create from them a 3D symbol. Complex three-dimensional objects must be created by assembling simpler 3D symbols. And a constructed three-dimensional object can no longer be rotated in 3D space, nor can the lighting be altered for the whole assemblage. Worse, when a fill has been applied to a three-dimensional object, the light source can no longer be changed without first removing the fill.

All things considered, Designer is powerful, but many of its features are clumsily executed. Many features have a ragged execution, with the parameters spread over many panels and buttons. Consolidation of a tools option into a single panel is advisable, and many relatively common things are missing from the interface.

For instance, there is no indicator of the zoom level magnification—only 1:1 is given any numerical value; nor is there any way to choose a specific magnification. One is compelled to use the preset icons to zoom in and out. One cannot zoom out from a full page view to see the whole scratchpad area outside the page if there is

nothing already in that area. Instead, one is reduced to using the horizontal and vertical scroll bars. The use of clicking to rotate through editing and drawing modes is sometimes frustrating, and text handling (as mentioned earlier) is slow. The lack of page-to-page text flow is a flaw.

On the plus side of the ledger, apart from all the features already discussed, there is the ability to label symbols and to manage them by labels or their properties. One can, for instance, select all the items labelled by the name Small Phillips Screws, or all the symbols with a blue interior fill. This feature can be used to generate a parts list. The program can also be used to assemble a standalone slide show presentation with transitional video effects. Another important feature is the ability to create master pages, which can be used as a template for the production of multiple page documents with a common background.

Aldus FreeHand

FreeHand is a PostScript drawing program from Aldus Corporation. It looks and acts like a cousin of CorelDRAW. It has a simple user interface, which, having been developed and refined in the Macintosh environment, is well-suited to Windows. It has powerful commands, and it has Roll-Ups.

Figure 7-56

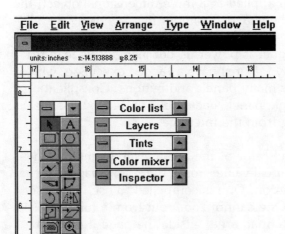

Aldus FreeHand's interface is reminiscent of that of CorelDraw.

Roll-Ups are the first thing that you notice when you begin to use FreeHand. There are Roll-Ups for all of the tools, a Roll-Up for the Toolbox, a Roll-Up for Color Mixer, a Roll-Up for the Color List, one for Type, one for Tints, one for Styles, and another for Halftones, yet another for Layers, and, most importantly, one for The Inspector. FreeHand is Roll-Up nirvana.

The Inspector is the main protagonist in FreeHand. It controls most of the characteristics of the agents in FreeHand. The Inspector contains a group of five miniature icons, the selection from which changes the functions or the focus of the Inspector. The fifth icon controls the page setup, as good a place to begin as any other.

Everything in FreeHand, starting with the page, exists on the pasteboard. When you run the program, the pasteboard is the first surface that you see. It is conceived to be 54 inches (or its unit equivalent) square. On it you place the page on which your work will be created. As the pasteboard is over 2900 square inches in area, there is room for multiple pages, e.g., 30 pages, if they are letter-size. Things that are drawn on a page can be printed, while things on the pasteboard surface cannot.

The Document Inspector sets up the page arrangement on the pasteboard. Initially, there is a single page set in the middle of the pasteboard. Added pages are arrayed from left to right, starting in the upper-left-hand corner. Page thumbnails can be dragged into different order in the preview window of the Inspector.

The Object Inspector is activated by the first icon on the Roll-Up palette. It provides vital information about the object. With checkboxes you can control whether the object will be entirely filled at points where it overlaps or intersects itself, or whether there will be gaps in the fill at those points. This especially affects type characters that have been converted to paths.

The second icon activates the Fill Inspector. You can select a fill type from the drop-down menu. There are nine categories of fill: None, Basic, Custom, Graduated, Pattern, PostScript, Radial, Textured, and Tiled.

The third option, the Stroke Inspector, provides information about the selected path and allows you to change its characteristics. There are five possible line strokes: None, Basic, Custom, Pattern, and PostScript. None and Basic are the same as in the Fill Inspector with regard to fill. A setting of None nullifies other attributes as well. Basic enables other stroke attributes. Custom is selected from 23 PostScript presets. Pattern provides 64 bitmapped patterns, and the PostScript setting is based on user-supplied PostScript language code.

The Text Inspector is brought up by the fourth icon. It controls such text items as columniation, leading (line spacing), special effects, kerning, paragraph indents, and spacing before and after paragraphs. Font details like type family, type size, and type style are set in the Type Roll-Up or from the Type menu.

Figure 7-57

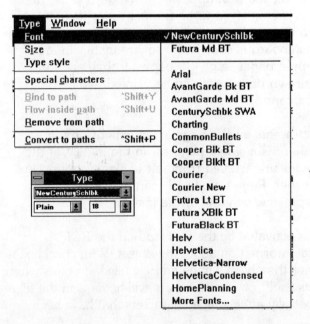

Type Menu and Type Roll-Up.

Text handling is very slow. Moving the cursor about in the text editing frame is excruciatingly slow. The lag between clicking at a location and the cursor's arrival there could be called tortoiselike, if the tortoise had a broken leg. On the positive side, text can be placed in columns and threaded from page to page automatically.

Text can also be bound to a path, of course. Better, it can be typed directly to the path. Better yet, text can flow from a text box to a path and thence to another box or path. And, after it has been bound, it can be edited as text. It can flow inside a path, and it can be skewed horizontally or vertically with regard to the path, producing some striking three-dimensional appearances.

Text can be made to flow around objects. The standoff distances determine how tightly to the object's outline text will be permitted to wrap. Objects containing blends are not subject to this feature, nor are groups. To make text wrap around either of those objects, you must draw a path around them and set the text wrap function for that path.

Binding text to an arbitrary path is as easy as typing.

Figure 7-58

As would be expected, text can be converted to paths for special effects. The zoom special effect is part of the Inspector's duties. Other PostScript effects must be imported, although you can do just about anything to text once it has been converted to paths.

Special effects such as outline, shadow, and zoom are built into the Inspector.

Figure 7-59

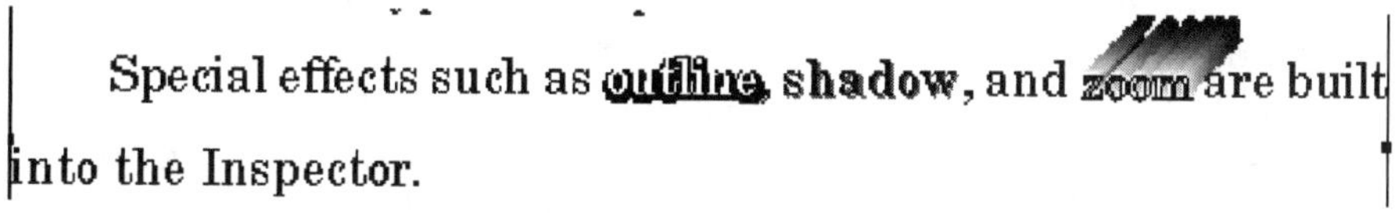

Special text effects from the Text Inspector.

Color handling is divided between two Roll-Ups, the Color List and the Color Mixer. The Color List is where the colors used in your drawing are stored. The Color Mixer is where you create the colors that you use. CMYK, RGB, and HLS are supported in the Mixer. Why it should be thought useful to fragment this function is not explained, and I cannot think of any reason or excuse for it.

The saving grace of the arrangement is something quite special: the first internal program implementation of drag-and-drop color. Colors

are added to the Color List after they have been created in the Color Mixer by dragging a color "swatch" from the color box in the Mixer to the Color List. You then drop the swatch into the list and it takes a place with a generic title Color-X, where X is a number sequentially applied from 1.

You can rename the colors you have created. If you are using a color matching system, then the color that you select from the matching system's palette will be added to the list with its proper system name. Colors can be dragged about in the list to change their order, and the list scrolls when it becomes longer than the Roll-Up's display area. You can duplicate colors in the list, or add new places in the list and then drag new colors into the existing swatches to change them.

The really remarkable thing about this drag-and-drop color management is that it applies to the drawing as well. You can drag color swatches from the color list to the drawing surface to apply those colors to objects in the drawing. An object does not even have to be selected to receive the new color. The drag-and-drop applies to text as well as to paths. So well thought-out is this feature that it works even with gradients, replacing the color onto which it is dropped and not the entire fill.

FreeHand can create separations. The procedure requires that your printer selection in the Control Panel be a PostScript device. The program then gives you the option of printing separations. Options selected in the Output Options dialogue affect how FreeHand processes the PostScript to prepare separations. Conversion of RGB TIFF into CYMK TIFF can be handled automatically.

The Transform Roll-Up contains the icons for the Move, Rotate, Scale, Skew, and Mirror functions. Moving an object can be accomplished simply by dragging with the pointer, but there is a nudge factor, set in Preferences, that allow the arrow keys to move an object incrementally. The current location of the cursor, by the way, is always displayed in the info bar, if you have activated it from the View menu. You can, therefore, arrive at your destination with some quick calculations.

Rotation can be accomplished either by dragging or by entering figures into the Roll-Up's boxes. You can set the center of rotation in absolute

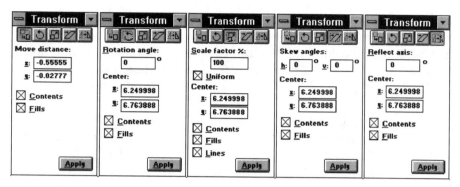

Figure 7-60

Transform Roll-Up palette controls the usual transformations.

x and y coordinates, either by clicking on the drawing with the mouse, or by direct entry. The amount of rotation is entered in degrees.

The Tool box rounds up the usual drawing instruments, with the rectangle, the ellipse, the line, and the polygon all present and correct. The Lines tool produces lines. Because the FreeHand, Pen, and Bezigon tools could also make lines, this simple tool seems out of place.

The FreeHand tool has three optional forms: simple freehand, which makes continuous curves or lines when dragged; variable stroke, which creates closed objects similar or identical to those created by the PowerLines tool of CorelDRAW; and calligraphic pen, which emulates the broad, slanted pen nibs used by calligraphic pens. The variable stroke option can be coupled with a pressure-sensitive stylus and digitizing tablet to draw very convincingly "natural" lines of unequal width. The variable-width calligraphic pen very closely simulates strokes made by a brush calligrapher.

The Pen tool is called the most versatile. With it you draw curves by clicking and dragging. The line is then pulled out from the node. You can create different types of nodes by using a modifier key with the tool. Cusp is the default style of node. The Alt key with the tool makes curve points, and the ALT and Right mouse button make connector nodes.

The Bezigon produces, surprise, Bezier-based polygons or paths.

There are three types of line joints in FreeHand: mitered, beveled, or rounded. Likewise, the three commonly used types of end caps are also here: Butt (square and flush to the end of the line), Round, and Square (extends beyond the end of the line a distance equal to half the line's width).

There is a Tracing tool in the Tool box. It will convert bitmaps into paths, and it works best, as do all tracing features in all programs, on high contrast or monochromatic images. The Trace tool will consume a lot of memory if you trace at the highest resolutions.

Magnification can be controlled from three places in FreeHand: the View menu, the Magnifying Glass in the Tool box, and the lower-left-hand corner. You can magnify the page up to 800% or reduce it to 12% of normal. When the Fit All view is active, you can drag objects from one page to another, whether or not the pages are contiguous. This is a valuable editing function.

There are three forms of Snap in FreeHand: Snap to Grid, Snap to Guides, and Snap to Point. Snap to Point allows you to position an object in relation to a snap point on another object in keyline (wireframe) mode.

There are three layers initially in a FreeHand document: Foreground, the active drawing layer, Guides, and Background. You can add layers as you like, and assign a color to objects drawn on each layer. Layers can be locked and made invisible, and placed in a different order by moving them about with the mouse in the Layers Roll-Up.

While I would not call FreeHand a drafting program, it can be used as an accurate drawing program to prepare scaled drawings and models. Its manual takes pains to point out the precision drawing capabilities of FreeHand, devoting a chapter each to accurately moving and rotating objects, drawing in perspective (five hundred years after the Renaissance, most of us should know already), and converting flat art to isometric projection (really rather neat).

One of the more valuable features is the Paste Inside command, which allows you to crop an object or an imported image by pasting it inside a closed path object. You can draw the path over the object to

be cropped, then cut the object, select the path, and choose Paste Inside from the Edit menu: the cut object on the Clipboard is then placed within the boundaries of the path, with a material that would exceed the boundaries defined by the path being cropped or hidden. You can recover the pasted image or object entirely by using the Cut Contents command.

Figure 7-61

Paste Inside command functions to crop an image pasted within the outline of an object, creating a vignette.

You can combine object paths to make new or compound objects. The Union, Intersect, and Punch commands perform variations on that theme. The most useful or dramatic is probably the Punch command, which can create a transparent section within a closed path, allowing the objects beneath to show through.

There are two viewing modes in FreeHand: the Preview, which shows the drawing as it will print, and the Wireframe, which shows only the outlines of objects. Wireframe's primary reason for existence is to speed up redrawing when moving about the pages. You will want a fast graphics adapter for FreeHand; working in wireframe mode can only show you a limited amount of information.

FreeHand may not be the most obvious choice for a drawing program, but it offers enough features to make it competitive with the better two-dimensional programs, and it is definitely the choice if you are going to work with PostScript. The drag-and-drop color and the Paste Inside command make the program all the more attractive.

Computer-Aided Drawing and Drafting (CADD)

CADD is the creation of working drawings to scale, from which manufactured objects can be made. Precision is paramount and ease of use is secondary, although one would think that true ease of use would augment precision. At any rate, the standard for CADD is AutoCAD. AutoCAD is really the gateway to a suite of programs and supplementary applications used by every high-end system.

AutoCAD LT by Autodesk

AutoCAD LT is the median drawing product from Autodesk. It is less than AutoCAD but more than AutoSketch. It resembles both of its siblings to some degree.

Upon opening, AutoCAD LT looks very much like AutoCAD. AutoCAD LT has many of the same commands and features of AutoCAD. There is a Windows Write readme.doc file of a long list of things that AutoCAD LT can and cannot do in comparison with AutoCAD.

AutoCAD LT for Windows is designed to be an out-of-the-box solution for users new to CAD who want an easy-to-learn yet powerful CAD program. AutoCAD Release 12 for Windows is a comprehensive design and drafting engine. The following is a partial

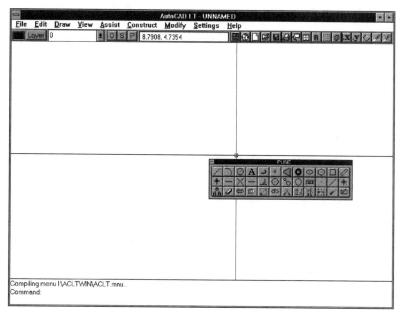

Figure 8-1

AutoCAD LT workspace.

list of features that are included in R12 Windows and NOT available in AutoCAD LT:

➤ High-end drawing and editing tools (e.g., advanced geometry creation options)

➤ Full 3D drawing and editing tools

➤ AutoCAD Development System (ADS) support

➤ AutoLISP programming language

➤ Dialog box programming

➤ Digitizer support (mole mode)

➤ Plotter and accelerated display driver support (no ADI in AutoCAD LT)

➤ Extended entity data support

➤ Region modeling

➤ Multiple sessions

➤ Geometry calculator

➤ Dynamic Data Exchange (DDE)

➤ Advanced Modeling Extension (AME) support

➤ AutoCAD SQL Extension (ASE)

➤ Open Database Connectivity (ODBC) support

➤ AutoCAD Visualization Extension (AVE)

➤ Render Window and Multiple Document Interface (MDI)

➤ Raster and PostScript Import

Like AutoSketch, AutoCAD LT has a flexible user interface. You can add buttons to both the Toolbar and the Toolbox. By clicking on an icon with the right mouse button, you summon up a dialogue box which offers you several options to customize, add, or delete a button. The scrolling list on the left is of the AutoCAD LT commands

Figure 8-2

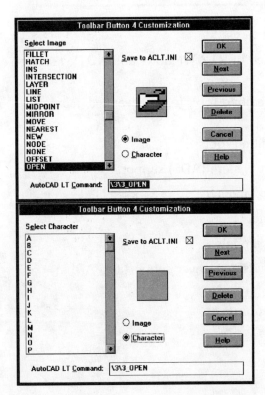

Toolbar contents and buttons can be customized.

supported by Toolbar or Toolbox. When you choose one command from the list the corresponding icon and command line prompt are displayed in their respective boxes.

With this customization you can create macros in the command line prompt that will be executed when a button has been clicked. If there are multiple parameters to be set in the macro, a space must be introduced after each parameter to signal a carriage return. The Toolbar can hold as many as 26 buttons in addition to three preset buttons. Rather stupidly, however, the number of buttons you can use is severely limited by the display size and resolution. If the resolution is insufficient, the Toolbar will be truncated and buttons that reside beyond the bounds of the truncation will not be displayed. Other programs make allowance for the size of the display and the resolution in order to rearrange additional palettes and ribbons.

Unfortunately, you are limited in choice of icons for the newly created button. You must choose an icon from the list of commands the button editor presents. Only icons already in use are displayed, and your new button will have an icon identical to one of a button already defined. You cannot add commands or set a null icon or blank button. It is up to you to remember which button has which function. The power to customize buttons is, therefore, next to useless.

Infinitely more useful is the power to create custom menus. Menus are created from menu files, which are text files that describe the menus and the menu items. Menus can have almost any number of commands, and submenus can be added to extend the scope of the menus. Hierarchical, popup, and cursor menus are available. And a powerful programming language, DIESEL, makes possible macro string execution from a menu command selection.

Also of great practical value is the ability to create scripts that can set up documents and create whole drawings. Scripts are merely lists of AutoCAD LT commands and their parameters stored in plain text (ASCII) files. These scripts can be run from the menu command. In this manner, all the tedious work can be taken out of many AutoCAD LT functions. Naturally, you can also remove much of the tedium associated with setting up documents by creating stationery or template documents with such things as drawing area and line types already defined.

Figure 8-3

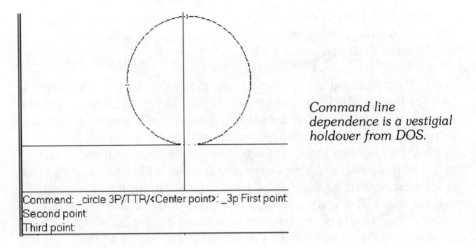

Command line
dependence is a vestigial
holdover from DOS.

As a hybrid, AutoCAD LT can be expected to satisfy some people and to dissatisfy others, depending on their expectations. Its fidelity to the AutoCAD file format is heralded by Autodesk as the principal attraction, but the retail price in comparison to AutoCAD must be another. Selling for less than $500, AutoCAD LT provides excellent value as an AutoCAD surrogate.

AutoCAD LT's graphic area, so-called to differentiate it from the actual drawing area, is not bounded by the familiar Windows horizontal and vertical scroll bars. This gives the user the utmost freedom in defining the drawing area, but it has the drawback of making movement around that drawing area, once it has been defined, a halting process.

Panning can be accomplished with the Pan tool menu command. There is no automatic scrolling with any tool in either AutoCAD LT or AutoSketch. The lack of automatic scrolling is a nuisance that slows down work considerably, especially if you are working in a magnified view. Even in tiled view, you cannot move the pointer beyond the edge of the active view. When drawing, this is an encumbrance.

You can pan and zoom simultaneously by using the excellent Aerial View tool, which is very similar to that used in AutoSketch, though not as refined. The Aerial View is a small windoid that shows a reduced view of the entire drawing. Within that view floats a box which defines the area currently displayed in the window. By moving the box about on the Aerial View, you can scroll to different regions of the drawing effortlessly, while always knowing where you are in relation to the rest of the drawing.

A definite improvement over AutoSketch is in AutoCAD LT's handling of text. Only True Type and .SHX fonts are supported in AutoSketch. AutoCAD LT supports PostScript fonts, and it does so in the conventional point sizes rather than in the ridiculous scaled sizes used by AutoSketch.

Figure 8-4

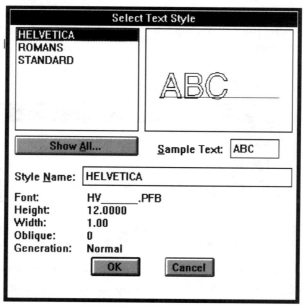

Typography now includes PostScript.

Text can be entered rotated or at an angle. It can also be given height or depth. Text can also be protected from hatching over when placed within a hatched object.

As in AutoSketch, there is no align command in AutoCAD LT. Like AutoSketch, AutoCAD LT uses attachment or snap points on objects, the grid, and drawing area snap points to align objects as they are being created.

AutoCAD LT cannot open AutoSketch files. In fact, despite the presence of 20 input choices in the Open dialogue box, AutoCAD LT can open only .DWG, DFX, and.SLD files. AutoCAD LT can import .DFX .WMF and Slide file formats, and it can export Slides, .DXF, WMF, .BMP, and PostScript. For those who need parts lists, AutoCAD LT can export database files with complete details about selected objects.

Unlike AutoSketch, which has only a rudimentary pseudo-3D capability, AutoCAD LT can create and manipulate real three-dimensional objects. In fact, it does so very easily: any 2D object can be converted into a three-dimensional one simply by changing the Thickness property of that object. All 2D objects have a default thickness of Zero (0). By giving the object thickness, it takes on three-dimensional existence.

Figure 8-5

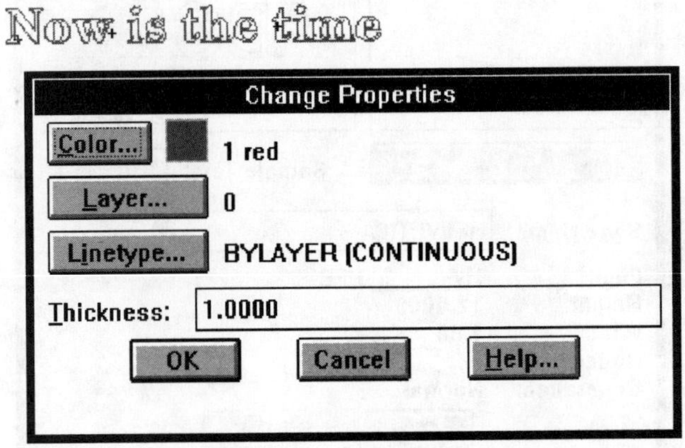

Now is the time

Change Properties

Color...   █ 1 red

Layer...   0

Linetype... BYLAYER [CONTINUOUS]

Thickness: 1.0000

OK   Cancel   Help...

Creating a 3D object is as easy as giving the object thickness.

While there are nine possible objects that can be drawn in three dimensions, including rectangles (boxes), solids (three and four sides only), ellipses, circles (cylinders), and polygons (regular, multisided boxes), there is no sphere. Unlike Micrografx Designer, which has preconfigured primitive objects, AutoCAD LT has no such objects. Neither does the program have a way of joining three-dimensional objects. However, there is no exclusionary principle in the universe of AutoCAD LT; you can assemble objects into spatial relationships that simulate continuous-surface solids.

Three-dimensional objects can be viewed from preset viewpoints, or you can choose the viewpoint by several means, by Axes, by Rotation, and by Vector. A Dynamic View can be established that has user selected Camera Angle, Distance, and other parameters.

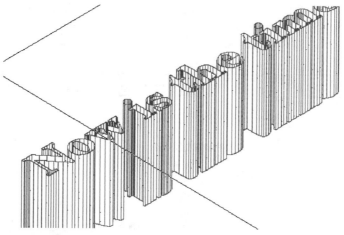

Figure 8-6

The resulting 3D text.

Neither two- or three-dimensional objects can be rotated in the Z axis of 3D space, only in the two-dimensional X and Y axes.

Like AutoSketch, AutoCAD LT supports all the commonly used dimension formats. In addition, the program can calculate areas and distances. The List command in the Assist menu will give those and other data about any selected object.

Also like AutoSketch, AutoCAD LT can construct Rectangular (columnar) and Polar (circular) arrays of objects. It also can Fillet and Chamfer lines, and there is an Offset command that creates a duplicate of an object which is placed at a certain distance from the original. This latter command can be used to create insets.

The 3D drawing tools are modest, as has been noted. Lacking, besides the sphere, is a freehand drawing tool. Polylines, lines that can have their parameters changed as they are being drawn, must be used. Thus, the width or color can be altered in the middle of creating an object. And you can switch between straight lines and arcs.

AutoCAD LT supports XREFS (external reference) file linking. This feature allows you to assemble a drawing by importing copies of other complete AutoCAD LT or AutoCAD drawings. The XREFS are embedded and linked to the current or master drawing in much the same manner that Windows uses OLE objects. An XREF can be changed, and the changes will then be incorporated in the master drawing. Each of the XREFS can be assigned a different view, and more than one copy of a particular XREF can be placed in a master drawing.

Figure 8-7

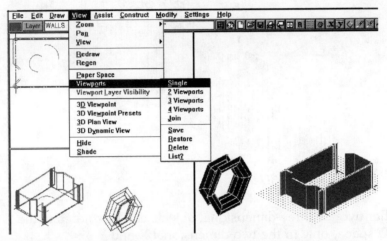

Multiple views (Viewports) can be set up with menu selections.

As implied, multiple views can exist in an AutoCAD LT document by creating viewports within the document. Thus, you can have plans, elevations, and 3D views of one part or of different parts of the same drawing displayed at once. Each view can be manipulated separately and its viewpoint changed. Changes made in the drawing in one viewport will be echoed in the other viewports.

Hatching in AutoCAD LT is as complete as you would expect it to be in a program of this level of performance. Most of the common engineering and architectural materials are represented, and you can create your own hatch patterns if you have the time and energy to learn the process. AutoCAD LT supports 256 colors and an unlimited number of layers. Colors and line types can be associated with particular layers, so that all objects drawn in a layer will have that layer's assigned color and line type.

AutoCAD LT supports Cartesian, Polar, and Spherical coordinates, as well as Surveying Angles and Engineering units. Coordinates can be relative to the preset system (World Coordinate System or WCS) or to a User Coordinate System (UCS) defined by the draughtsman in either two or three dimensions. The origin can be reset, and the familiar AutoCAD coordinate icon can be turned on or off to act as an index.

All things considered, AutoCAD LT is a large step up from AutoSketch, both in power and in programming accuracy, even if the user interface is too dependent on the command line. Some commands have no menu or toolbar/box equivalents, and even some of the commands that can be initiated from the menu or toolbar/box have parameters that must be set successively in the command line.

 # AutoCAD Release 12 for Windows

AutoCAD is the Big Kahuna of CAD, the program against which all others are measured. AutoCAD is not really one program, however, but more of a front end for a collection of programs that interact to produce the AutoCAD environment.

AutoCAD R12 for Windows is massive. The package alone is intimidating. The manuals constitute an encyclopedia-sized set of 10 reference volumes, with a total of 3359 pages, not counting pages for volume indices, Bug Reports, Wish Lists, and submission forms for Your Best Work.

AutoCAD for Windows is even more dependent on the Command Line than are AutoSketch and AutoCAD LT. This is to be expected, because AutoCAD has so many more commands than either of the others. AutoCAD is, therefore, only an imperfect Windows application, in that it does not make full use of the Windows interface.

Like both AutoCAD LT and AutoSketch, AutoCAD has a flexible interface. In fact, it uses the same model as AutoCAD LT. In this, it is inferior to AutoSketch, which has a far more useful Toolbar/Toolbox customization routine. If a command does not appear on the scrolling

Figure 8-8

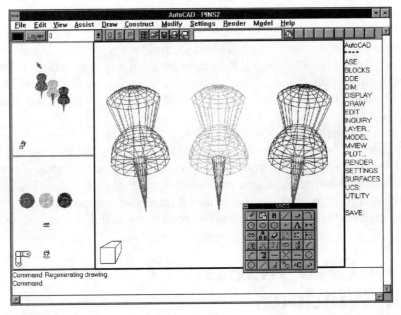

AutoCAD's user interface is superficially Windows compliant, but it's real power is still command line driven.

list, then there is no way to easily create an icon for it. And, if a command does appear on the list, the chances are that it already has been placed in the Toolbox. And, even more stupidly, if a command name in the list is selected and the complementary icon is displayed, the actual command itself is not automatically entered into the box where the command line phrase is written. That much, at least, ought to be assumed.

As in AutoCAD LT, menus also can be customized. In AutoCAD, however, some of the menus can be toggled between iconic and text display of the commands. Icons have no identifying blurbs, leaving the user to guess at their meanings if they are not already familiar, while items that have submenus display those submenu items only as text. More useful are the iconic menus; these display graphic examples of the menu item selected, and are best used for adding hatchings or blocks to libraries.

All menu modifications are rather more complex than ought to be the case. An object-oriented menu construction interface would be more

Figure 8-9

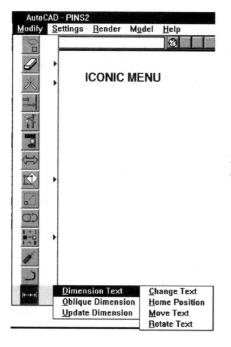

Icon based menus are colorful curiosities.

valuable than the presently used text files composed of a mixture of AutoCAD command language, DIESEL, and AutoLISP programming combined with the optional slides and icons constructed separately in AutoCAD and in icon or bitmap editors.

AutoCAD, of course, has many features that are not available in either AutoSketch or AutoCAD LT, not to mention other CAD or drafting programs. It can, for example, save drawings in more than the standard .DXF and .DWG formats. You can save a graphics screen as a Device Independent Bitmap (DIB). This is the equivalent of making a screen capture; every part of the screen is saved, including the toolbar and command area. Additionally, you can save in Filmroll format, which is used in AutoShade to create rendered 3D scenes.

The Open command suffers from the same peculiarities as does its counterpart in AutoCAD LT: of the many file formats shown in the Open dialogue box's scrolling list, only the .DWG, .DXF,.IGS, .SLD, and .FLM formats can actually be opened. What is the purpose of displaying the other formats if they are untouchable?

There are two Video Display drivers supplied by Autodesk, the Windows Driver and the Windows Accelerated Driver. The Accelerated Driver is supposedly faster than the plain Windows driver. The Aerial View works only when the Accelerated Driver is used. As far as I can see, the only reason to use the Accelerated driver is to gain the Aerial View.

One of AutoCAD's most important features is ASE, AutoCAD Structured Query Language Extension. AutoCAD can read data directly from databases, and data from AutoCAD can be exported to databases to create, for instance, parts lists or materials bills. AutoCAD uses the same interface with all compatible databases, among which are dBase, Informix, and Paradox.

The integration of databases with AutoCAD objects or entities is an important feature, but it is less important in the Windows release of AutoCAD than in the DOS versions. Its presence in R12 for Windows is, I suspect, to preserve compatibility with already developed database links from previous releases. The fact that AutoCAD also supports OLE (Object Linking and Embedding) and DDE (Dynamic Data Exchange) probably means that the ASE module will be phased out in the future.

DDE, invoked from the Edit menu, will (when fully implemented by other Windows applications) allow programs to exchange and update data in one another. Data from a spreadsheet or database can be linked to a drawing: when the data in the spreadsheet is changed, the drawing will be automatically updated, or, when the drawing is changed, the data in the spreadsheet will be changed to reflect it.

If DDE becomes fully operational, then the ASE will either be subsumed or it will be cut loose. Since the phenomenal growth of Windows is likely to continue, I would be willing to bet that ASE will not survive in present form. More likely to survive is the built-in AutoLISP interface. The language can be used to write standalone programs that interact with AutoCAD. It can be used to create new AutoCAD functions that appear to be part of the program. AutoLISP resides in AutoCAD in interpreter form. AutoLISP commands can be entered at the command line for immediate processing. On the AutoCAD supplementary CD-ROM disc there are many programs that can be used without modification.

AutoCAD supports OLE (Object Linking and Embedding) as a source only. AutoCAD drawings can be linked or embedded in client applications, such as word processors, and can be updated from the clients.

As might well be expected, AutoCAD adds much to the menus that it shares with AutoCAD LT. The View menu offers more choices, but they are not as self-apparent as those in AutoCAD LT. Where AutoCAD LT has reduced the creation of multiple viewports to a single action of selecting a number from the menu, AutoCAD requires the user to select the number and then to draw the boxes on the screen by picking diagonally opposed corner points into which all of the views will be placed. This is flexible, but it is also extra work.

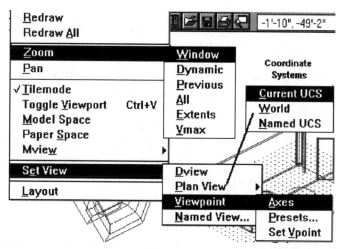

Figure 8-10

Hierarchical menus conceal the Viewports that AutoCAD can produce. Composite shows alternate coordinate systems and Zoom options.

In the Assist menu, AutoCAD has sensibly grouped all of the Object Snaps into a hierarchical submenu, but it is not apparent that none of these can be chosen until you have first selected a drawing tool, such as Line.

As in AutoCAD, there is no indicator of which snaps have already been set and which are not set. Typically, if an option has been set, it would have a checkmark or some other marker to show that has

Figure 8-11

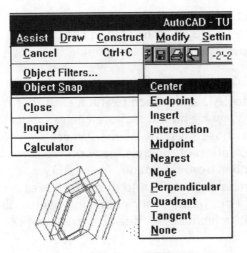

Object snap is set in the Assist menu. These settings affect the current tool and operation.

already been activated. Selecting an option that is already active should, as in other programs, render the option inactive.

A very useful feature in the Assist menu is the Object Filters command. This command brings up a panel in which you can set the attributes by which objects will be selected in a drawing. The choices and combinations range from the simple (ARC, LINE, LAYER) to the complex (BLOCK, BLOCK ROTATION, SHAPE, VIEWPORT). You can string the attributes together in logical sequences with the Boolean operators, and you can compile lists of filters that fit your needs to be used repeatedly. Each list can be saved and recalled for later use.

Because I have faulted both AutoCAD LT and AutoSketch for lacking an Align command, I ought to mention that AutoCAD does have an Align command. It is not, however, the tool that I would have wished it to be. Align moves objects in two or three dimensions and performs revolutions of the objects into the bargain. If a group of objects not aligned to one another is selected and the Align command used on the group, the objects will be shuffled about in relation to points picked out on the drawing surface. Their original misalignment will not be corrected, and, indeed, it might be worsened as objects are rotated.

AutoCAD provides two basic ways to create 3D entities: by creation of 3D surfaces, and by creation of 3D solids. Solids are generally the province of the Region Modeler or of AME, while 3D surfaces are found in the Draw menu. The two forms are handled differently by AutoCAD.

Figure 8-12

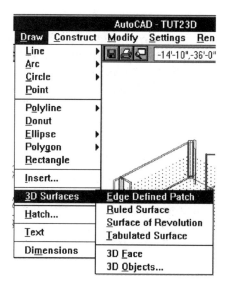

3D surfaces are one form of three-dimensional drawing in AutoCAD.

Three-dimensional surfaces can be constructed one vertex at a time, or they can be made from primitives. You can model more complex objects by combining the primitives or by making wire mesh, ruled, or tabulated surfaces, or by revolving a surface around an axis.

Figure 8-13

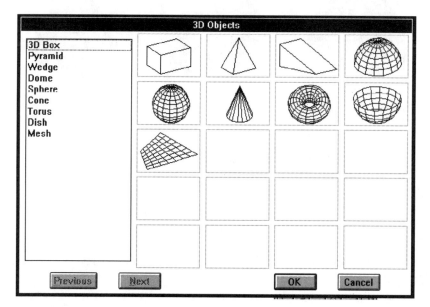

3D primitives provide ready to use basic forms.

The Region Modeler works with closed polygons or other closed 2D entities. If you have purchased AME, you can extrude 2D objects into 3D solids. This is not the same as giving an object thickness. Three-dimensional entities created with the drawing tools are not subject to the modeler's commands. Like AutoCAD LT, AutoCAD can create rectangular or polar arrays of objects, but AutoCAD takes the ability into the third dimension, making models easy to reproduce.

The rendering that is built into AutoCAD is sufficient for checking your work and for demonstration purposes. It is not photo-realistic, however. You can select Shading, Hidden Line, or Rendering from the Render menu. Only 256 colors are available, so the results from rendering are not particularly good. Users of AME have access to spotlights. All AutoCAD scenes can have specular reflections. You can also select how light will behave.

Figure 8-14

Smooth rendering is sufficient for simple objects.

Finished renderings or shadings can be exported in four bitmap formats (TGA, TIFF, GIF, and RND) for use in presentations or for touchup in paint or image-editing software.

As a Windows product, AutoCAD has come a long way from its roots in DOS, but much of its new growth is still in the DOS pastures. It is not a satisfying Windows application, barnacled over by the command line and so many other creatures of its long DOS existence. However, AutoCAD

is still the definitive 3D CAD program in DOS or Windows. Remember, the right mouse button can be used instead of the Enter key.

Ashlar Vellum

Vellum is the fine parchment made from prepared hides. Ashlar are the squared blocks of stone used in the masonry of medieval castles. The title, intended to imply tradition and craftsmanship, seems inappropriate when attached to such a nontraditional product. Vellum is a 2D and 3D drawing and drafting program that breaks new ground in simplifying 3D drawing, using a smart cursor called the Z Drafting Assistant. But Vellum holds fast to an antiquated protection system, the hardware key.

Vellum has an attractive Windows interface, simple and uncluttered. So intent has Ashlar been to reduce the rank growth that can accumulate in some programs that they have pruned away some things that might be considered essential—the rulers, for example. While the Drafting

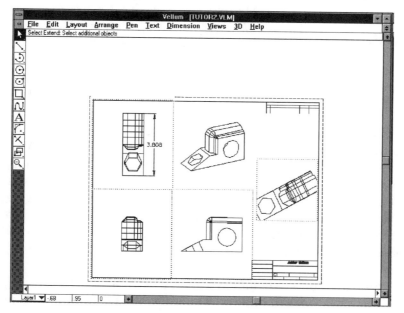

Figure 8-15

Vellum's interface is clean and well-developed.

Assistant is excellent, rulers provide an irreplaceable fixed reference. In 3D, you can live without rulers, but not in 2D.

The Drafting Assistant gives you information that in other programs is rather harder to come by than ought to be the case. Drafting Assistant acknowledges midpoints, endpoints, perpendicularity, alignment to axes, tangentiality, the intersection of construction guidelines extended from midpoints, vertices, or other points, angular presets (defaults of 90 and 45°), and other helpful relations. There are verbal as well as graphical cues to the states of the relationships found. The Drafting Assistant can be used to create construction lines, either temporary or permanent, the latter of which will remain until manually deleted.

Figure 8-16

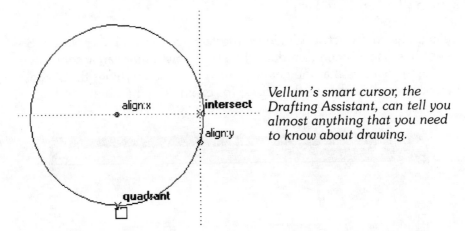

Vellum's smart cursor, the Drafting Assistant, can tell you almost anything that you need to know about drawing.

The location of the drawing plane is a troublesome matter in most 3D drawing programs, and is problematic in the rest, but in Vellum the drawing plane is not really a plane: it is an entire dimension. You can draw anywhere in the dimension that lies along the axis perpendicular to the plane of the screen. This simplifies drawing; you have to make fewer changes of viewpoint and orientation to shift your work to another plane. When you do want to change planes, it is also much more easily done than in other programs.

Views are based on the common Sheet, Model, and Detail paradigm. There can be more than one model per sheet, and there can be more than one view per sheet. And additional sheets can be added with their own models or based on models in another sheet. Views are generally interactive or associative, with changes made to the active model being displayed in all views simultaneously. Crosshatched, dimensioned, and dissociated views are the exceptions.

Figure 8-17

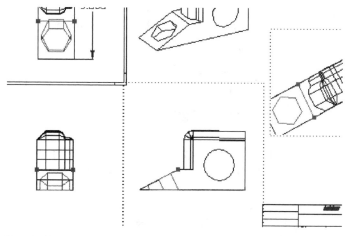

Views are ordinarily interactively associated. Changes in one are carried through into others. Dissociated views are unaffected.

Dissociated views are those that are no longer interactively connected to the model and to other views. Flattening a view will dissociate that view from other views. Flattening takes a three-dimensional view of the model and projects it back into two dimensions. This is done primarily to prepare a hidden-line version of an isometric view.

The standardized crosshatching patterns are available. Hatching applies the currently selected crosshatch to the area immediately without calling the dialogue box. Crosshatching can only be applied to closed areas. Dimensions, like crosshatching, apply only to view into which you enter them. You can select the precision and the form from hierarchical menus. You can also specify the placement of text relative to the dimension lines. Dimension lines and their end forms, arrows or brackets, can be selected. Tolerances can be set for dimensions.

An important standard form of dimensioning, GD&T (Geometric Dimensioning and Tolerancing), used to assure that interchangeable parts can be made by and obtained from different sources, is

Figure **8-18**

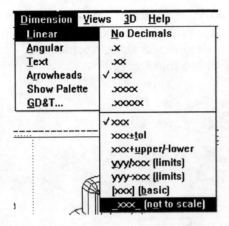

Dimensioning is simplified by menu selections for types and precision.

included. The use of GD&T also introduces the concept of a Bonus Tolerance, by which the permissible hit spot is expanded.

There are five preset views in Vellum: isometric, trimetric, front, top, and right. You can rotate in three dimensions any view with an on-screen trackball to create a nonstandard view. The primary view of a drawing begins at the sheet level with a top view of the model. The sheet view can be changed in any way desired. However, when new views are created, the sheet view reverts to the top view, and all subsequent changes to the viewing angle must be made in the separate view windows.

Figure **8-19**

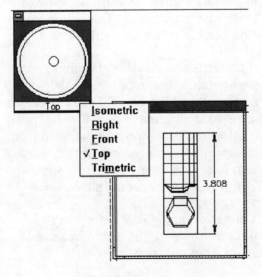

Standard views are available from menus, but the trackball has its own menu to toggle views. Rotating trackball with mouse rotates the drawing in the view.

Vellum's drawing tools are typical. Vellum supports NURBS (Non-Uniform Rational B-Splines), a form of Bezier curves that can be edited at individual points without affecting the remainder of the curve. There are also vector splines available.

There are two- and three-point arcs, ellipses, and circles, rectangles, inscribed and circumscribed polygons, lines, connected lines, parallel lines, and double lines. In addition there is chamfering and filleting, and there is a smart tool that will complete corners by extending and trimming lines automatically.

Figure 8-20

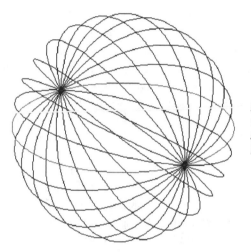

Lacking primitives, you must use the tools at hand to make solids. Here a rotated circle becomes a sphere.

Drawing in three dimensions is less confusing in Vellum than in other programs, but it's not perfect. There are three basic means to create 3D figures: by manually drawing, by extrusion, and by revolution. There are no predefined primitives. Therefore, spheres can only be created by revolving an arc around an axis that intersects its center. Boxes can be made only by extrusion or by direct point-to-point construction.

Extrusion and revolution can be described by terms entered into the related dialogue box or by picking points and dragging with the mouse. You can extrude both solids or holes, because there are no real surfaces or solids in Vellum. Vellum creates only lines.

Even the connected line tool creates individual line segments after the double click. Every surface in Vellum is only apparent. As a

consequence, objects in Vellum have only apparent volume. You cannot color fill a Vellum surface; only crosshatching is possible. Vellum objects in AutoCAD are just lines arranged in three-dimensional space.

Text is handled adroitly by the normal Windows menu. PostScript and ATM are supported, which is as it should be. There are no disappointments or surprises here, as there are in AutoCAD or AutoSketch. However, plotting from Vellum requires that the plotter fonts will be used.

One of the more important features of Vellum is the use of Parametrics, the process by which a figure can be described in general terms and then precisely scaled from text file descriptions of the exact dimensions. A product that is to have the same form but to be made in different sizes can be drawn once with its dimensions described parametrically; then separate scaled draftings can be produced from the same generalized drawing by the use of different text files containing the relevant dimensions.

Vellum has a 2D analysis feature, which calculates area, perimeter, weight, inertia, and center of gravity for selected objects. This is similar to the AutoCAD region analysis. Items to be analyzed must be in a plane parallel to the work plane and must be closed. Internal regions (e.g., holes) can be excluded from the analysis by selecting them.

The documentation for Vellum is supplied in a ring binder, but you must assemble the manual from separate packages of pages, those for

Figure 8-21

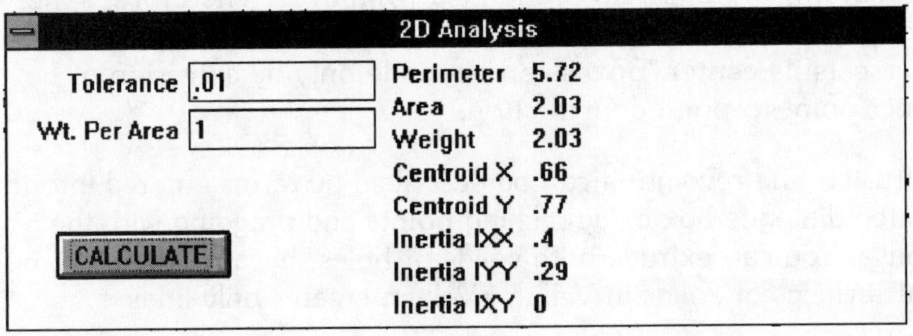

	2D Analysis	
Tolerance .01	Perimeter	5.72
Wt. Per Area 1	Area	2.03
	Weight	2.03
	Centroid X	.66
	Centroid Y	.77
CALCULATE	Inertia IXX	.4
	Inertia IYY	.29
	Inertia IXY	0

2D analysis provides some physical data based on geometry and materials.

the 2D version and those for the 3D version, the latter of which must be interleaved with the former to construct a finished manual. This is a bother. Manuals should come already assembled.

Additionally, the manual is not entirely accurate, nor is it complete. There is no section concerning product support. Nowhere is there a telephone number to which you can call for technical assistance. (The telephone number for Ashlar technical support is given in a NotePad README.TXT file that appears on the desktop in the Ashlar group.)

About the hardware key: ordinarily, I would simply advise against buying any software using such a protection scheme, but Vellum is innovative enough to warrant recommendation anyway. This limitation is against the trend of greater integration of software functions and cannot be expected to survive. Besides, there are many ways to defeat this type of protection. In a time when almost every other publisher has removed protection from their software, Ashlar's continuance of the practice is all the more conspicuously out of step.

Vellum has outstanding capabilities for work in three-dimensional space, but without opportunities for expansion. It is superior to AutoCAD in every aspect of the program's design, but the lack of access into rendering and modeling software may be its most serious flaw. Vellum goes its own way, and if the end that it reaches is sufficient for your purposes, then it is excellent in that degree.

Three-dimensional visualization and presentation

T HIS is a category that is somewhat difficult to define. The programs in this category must be able to put the viewer into the three-dimensional world that lies beyond the computer screen. This is the world that is called cyberspace or virtual reality. You can use this virtual reality for any task requiring the simulation of real space, but most often it is used to provide for the viewer a chance to see from any perspective in current time what a planned object or building will look like when realized.

⇨ Virtus WalkThrough

This is one of those programs that defines its genre. You must buy this program, even if you only use it to run the prerecorded "walks" (as the animated navigations through WalkThrough's 3D world are called) that come with the program. Virtual reality is unlike anything that you could have seen or produced on a microcomputer just five years ago.

The world of WalkThrough is a flat earth in which there is no gravity, and space is the modeling clay from which all objects are made. You fabricate everything that is in that world except for the flat earth and the unseen sun that illuminates it. There are five laws in that world, which you violate only at your own risk. Everything else is up to you.

WalkThrough provides a means by which you can quickly turn a plan into a virtual reality. While there are programs that will take the

Figure 9-1

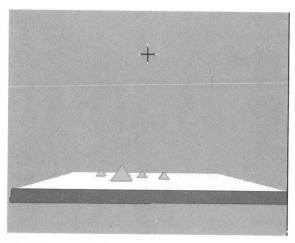

WalkThrough's flat Earth.

output of a three-dimensional CAD program and turn it into a beautifully rendered surface model, they take hours to complete their work, not counting the weeks spent creating the rendered objects. And then you will have but one frame, one view of that scene. WalkThrough can give you the basic forms and more than enough of the experience of the fully rendered scene in a tenth of the time, and it will be fully three-dimensional and interactive. You can go anywhere you choose in that world.

On the practical side, you can find out if the kitchen sink is close enough to the refrigerator, if there is enough room between the range and the island, if there are enough cupboards, and if they are at a convenient height. You can design the landscaping to take advantage of the natural contours of the lot, and then walk through the garden to see if it is the way you want it. Everything can be where it will be when built.

The size of the world is limited to 65,536 units (2_{16}), but the units can be anything from angstroms (one ten-billionth of a meter) to parsecs (approximately $17.6 \times 10_{12}$ miles, or 28,380,000,000,000 kilometers). At the atomic scale, you could model a molecule. At the parsec level, you could model nothing smaller than, say, a nebula.

If you set the unit to inches, your world will be 65,536 inches in diameter, slightly over one mile—wide enough, certainly, for most

Figure 9-2

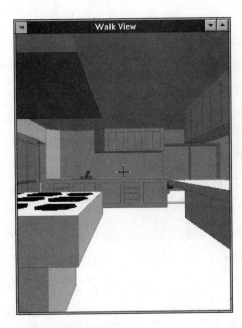

Interior design is a perfect use for WalkThrough.

practical designs. The inch represents the resolution of the design, as well. That is, you will be able to draw down to the inch any detail that you wish. Objects smaller than an inch will not be visible.

The program has two basic windows on opening: the Design Window, where you actually design the objects that will occupy the space of WalkThrough, and the Walk or Navigation Window, which presents the rendered 3D view of the WalkThrough world. The Design Window can be toggled to show Top, Bottom, Front, Back, Left, and Right views of the drawing surface, or you can have as many as the six client views open. There is but one Navigation Window, but that too can be formatted to your needs. The Navigation or Walk Window can be set to provide a variety of view formats. By default each of the two main windows occupies half the screen, Design on the left and Walk on the right. Either can be expanded.

The Design Window is very much like the drawing window of any other drawing program: there are rulers on the top and the left edges of the window and scroll bars on the bottom and right edges. You can, if you want, have snap points and a grid, each with user-selected values.

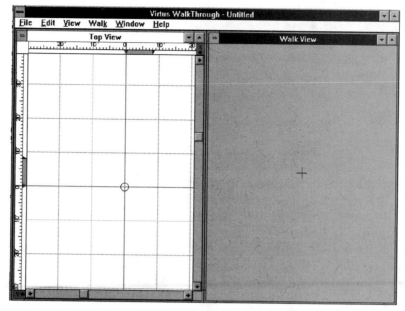

Figure 9-3

WalkThrough's default window arrangement, Design on left and View on right.

The drawing tools in the floating toolbox arrayed to the very left of the screen are very much like the tools you would find in other drawing programs. There are tools to draw polygons, a tool to draw triangles, a selection tool, and a tool to change the current color. Then there are the tools that you haven't seen before.

There are three tools that control the opacity of objects: one to make them totally opaque, one to make them partially opaque or translucent, and one to make them transparent. There is a tool with an icon of a building facade, which will toggle on the Surface Editor. And there is a tool to turn on the Tumble Editor.

The Surface editor is used to add surface features to walls and other plain objects in the drawing window. Surface objects are attached to other objects, and, unlike the ordinary WalkThrough objects, they have an infinitesimal thickness by definition, so that they appear two-dimensional even in the three-dimensional walk view.

Figure 9-4

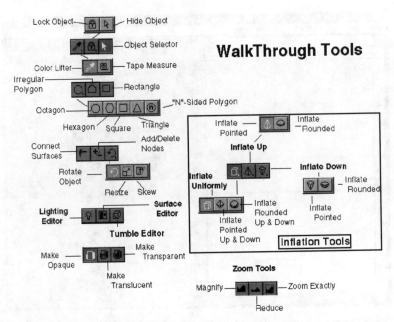

WalkThrough's design tools identified.

The Tumble Editor, indicated by the icon of the cube with a severed corner, is used to create objects that are not simple primitives in the Design window's objects menu. The Tumble Editor allows you to slice away portions of an object to create new surfaces on the object, thereby altering its shape. You can also change other properties of the object, such as its color, while in the Tumble Editor.

Figure 9-5

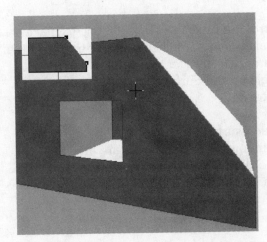

Tumble Editor. Effect of slicing one corner from the block. Design View is inset.

You can also change the shape of an object by adding handles to its outline. Objects can be rotated, scaled, or skewed with the commands accessed by the transformation tool. The eyedropper tool can be replaced with a tape measure that will give you the distance between any two points. The view magnification can be increased or reduced with the icons at the bottom of the toolbox.

The Design window also shows the Observer in relationship to the objects within the WalkThrough world. The Observer is your eye as you are wandering through the WalkThrough world. Because you cannot actually go into the Virtus world, the Observer goes for you.

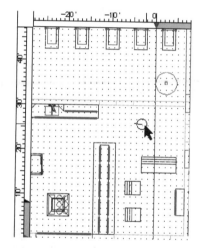

Figure 9-6

Observer is indicated by arrow pointer.

You control the movements of the Observer in the Design windows by simply clicking on it and dragging. The Observer can be moved in any view, but only in directions that lie parallel to the plane of the screen in the current view. If you are in a top or bottom view, you can move the Observer laterally. If you want to move the Observer up or down in elevation, you must change to one of the other views.

This is important, because it touches on the relationship of the third dimension to the current view. All things in the Virtus world have depth; because you can see only two dimensions at a time in the Design window, you must keep track of that missing third dimension with a mental image. To make this easier, Virtus supplies a visual aid, the Virtus Cube, which can be used as a reference.

The trick is to remember that when an object is drawn in the Design window, it is drawn not only in the two dimensions that you see on the screen, but outward from or backward into the screen as well. *Depth is always perpendicular to the current view.* To set the depth that a new object will have in the third dimension, you must set the depth sliders that flank the Design window. This is where the process can become confusing, because *the depth sliders that are visible in any particular view will not affect depth perpendicular to the screen;* they affect the two dimensions that are current.

Figure 9-7

Depth window.

Alternatively, Virtus supplies a Depth window, which provides a depth slider for the currently intangible axis, but it is good practice to shift views to make depth changes until you are comfortable with Virtus' notion of depth.

Virtus calls this process of giving a third dimension to a two-dimensional planar object inflation to depth. There is another important aspect to this inflation. When the inflation occurs, you can choose how the object will be shaped by the process. There are three basic forms that inflation can give to an object: extruded, pointed, or domed.

The extruded inflation simply extends the drawn shape back into the third dimension. Pointed inflation draws the object with a conical or pyramidal projection into the third dimension. The direction of the inflation can be up or down (backwards or forwards) to create a cone

Figure 9-8

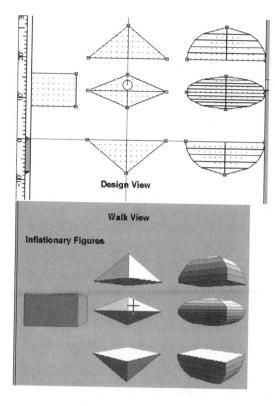

Examples of Inflation to Depth. All figures were drawn in Top View, with different floors. Top figures inflated up, middle figures inflated uniform, and bottom figures inflated down.

or pyramid, or bidirectional to create an object that is diamond-shaped or pointed on both ends. Domed inflation is a variant of the pointed inflation, causing the object to be rounded at the point. If you select domed in both directions, then the object created has a spherical shape.

The last editor in WalkThrough is the Lighting editor. The Lighting editor works with either the World lighting or with Object lighting. World lighting is applied to everything in the Virtus world, not surprisingly. It applies to everything, inside objects and outside. By default, objects contained in other objects, like the furniture in a house, have the same lighting as the containing object.

One limitation is that you cannot show a scene at night, even if you turn off the ambient light. To make things dark, you must darken the background color, which makes the sky a different color. Turning off ambient World lighting will then make the objects dark, also.

Figure 9-9

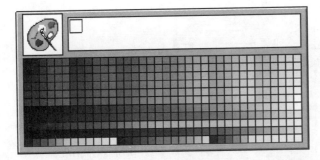

Color Picker.

I know of no way to make an object luminous. Conversely, there are no shadows in the Virtus world. While objects are correctly shaded with regard to the light sources, they do not cast shadows, nor can they shed light to become sources of illumination.

Virtus has supplied a library of some objects that can be added to your own Walks. There is a library of stairways, which can be tiresome to construct, because you must make and place each of the steps individually. And there is a library of mannequins in various poses; these can be imported into your drawings to give scale and

Figure 9-10

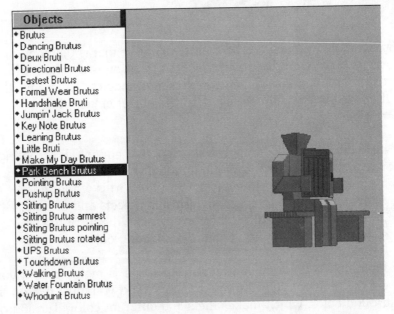

Objects
- Brutus
- Dancing Brutus
- Deux Bruti
- Directional Brutus
- Fastest Brutus
- Formal Wear Brutus
- Handshake Bruti
- Jumpin' Jack Brutus
- Key Note Brutus
- Leaning Brutus
- Little Bruti
- Make My Day Brutus
- Park Bench Brutus
- Pointing Brutus
- Pushup Brutus
- Sitting Brutus
- Sitting Brutus armrest
- Sitting Brutus pointing
- Sitting Brutus rotated
- UPS Brutus
- Touchdown Brutus
- Walking Brutus
- Water Fountain Brutus
- Whodunit Brutus

Mannequin Library.

some life to architectural Walks. You can also use the furnishings that are in the sample Walks provided by Virtus.

There are layers in WalkThrough; they appear in the layers list in the toolbox area. They can be moved about in their order by shuffling the names in the list with the mouse. Each layer has a pop-up menu that can be activated by clicking on the layer's name in the list and holding down the mouse button.

There are five laws or commandments that have been handed down from Virtus Mountain and which you must obey during construction, lest you cause funkiness. (Funkiness is any computational error due to violation of the laws that results in odd display behavior.) The laws are as follows:

❶ Do not overlap objects on the same plane. Overlapping is bad karma.

❷ Do not create objects that are not convex. Objects that are not convex must be constructed from smaller convex objects with openings placed in their common walls.

❸ Speed of movement in a Walk is inversely related to the amount of detail in the Walk. The more objects that you place in a Walk, the harder the computer has to work to render them in correct order, with the consequent slowing of motion.

❹ Transparent and Translucent objects or surfaces slow processing, because the computer must apply the transparent or translucent effect to all objects that can be seen through the object or surface.

❺ All objects have depth.

It is wise to obey the local customs. If you simply jump in and start building willy-nilly, you are more than likely to create problems for yourself.

You can speed up the display somewhat by selecting the Flash Graphics option in preferences. This option allows WalkThrough to bypass Windows GDI and to write directly to the Windows display. Also, you can choose to have objects displayed in wire frame or plain white fill modes. These alternatives are useful during the development and testing of a Walk.

When the Walk window is active, the toolbox contains the background color bar and a zoom lens adjustment slider. This allows you to zoom in and out from the current viewpoint as though you were using a zoom lens on the camera. This is a convenient way to look at details without having to move the Observer forward. There is also an orientation cube that shows where you are relative to the scene and its contents. At the very bottom are the controls for recording or playing back your movements.

You can record your peregrinations through Virtus land. These Walks can be played back as self-running demonstrations or presentations, taking the viewer through the finished artifice, simulating a videotaped or QuickTime tour of your project as it will look when built.

You can import DXF two- and three-dimensional files, but the 3D objects do not translate well. WalkThrough has a nice Snapshot utility that can capture windows or screens and save in Bitmap, TIFF (with or without compression), EPS (with or without preview), and Illustrator formats, as well as create Animator Pro formatted files from recorded Walks.

For all of its power, WalkThrough comes with a very slim manual, because the program is so easy to use. The tough concepts are very clearly explained. The manual's authors, Eric Olson and Alan Scott, have a light touch; they are to be congratulated. Buy this program!

Virtus WalkThrough Pro

WalkThrough Pro, a more advanced version of WalkThrough, exists on the Macintosh and is being ported to Windows. It permits the realistic rendering of surfaces and the mapping of textures to rendered surfaces. The scale is also more precise, allowing creation and rendering of objects down to $\frac{1}{64}$ of a unit.

trueSpace from Caligari

trueSpace was originally developed as an Amiga product. Given Commodore's mishandling of the Amiga in the North American

Figure 9-11

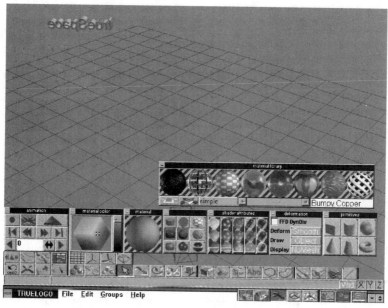

trueSpace Workspace. Menubar can be relocated to top.

market, that trueSpace has survived says something about its durability, if nothing else.

This could be another one of those "must have" products. It is a designer's product, one with artist's rather than draftsman's sensibilities. It does not provide the kind of visual feedback that lends precision to drawing. There are no rulers, nor is there a display that shows distance, angle, or coordinate location of the cursor as you draw. While you can enter measurements into Object Info dialogues, this can be a sorely inadequate means of assigning precise dimensions to an irregularly shaped object. It can be done, of course, but it is not easy.

The user interface of trueSpace is a bit eccentric; the default locations of the menu bar and toolbar are at the bottom of the screen. The toolbar in trueSpace is another problem area, whatever its location. Tools are grouped into clusters according to their spheres of influence, so to speak. There are Window tools, and there are Object tools. There are Point tools, and there are Eye tools. Many of the tool groups have flyout icon menus, and many of those flyout menu items have function panels. To add to the complexity, many of

Figure 9-12

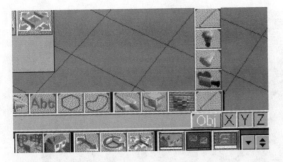

Light tools: Add Infinite Light, Add Local Light, Add Spotlight, Camera.

the flyouts and function panels are identical across the tool groups, leaving a confusing web of controls from which it is not always obvious how a tool will affect the drawing.

trueSpace suffers from the same sort of command structure complexity that mars Designer: the proper order of operations to accomplish a task is not obvious, and the same icons seem to have contradictory definitions in differing circumstances. An iconic tool should have the same function everywhere in a program, and a general tool, such as the Camera, should have a global effect.

trueSpace is a three-dimensional stage onto which you introduce actors of your own creation. The actors are created on the stage, drawn with the tools that trueSpace provides. There are tools to create 3D primitives; each of these primitives can be modified by distorting their surfaces, pulling, pushing, and twisting as needed. There are tools to draw splines and polygons. You can use polygons to punch holes into other polygons. Splines and polygons can then be converted into 3D objects. Holes are preserved in three dimensions.

The Sweep tool is really an extrusion tool. A Sweep command creates a new surface (called a floor) a specified distance from the original

Figure 9-13

Primitives Tool

Primitives Tool and Primitives Panel.

Splines Tool

Figure 9-14

Splines Tool and Paths Palette.

floor, and then connects those two surfaces along their corresponding edges. Sweeping in trueSpace can be performed repeatedly, with a concatenation of results. You can also modify the newly created surface (by rotation, editing of points, etc.) to make the succeeding extrusion different than its predecessor. The entire series of extrusions will be remembered by the program and can be executed or saved as a Macro Sweep, which can be applied to other objects.

The Tip tool is a specialized form of extrusion that sweeps a polygon to a point. Tipping is a terminal sweep; a point, which is the result of a Tip sweep, cannot be swept.

The Lathe tool rotates a polygon or spline around an axis to form a 3D shape. You can alter the segments of the defining polygon or spline, set the radius of the shape to be created, and set the degree of rotation. You can also specify a helical path along which the Lathe tool will create the new solid.

Figure 9-15

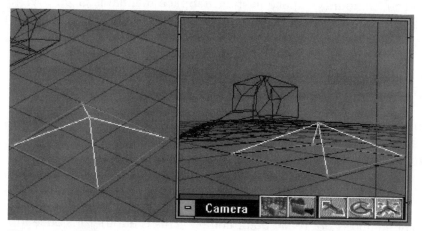

Tip tool extrusion.

Figure 9-16

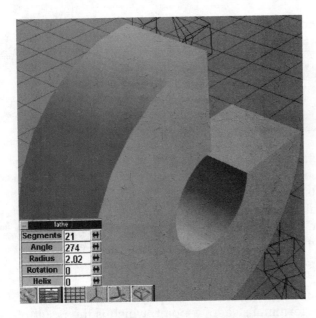

Rendered Lathe result.

The Bevel tool is another modified extrusion, similar to the Tip tool, except that the solid created is not pointed but truncated. The selected original polygon is duplicated, and the duplicate is scaled down proportionally the farther it is moved from the original. The sides of the solid are then formed by connecting the two floors with polygons along their edges.

A sizable amount of space in the trueSpace manual is given over to the concept of Navigation within trueSpace's stage. There is not only Navigation within the work window, but Object Navigation for movement of an object, and Point Navigation for operations on points. One could wish that a more generalized means of affecting actions were provided.

There are three coordinate systems in trueSpace: the world system, the object system, and the screen system. You can switch among them as desired. Every object, indeed, every point, has its own coordinate system and axes. You should make certain that you have selected the proper coordinate system before performing any action.

Point editing is not really point editing. This is another instance in which the nomenclature fails. Point editing can be applied to surfaces,

to vertices, to edges. Often it is not really clear why a surface is not an object, or why an object should be edited in Point editing. It is a case in which it takes familiarity to breed respect, or, at least, acceptance.

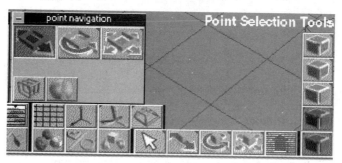

Figure 9-17

Point editing is preceded by point selection. Tools are right, top to bottom, Vertices Selection, Edge Selection, Face Selection, Context Editing. Left, Point Navigation Tools: Point Move, Point Rotate, Point Scale, Slice, Separate.

You can create compound objects in trueSpace, allowing the production of complex surfaces, such as a human face. You can also slice an object to create a surface. As with simpler operations, you must wade through a dense series of concepts and peculiar operations before these activities can be mastered, but the attention is repaid amply in the results.

Surface mapping is accomplished with Painting tools. Materials are applied in a fairly straightforward manner. The Paint Object tool applies a material to an entire object. Optionally, you can also paint individual faces with materials. Textures can be applied over a painted surface with degrees of transparency, allowing underlying colors or images to show through with varying clarity. Bump maps can also be applied, creating a simulation of an uneven surface by using adjacent areas of high contrast. Areas supposedly higher in elevation above the surface will have brighter pixel values than lower areas.

The actual mapping to the surface is determined by the UV projection used for any object. UV projections are Planar, Cylindrical, and Spherical. The term UV represents the mode of coordinate location, U for the horizontal numerical value from a given point and

Figure 9-18

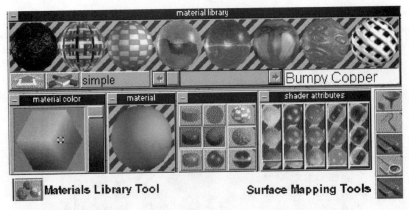

Painting of surfaces is handled by tools (lower right corner). Materials, colors, shading, etc. are determined by panels.

V for the vertical distance from the point. Planar mapping applied to the texture maps a flat image to a surface, like the picture on the front of a cereal box. Cylindrical mapping applies a map to the surface in curvilinear manner, as in the label on a can. Spherical mapping applies an image as though to a globe.

Figure 9-19

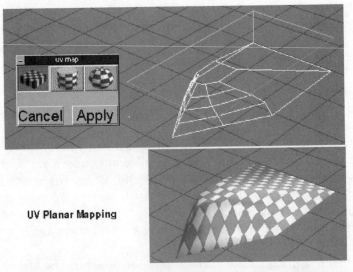

UV Planar surface mapping is indicated in the workspace by a flat surface suspended over the object. Mapping is draped over the object like a tablecloth with only minimal distortion of pattern.

Figure 9-20

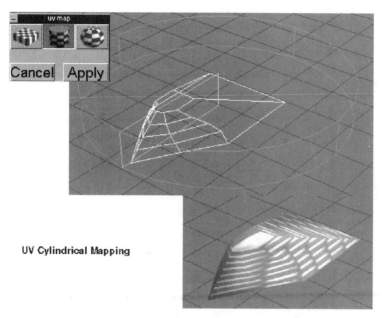

UV Cylindrical Mapping

UV Cylindrical surface mapping is shown by cylinder enclosing object. Mapping is wrapped around object and conforms to surface irregularities.

After you have overcome its manual and its iconic tools, the view in trueSpace is striking. The realistic rendering of three-dimensional surfaces is extremely persuasive. Actors within trueSpace's stage animate the scene. You can move the actors about on the stage, using the mouse or user-defined paths, and the actors themselves can be altered to provide subordinate motions. Objects can be made to orient themselves automatically to the plane of motion. And the whole can be viewed from any angle.

Simple animation, the movement of a character from one place to another, can be accomplished by placing the character in the starting position for frame 0, and then moving the actor to the ending position for the final frame. The program will then make all of the intermediate frames as needed to produce the movement indicated in the prescribed number of frames.

One rather neat effect is the ability to use one object in an animated sequence as an extruding tool. That is, you can cause an object to be

Figure 9-21

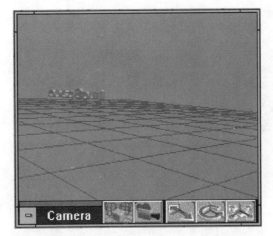

Camera view (as actual animation will appear) of rendered actor at frame zero.

forced through an opening in another object as though the first object were made of some malleable matter. The effect is similar to the forcing of icing through a decorative tip on a pastry bag. Unfortunately, you cannot move around in a rendered scene, only in its wireframe rendition. To move through a rendered scene, you must create an animation and then render the animation to a file.

Figure 9-22

Deforming by lattice can produce the Pastry Bag Effect, simulation of the squeezing of an object through an opening in another object.

There is an Undo command, as well as a Redo. Undo does not affect some actions, such as the placing of a new camera or the introduction of a new object. Those types of actions can be undone only by Erasing the object or camera. Other actions, such as Sweeping, can be undone and then redone multiple times to produce a cumulative effect.

Among the utilities in trueSpace, there is the Grid, which can be set from the Grid Snap panel, accessible by right-button clicking on the Grid icon. The grid can be set and enabled or disabled for each of the three axes. trueSpace also has a Mirror command that reverses the geometry of the selected object. All of trueSpace's commands or tools can be activated from the keyboard by hot keys. Hot keys can be customized.

All things considered, trueSpace is a remarkable tool for three-dimensional design and animation, despite its quirky interface and poorly executed manual. trueSpace is an attempt to make drawing in three dimensions as easy as it has been in two dimensions, and it succeeds to a fair degree. If you are willing to take the time that learning trueSpace will require of you, and if you are willing to accept the redefining of some conventions, then you will have a very powerful tool.

Painting and image processing

IMAGE processing program" is really a new name for the type of software that began the revolution in computer user interfaces, the paint program. MacPaint and its descendants are bitmap editors. They work on graphic files that are made of pixels rather than vectors. When the paint programs began to be capable of loading or creating images that contained grayscale information, then they became capable of photographic image processing.

If a paint program can create a mask, called a frisket in the photo editors, then it is a full-fledged image editor. The presence of the ability to control gamma, brightness, contrast, hue, and saturation is another tip-off that your paint program is really an image editor. If your image editor allows you to create new documents, then it is a paint program. Image editors with paintbrushes, erasers, air brushes, selection lassoes, and customized brush sizes are paint programs.

⇨ Fractal Design Painter

Fractal Design Painter is not just another painting program. That is evident the second you see the package. Painter is packed in a paint can. This is not a mockup of a paint can, but the real thing, the kind that you would expect to find containing a gallon of Sherwin-Williams semi-gloss. When you open the can, the inside actually smells like latex paint. You immediately get the idea that this product will not disappoint, and you will be right.

Fractal Design Painter carries the subtitle "the Natural Media" painting program. The goal is to so perfectly imitate the real-world

tools of the atelier that the artist will feel as comfortable before the computer screen as before the easel. The software makes the actions of those tools on the monitor produce results that rival those of real pens, paper, brushes, paint, and canvas.

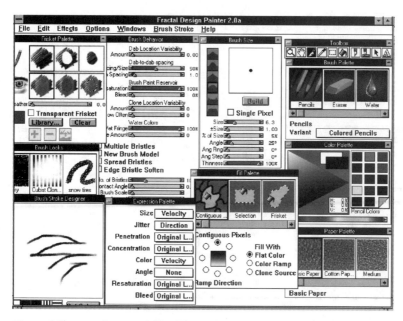

Figure 10-1

Fractal Design Painter's tools are located in floating palettes, sections of which can be torn off and distributed about the work area.

It may not seem appropriate to couple a software review so intimately with a particular hardware product, but Painter depends on a pressure-sensitive graphic tablet. It works best with a Wacom (or similar) tablet. If you are going to use Painter with a mouse, be prepared to do a lot of switching between menus and the painting in order to duplicate the effects that a tablet can produce almost offhandedly.

Painting with a normal bitmap painting program is mostly a process of changing the colors of the pixels of the image display. The process is similar to the woodcut or, at best, to the silk screen. The effect produced can be every bit as good as that produced by the printing press. Painter is designed to produce results that can be mistaken for physical media.

Figure 10-2

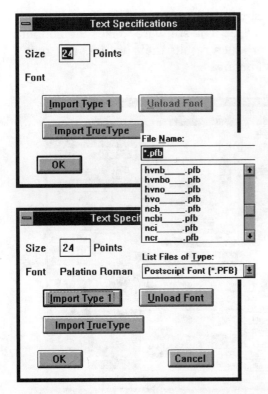

To use text, you must double click the text tool, opening the Text Spec dialogue. Import a font (superimposed font list) from cryptic list, and then click OK when font you want is loaded.

Painter makes underpainting possible. This is reason enough to adopt it. Making paint that is semitransparent is not a great leap in itself. But making electronic brushes that act like real ones is a great leap forward. Although the stylus of the tablet does not have the tactile response of the brush, the result is close enough to the real thing that you can feel justifiably amazed.

Painter employs palettes to provide access to commands and features. The palettes are activated from menus, and the individual tools of a palette can be torn off and placed on the desktop as you would any real tool. There are pencils, crayons, charcoals, chalks, brushes, pens, air brushes, felt-tip markers, and tools that simulate water drops and watercolor brushes, not to forget the Eraser. There are even tools that mimic the styles of certain artists or schools or painting, such as the Pointillist Suerat or the Impressionist Van Gogh.

Each tool has its own palette of specially designed colors that represent the colors that the real tools would produce. This is a

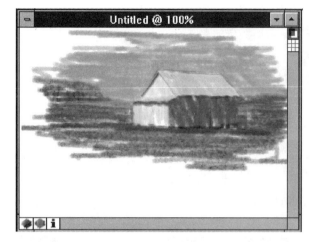

Figure 10-3

Special effects produce an attractive effect.

Figure 10-4

Experiment with a duplicate image to avoid ruining the original.

Figure 10-5

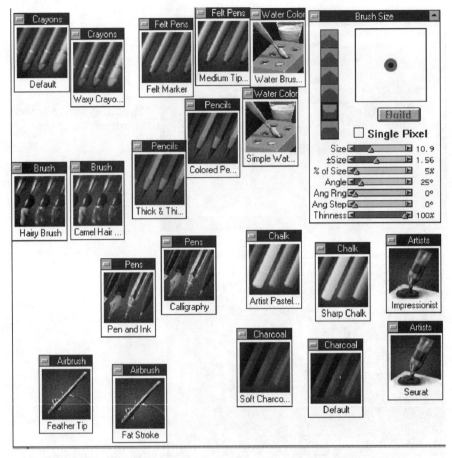

You want a choice of painting implements? Painter inundates you with every graphic instrument imaginable.

suggestion, not a limitation; any palette of colors can be used with any tool. You stand less of a chance of being disappointed with a tool if you follow the suggestion.

Each tool recreates the effect that its real-world counterpart would produce on a variety of surfaces. Those strokes are remarkable counterfeits of the originals; their appearance is convincing.

There are six different categories of the Pencil Tool and nine types of Water Color brush. Besides the standard No. 2 pencil, there are

colored pencils, thick and thin pencils, sharp pencils, a single-pixel scribbler, and a 500-lb. pencil, which is much larger than even the fat pencils you used in the first grade. The difference is not just in the size of the "lead" of the pencil, but in the very nature of the pencil's action. Each variation of each tool has its own peculiarity that other tools, even of the same general type, cannot exactly match.

The faint image left behind by the Eraser is a small effect, but it is nonetheless remarkable for its fidelity to the result from a real eraser.

Magnified pencil strokes

Pencils in other programs make a uniformly black line, but Painter's pencil is as close to electronic graphite as can be.

The conceit of the natural media is carried through from the choice of surface and the absorbency of the paper on which to paint to the use of "wet" or dry "paint." When you use the "wet paint" option, the effect of dragging a brush across a colored area is decidedly different from the effect of the same brush across "dry paint." Some brushes (watercolor brushes) will have no effect unless you are working in the "wet paint" mode. And if you have chosen an absorbent paper to work on, then the "wetness" of the paint will interact even more strongly with the surface texture.

Painter's special features cannot be saved in the normal formats that are used by other programs. Wet paint must be saved in Painter's own .RIF format. The .TIF format will preserve features such as friskets in the alpha channel. If you "dry" "wet" paint, you can save the file to .TIF, and when the file is opened, you can make the paint "wet" again.

Painter is a perfect photo editor. There are tools in Painter that do not exist elsewhere, not even in Photoshop or PhotoStyler. Even the ordinary tools for image editing can have offbeat effects. The Brightness and Contrast controls may be the only tools that work in the same old way.

You might not have ever thought to alter the light source for a two-dimensional image as if it were three-dimensional, but you can with Apply Lighting in Painter. You can change the position of the light sources, both ambient and local, as well as the source colors. You can add new light sources, redirect them, and move them about.

Figure 10-8

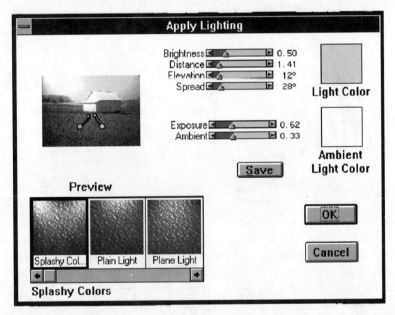

Applying 3D lighting to two-dimensional images is just one of Painter's extraordinary effects.

There are different types of lighting, ranging from a gradual light to spotlights. You can achieve very naturalistic lighting or lighting that is wholly surrealistic. There is a Billboard lighting effect, with multiple lights shining down on the image, and a crepuscular Half Dim light that simulates the shadowless light of twilight. Many 3D rendering programs do not have such a variety of preconstructed lighting scenes. This is an exceptionally creative tool.

Figure 10-9

Billboarding effect is dramatic.

Figure 10-10

Half light of an evening sky can be simulated.

Friskets form the basis of many image editing tasks. Painter has numerous ways to create friskets. You can use the Magic Wand to select a color or range of colors by dragging in an area to define the frisket. You can use the freehand knife tool to outline a selection that will become a frisket, or you can use the straight line knife to make a selection for a frisket.

You can have multiple friskets in the same image. One frisket can be used to punch an opening within another frisket, and you can add to

Figure 10-11

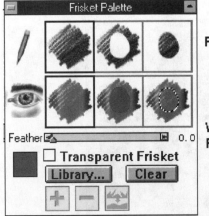

Frisket Knives

**Window
Frisket Popups**

*Frisket creation and
control tools. Popups
are the same as on the
palette.*

Figure 10-12

*Two methods for same
result, using frisket to
restrict changes to area
within selection. Top
uses paint inside
function (note icons in
lower left corner of
frame) with transparent
mask, while bottom
shows mask (note icons).*

or subtract from a frisket to adjust the shape. Friskets can be scaled, rotated, and feathered at the edges to allow them to be antialiased into the image.

Text in Painter is treated as a frisket. You import outlines into the Text Frisket tool by choosing a font file, either PostScript or TrueType, from those stored on the hard drive. Once a font has been chosen and imported, you type into the image. When you have completed typing, the text characters become individual friskets that can be manipulated like other friskets.

Cloning is another frequent activity in image editing. Painter goes beyond the usual touch-up technique that is used in other programs. There are 12 cloning tools in Painter: Pencil Sketch Cloner, Felt Pen Cloner, Hairy Cloner, Oil Brush Cloner, Chalk Cloner, Hard Oil Cloner, Van Gogh Cloner, Melt Cloner, Driving Rain Cloner, Straight Cloner, Soft Cloner, and Impressionist Cloner. Each will copy an area in its own unique manner. Only the Straight Cloner will make an exact duplicate of the original area.

The most remarkable feature of the Cloners is that you can clone to a different destination document than the original. The ability to

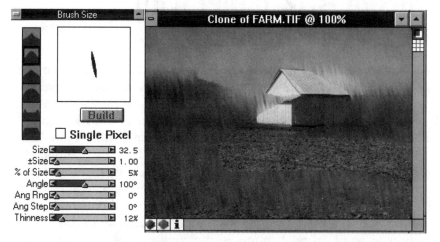

Figure 10-13

Driving Rain Cloner creates a blurred image similar to that that would be seen through a fogged window pane. Note effect as if someone had rubbed a finger across the filmy pane.

move areas between two different documents without copying or dragging is extraordinary.

Painter also has a Clone command, which duplicates an image in a new window. Thereafter, the original and its clone have a special relationship. You can paint in the clone and transform its appearance while retaining the subject.

Painter can read and save in TIFF, RIF (its own Raster Image Format), PICT, PSD (Photoshop proprietary format), BMP, PCX, TGA, and EPS. Only RIF and TIFF retain the alpha channel information. Only RIF retains all special image information.

Painter can record your motions as you paint, and the whole "session" can be replayed like a full-motion video. There are sessions supplied as demos. You can use your own sessions as demos.

What is wrong with Painter? Little. It does not retain tool settings from session to session. If you want a particular brush to use again, you must save it as a brush. Colors are not automatically retained after being mixed.

Wacom ArtZ tablet with pressure-sensitive pen

The Wacom ArtZ tablet, UD-0608-R, is a "laptop" digitizer, smaller than the normal 12 × 12-inch tablet, but just as useful. The unit is 9.6 inches by 13 inches, only 0.5 inches thick, and it weighs about 2 pounds. The active work area is 6 × 8 inches. The work area is sufficiently large and the resolution is fine enough (more than 1200 lines per inch) to make it a perfect companion tool for painting programs. It can operate in either an absolute or relative mode. In the absolute mode, the active surface is keyed to the display area with a one-to-one correspondence. Picking up the pen and placing it at a distance from the first point moves the cursor directly to the touchdown point. In relative mode, the cursor moves as it does with the mouse: lifting the pen from the surface and placing it elsewhere on the surface simply continues the motion from the previous point.

The pressure-sensitive pen is light and cordless. It is the size of a ballpoint pen, with slightly less heft. There is a single button mounted on the barrel, but the tip is the principal "clicking" agent. Pushing the tip on a window element and lifting is the equivalent of placing the mouse cursor on the element and clicking once. Tapping the tip to the tablet twice is the same as double clicking.

If the pen tip is in contact with the tablet surface when you click the side button, there will be a cancellation of clicks. The pen tip will be preferred. It is better to keep the pen tip off the surface of the tablet; this will return a clean double-click to the system every time with just a single click of the barrel switch, making it a genuine shortcut.

In addition, there is a feature called "double-click assist," which locks the cursor position to the first click location unless the pixel tolerance is exceeded. The assist also helps to differentiate between double clicking and click-and-dragging, which can "look" the same to the software. There is also a handwriting mode that ensures continuous input to the system from the pen stylus, despite variations in pressure or speed.

The tablet can also be configured to work with a puck. The mouse and tablet are both active, so that you can change pointing devices at any time. Input from the tablet is spooled to the mouse driver, making simultaneous use possible. The only caveat is that you must not lay the stylus down on the tablet, lest a continuous feedback loop be established that prevents the mouse from operating the cursor. A nice weighted and felted pen holder is supplied with the tablet to hold the stylus when it is not being used.

The setup of the tablet is almost automatic. The performance of the tablet-and-stylus combination is virtually flawless. The single bug that showed itself was caused by a conflict between the Microsoft Pen Windows elements that are used by the tablet and Microsoft Windows Write. Write will not run while Pen Windows is active.

The use of a pressure tablet with pressure-sensitive software is as close to natural drawing as you can get with computer-aided drawing. The making of tools that permit the use of transmitted light to create artwork on computer is a phenomenal achievement. The combination of tablet and Fractal Design Painter fulfills this desire of artists to be able to paint with light.

 # Fractal Design Dabbler

Fractal Design Dabbler is a painting program with many of the characteristics of Painter. It should not be thought of as a substitute for Painter, however, but more as an introductory product. It can also be viewed as the tyro's Painter. It has been suggested by one reviewer that Dabbler be thought of as the current standard bearer of painting software, the proper successor to MacPaint as that one piece of inspired software which demonstrates what can be done with a computer.

Figure 10-14

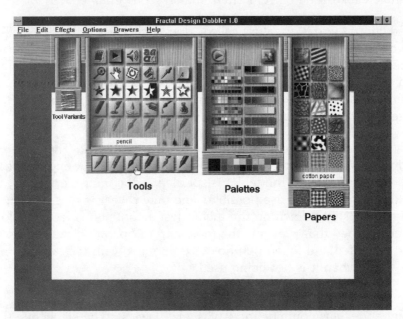

Changes to Elevation, Brightness, Distance, Spread, Ambient light strength and Exposure made with sliders are shown in thumbnail.

Dabbler has some elements of that "right stuff" of software, personality. Like MacPaint, it is easy to pick up and use without knowing anything about it, and it gives a certain pleasure in what can be accomplished without really trying. Dabbler uses the conceit of being an artist's paint box, the container with its drawers and lids, into which the itinerant artist will put his supplies. Dabbler uses the metaphor quite literally.

Dabbler has drawers which, when clicked on, will slide open to reveal their contents and, when clicked on again, will slide shut. The animation is clever, and it is accompanied by appropriate sound effects. The contents of the drawers are the tools and supplies of the artist. Rather in defiance of the metaphor, there is a wastepaper basket into which unsatisfactory works can be discarded, accompanied by the sight and sound of crumpling paper.

Figure 10-15

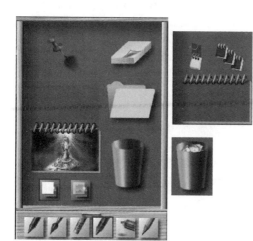

Sketchbook drawer contains thumbnails of your works in sketchbooks, with waste paper basket for failures, tracing paper, folder to file away work, new paper pad. Closing sketchbook reveals others under cover flap.

The tools of Dabbler are similar to those of Painter, although without that program's almost infinite possibilities of variation. You can move tools into and out of the drawers and line them up in the toolbar. Only a select few tools are active at a time. Choosing a new tool from a drawer means that one already in the toolbar must be sent back into the drawer whence it came. This process follows a rotation that seems fixed.

Unlike MacPaint, which was small and ran on a minimum of hardware, Dabbler is humongous and needs all of the computer that you can give it. Nothing, absolutely nothing, can run simultaneously with Dabbler. It wants all of the memory. And, because of its animation and sound effects, it demands a fast and powerful

486 computer to make it run at a tolerable speed. The typical home computer does not make a good base on which to run Dabbler.

 # Fractal Design Sketcher

Sketcher is Painter dressed in gray. While Painter is distributed in a paint can, its humbler, more casual sibling is distributed in a cigar box. All that is missing is the latent smell of tobacco. What use is there for a grayscale version of the best color painting program in the world? Certainly, you can do everything in Painter that can be done in Sketcher and then some, but, if you want to work mainly or exclusively in grayscale, why use Painter? By eliminating color, the program becomes smaller, the overhead becomes more manageable, more computers can be used, and the price drops.

Sketcher is virtually identical to Painter in most respects. It has the same tools, the same commands, and the same way of managing

Figure 10-16

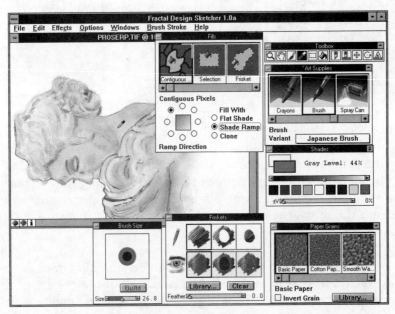

Sketcher's interface is almost identical to that of Painter.

tools and commands. Sketcher should be run in 256-color mode, because grayscale display technology is almost universally limited to 8 bits or 256 levels of gray. The program is faster in 8-bit mode. This program comes closer to being the new MacPaint than does Dabbler; it has nothing to apologize for in being a grayscale editor.

Image processing

Image processing has come to represent a considerable portion of graphic workstation usage. The task of the image editor is to provide the tools that will improve scanned photographs. These include certain filters or effects that can operate on the pixels of the scanned image in groups or singly relatively. Almost all programs contain a common set of these filters that affect change contrast, brightness, color saturation, sharpness, and noise. Some programs allow alteration of the gamma. Usually the user will want to reproduce effects from the darkroom. These include cropping, enlarging, dodging, burning in, and more complex effects.

Exposure is the fundamental aspect of photography, and the one most frequently in need of correction. Overexposure of a negative causes a darkening of the negative, and lightening of the print; underexposure of the negative causes lightening of the negative, and darkening of the print.

Dodging is the darkroom technique by which image detail is retrieved from an area of a photograph in which it would be lost during normal printing due to the original underexposure of the negative. Print exposure in a selected area is decreased by lessening the amount of light that reaches the paper.

Burning is the complementary darkroom technique by which selected areas in a print are darkened relative to the remainder of the photograph by increasing the exposure of the areas while shielding or masking the other portions of the print. The technique is used to retrieve detail that would be lost in an area of the negative which had been overexposed.

Adobe Photoshop

Adobe Photoshop is the 500-pound gorilla of photimage manipulation software. It is the professional's choice for touch-up and enhancement of scanned images. While there are many other competent image-processing programs, none can claim to exceed its number of features, file format support, or complexity.

Photoshop incorporates an almost inexhaustible number of tools and tool options to change or to create color images. The protracted

Figure 10-17

Adobe Photoshop has a familiar toolset. There is nothing enigmatic about its icons.

loading of the various tools at startup gives a fair impression of the wealth of the program's resources. I doubt that anyone has found the program lacking in any important aspect. The fact that the program is modular and has spawned a whole new genre of miniature, external programs called plug-ins is one reason for this completeness.

Even before attempting to use the program, however, the manuals insist that you calibrate your monitor. This is perhaps not so much a warning as a signal to professionals that it is, indeed, up to their standards.

Actions performed on images using Photoshop proceed in a comfortable, familiar fashion, despite being electronic. While the professional user will feel comfortable with the program, the novice user will find the program's many palettes, dialogue boxes, and hierarchical menus intimidating. To help with this disparity in the level of proficiency of potential users, an excellent tutorial manual is provided, which addresses both the operation of the program and the techniques and terms of image manipulation.

The basic workspace of Photoshop covers the monitor. On the left is the toolbar, and at the bottom is the Status bar, in which help comments and file size are shown. Both of these are active by default, as is the Brushes palette, but all palettes and bars can be hidden to make use of the full screen area for image display and editing.

The toolbar contains the usual drawing and painting implements, three selection tools (Marquee, Vignette, and Lasso), Magic Wand, Cropping Tool, Text, Grabber, Magnifying Glass, Paint Bucket, Gradient Fill, Line, Eyedropper, Eraser, Pencil, Airbrush, Paintbrush, Rubber Stamp, Smudge, Sharpen/Blur Tool, Dodge/Burn Tool, Foreground/Background Color, and Painting and Screen Mode buttons.

Photoshop offers seven menus for tools and commands (File, Edit, Mode, Image, Filter, Select, and Window) and an eighth Help menu.

The selection tools are very flexible. In addition to the regular selection tools, the Magic Wand is also a selector. It operates on pixel color, pixels of colors of similar hue distributed throughout the image, or pixels in addition and adjacent to the color designated. Combined with

commands from the Select menu, the power of selection can be very precisely controlled. Selection is the basic function that makes possible the use of Masking, one of Photoshop's most powerful features.

The Cropping tool is used to isolate a portion of the image and to eliminate areas outside the selection.

The Text tool, also called the Type tool, is used to enter text into an image. All the familiar attributes can be set. An interesting attribute is anti-aliasing, which softens the edges of text.

The Grabber moves the image about in window as if the scroll bars were being used. With the Ctrl key, the Grabber changes temporarily to the pointer.

The Magnifying Glass is the all-purpose zooming tool. A clicking with the zoom tool in the normal mode (a plus sign inside the cursor) causes a doubling of the present magnification up to 32:1. Using the Alt key with the zoom tool (a minus sign in the glass) results in a reduction of the magnification down to 1:16. An area can be centered in the magnified view by clicking and dragging diagonally. Holding down the Shift key produces the pointer.

The Paint Bucket is used for area fills. It has options for Tolerance, Foreground Color or Pattern Fill, and anti-aliasing. Tolerance is a value for the pixels having a color within the numerical spread of color designated in the box.

The Gradient Tool is used to create graduated fills, with the foreground and the background colors as the starting and ending points. The Shift key modifies the tool by constraining the direction of the fill to 45 degrees or its multiples.

The Line tool is used, not surprisingly, to draw lines. Lines can be customized for width and be drawn with or without arrowheads at the starting or ending point.

The Eyedropper is used to pick up or sample a pixel's color, which becomes the currently active foreground color. Used with the Alt key, the Eyedropper will select a new background color.

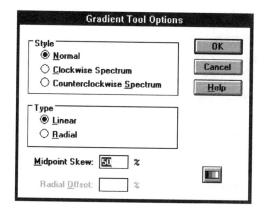

Figure 10-18

The Gradient Fill can proceed directly from the starting to ending color through shades of the two colors, or it can proceed through the spectrum in anticlockwise or clockwise direction around the color wheel.

The Eraser has two modes of operation. The basic eraser function is to wipe away anything beneath it, replacing it with the current background color. With the Alt key depressed, the Eraser becomes a Magic Eraser, which acts to restore the area beneath it to its condition at the time when the image was most recently saved.

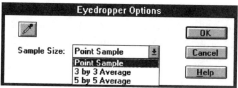

Figure 10-19

The Eyedropper can be customized to sample pixels or averages of pixels.

The Pencil is a freehand drawing instrument with several options to vary its effect. The most interesting is the Fadeout option, which decreases the intensity of the Pencil's impression as the line is lengthened. This option is available for all painting tools.

The Airbrush's options are the same as for the other painting tools, but its effect is cumulative. The density of its paint becomes greater the longer that it is applied to a pixel or the more passes that it makes across a pixel.

The Paintbrush is the basic bitmap editing tool in Photoshop. The options are the same as for the Airbrush. At this point, it is appropriate to consider the Brushes palette.

The Brushes palette establishes the most basic features of the painting tools (Airbrush, Paintbrush, Pencil, etc.) and many of the

Figure 10-20

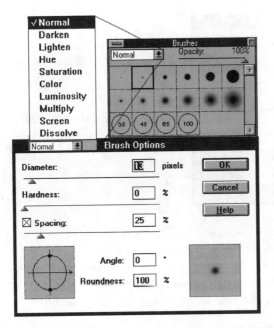

*Brush Palette and Brush
Options Dialogue.*

effects in Photoshop. The shape of the brush, its size, and the opacity
of its paint can be set, as well as the manner in which it acts on the
pixels of the image.

The Rubber Stamp tool paints with a copy of a neighboring area in
the image. For instance, this tool can be used to reproduce a pattern
or a background to repair a damaged image. Or it can be used to
clone an area without using a selection tool, which can leave artifacts
or fringing. The tool can be further modified by choosing the method
by which the parent area is chosen and reproduced.

The Smudge tool (the fist with index finger extended) is used to smear,
as though one were dragging a finger across wet paint. The effect is
to smear the paint at the point of first contact in the direction of the
drag. If the Finger Painting option is selected, then the foreground
color is substituted for the color beneath the cursor at mouse down.

The Blur/Sharpen tool (symbolized by the water drop or chisel,
depending on mode) is used to decrease or increase the contrast of
the pixels beneath it. The effect is to soften or to sharpen focus.

The Dodge/Burn tool is used to simulate the technique of reducing or increasing exposure of a print in the darkroom by either interfering with the light above an area that was overexposed on the negative (dodge) or allowing longer duration exposure (burning in) on an area which had been underexposed on the negative. The effect of each increases with time.

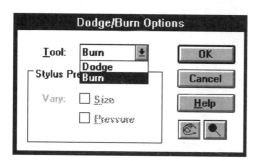

Figure 10-21

The Dodge/Burn tool likewise has a dual personality, set in the dialogue.

Immediately below the tools, the active foreground and background colors are displayed in swatches. Clicking on either brings up the color picker. The Photoshop color picker shows the spectrum on the center right and the specific area of the spectrum on the left. Thus, one can move the sliders to concentrate on any particular color range, with the colors in that range being displayed in the square.

Just below the color box are the controls that toggle between normal painting mode and the Quick Masking mode. A mask has the effect of creating a stencil or punch, through which another layer (or channel) can be allowed to show or can be removed while the rest of the image is untouched. The Quick Mask allows the creation of one mask, while the Mask Mode allows multiple masks. Quick Masks are temporary, while multiple Masks are saved and become permanent channels of an image.

Channels are 8-bit level grayscale images that are part of the total image. RGB images contain three color channels (one each for the red, green, and blue values in the image) and one for the combined image (the RGB channel). When a mask is created, it goes into a new and separate channel, which then becomes part of the total image according to the commands that are executed on it in combination with the other channels. Masks also can be used in other images.

175

Figure 10-22

Each of the channels of which the image is comprised can be viewed and edited separately.

Starting with two files, BLUES.JPG and LEAF.EPS, that are contained in the Tutorial folder supplied with Photoshop, we can show some of the effects available using masks. The BLUES file will serve as the basic image on which the effects will be worked. By creating a new channel, we prepare the image to receive the mask which will be formed by the LEAF image. Using the Place command from the File menu, we can import the LEAF file directly into the channel without having to open and copy it as a separate file. The EPS file is opened and placed in the center of the document.

By clicking the mouse when the gavel cursor is visible, the LEAF is deposited in the channel and automatically becomes selected as a mask. Changing to the RGB channel, we can see that the "crawling ants" of the selection are visible, defining the mask. Now, choosing Calculate from the Image menu and Add from the submenu, we can use the mask to create a new image from the BLUES file by specifying the sources in the dialogue.

The new image is created from the mask and the BLUES RGB image. The black area of the mask has been filled with the BLUES image, and the white areas have been masked out.

An important use of the mask or discontinuous selection is to restrict the application of an effect to a particular region of a picture. One might isolate the regions of flesh in a portrait, then use the Inverse

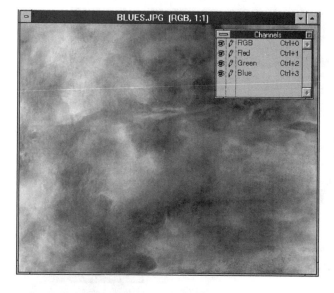

Figure 10-23

RGB image with four channels.

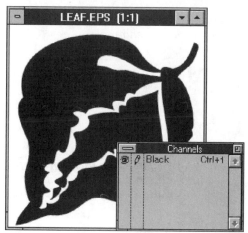

Figure 10-24

EPS image with one channel.

command from the Select menu to protect the skin from any effect that was applied to remaining areas of the picture. In that way, color in clothing can be changed, contrast altered, and special effects applied without changing the fleshtones.

Another use of the mask is to restrict the area into which an image can be pasted into another image. The selection can be filled with another image, but the remainder of the original image is protected

Figure 10-25

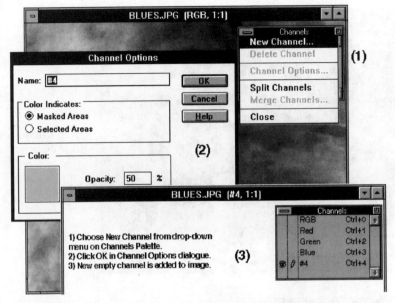

Process of adding a new channel to RGB image begins with Channels Palette and ends with new, empty channel.

Figure 10-26

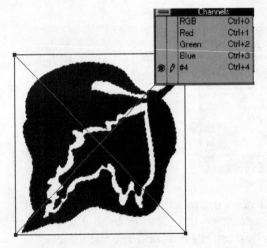

Placing EPS image in empty channel eliminates opening, cutting, and pasting of image.

by the mask. In this example, the LEAF selection has been filled with a sunflower cut from a third image and pasted into the selection.

If you choose Paste Behind, the image in memory is inserted between the mask and the background. The position of the pasted image can

Figure 10-27

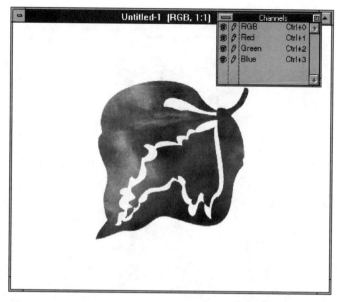

The new image, same size as the BLUES image.

be adjusted; its opacity and the manner in which the composition is to be managed are set in the brushes palette. Before the pasted selection is deselected, other options such as Defringe can be specified.

Defringe softens the edges of the selection so that the line of demarcation between the background and the selection is less evident. After the composition is correct, the selection is permanently placed in the image. Other effects can be applied to the image at that time.

In the case of the bumblebee and the sunflower, the sunflower is too sharply focused. Before the sunflower was added, there was a blur of motion from the bee's right wing below and to the left of the bee's body. This has been obscured by the sunflower. By selecting that area of the sunflower and choosing Motion Blur from the Blur submenu of the Filter menu, that effect can be restored. Also, the rest of the flower can also be blurred slightly to make it recede more into the background.

Besides Add, there are ten other possible effects in the Calculate submenu under the Image menu, Blend, Composite, Constant, Darker, Difference, Duplicate, Lighter, Multiply, Screen, and Subtract.

Figure 10-28

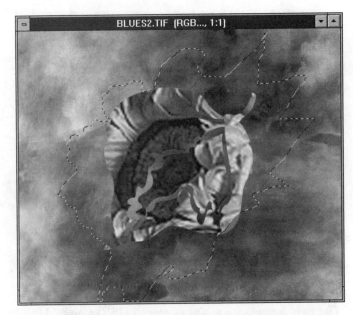

*Using the LEAF as a kind of stencil, the SUNFLOWER
can be revealed through the BLUES. SUNFLOWER can
be moved behind both the stencil and the overlaid image.*

Figure 10-29

*Area within selection can be
blurred directionally, as if by
motion, to recapture the effect
of the bee's wing movements.*

Other commands in the Image menu include those for orientation
(Flip horizontal, Flip vertical, Rotate 180 degrees, 90 degrees
clockwise or counterclockwise, or Arbitrary or Free rotation), plus
those for physical alteration of the image's proportions or aspect
(Scale, Skew, Perspective, Distort), and for changes in the Image Size
and Canvas Size.

Figure 10-30

More realistic result of blurring.

Figure 10-31

Composite uses three sources, one a mask, to make final
image.

Figure 10-32

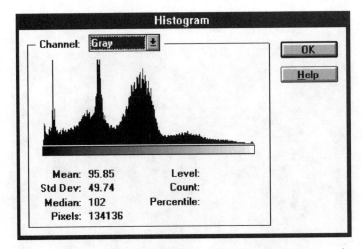

The Histogram allows inspection of balance prior to and after adjustment of distribution of values in image. A count of pixels having particular values is displayed.

A Histogram display is also available. The last command, Trap, is used in color separation of CYMK images to specify the amount of overlap of colors in the channels to compensate for misregistration of the color plates in the press. The trap value is determined by the amount of misregistration that the printing house normally can expect from its machines.

The File menu is long. Not only can you Open files in 15 specific formats, you can Open as a suspected file format. Among the supported formats is one, RAW, which makes no assumptions about format and can be used to open many files that have defective or missing file headers. Using the plug-in feature, the standard Photoshop configuration opens and writes Photoshop 2.5 (.PSD), Amiga Deluxe Paint Image File Format and Hold and Modify (.IFF,.HAM), Microsoft Bitmap or Run Length Encoded (.BMP,.RLE), CompuServe Graphic Interchange Format (.GIF), Adobe Illustrator and Encapsulated PostScript (.AI,.EPS), Joint Photographic Experts Group compression format (JPEG,.JPG), MacPaint (.MAC,.MPT), ZSoft PC Paintbrush (.PCX), Kodak Photo CD (.PCD), Pixar (.PXR), PixelPaint (.PXI), Raw (.RAW), Scitex Continuous Tone (.SCT), Targa (.TGA,.VDA,.ICD,.VST),and Aldus Tagged-Image File Format (.TIF).

Photoshop has eight modes of image handling and display. These modes determine the actions and the tools that can be applied to an image. By choosing a different image mode than the one in which the image was opened, Photoshop will convert the image to the designated format. Conversion can also be made at the time an image is saved. Photoshop supports Bitmap, Grayscale, Duotone, Indexed Color, RGB, CYMK, Lab Color, and Multichannel formats.

Bitmap is the simplest form of digital image, black-and-white pixels alone. Other image forms can be converted into bitmaps, but first they must be converted to grayscale: grayscale is the only form that can be directly converted to bitmap.

Grayscale images are color images from which only the values for luminosity or brightness are retained. Values for hue and saturation are discarded. It is possible to convert a black-and-white bitmap to grayscale, but, unless the scale of image is reduced so that pixels can be combined to form areas of gray, the result will be useful only for hand editing.

Duotone is a catchall category that includes true duotones, as well as monotones, tritones, and quadtones. Monotones use one nonblack ink to print the image. Duotones use two inks, tritones three, and quadtones four inks. The ink colors can be specified in the conversion dialogue.

Indexed color is the mode for 8-bit images. It creates a color lookup table for the image, in which the colors are limited to 256. Depending on the method in which you have Photoshop create the table, the relative fidelity of the reduced palette image to the full spectrum image will be determined.

RGB mode is the most common color mode for true (24-bit) color images. The color model is that of the familiar red, green, and blue used in most electronic color displays.

CYMK (Cyan, Yellow, Magenta, and Black) images are 32 bits deep (four channels of eight bits each). It is the mode used by printers for color separations.

Lab color creates three channels: luminosity, "a," and "b." It is most useful when a change in the brightness of pixels is desired but the actual colors are to remain the same. The "a" channel contains information for green to magenta and the "b" channel contains the blue to yellow data. Lab color mode is mainly a temporary one and after the luminosity has been adjusted, the image is usually converted back to RGB or CYMK. It is also useful for transferring images between computer platforms or for printing to PostScript color printers, because the mode is device-independent.

Multichannel color mode is produced by adding a channel to a grayscale image or by removing a channel from a 24- or 32-bit image.

The Filters provided with Photoshop cover most of the types of effects that you would wish to have available. There are three different forms of Blur, Gaussian, Radial, and Motion. Blur is a softening of edges and a removal of noise. Gaussian blur is fog effect. Gaussian blur refers to the Gaussian or Normal distribution curve. Motion blurring can be directional and limited to a specific length. Radial blurring is similar to the effect that a rapid zoom has in photography.

Unlike the simple Distort command under the Image menu, the Distort filter has nine variations in its submenu, and each variation has options. Displace has practically infinite variability, since it relies on a user-specified and user-modified displacement map to perform its effects. The displacement map is used to assign values to the direction and amount of movement of the pixels in the original image.

Pinch, the second command in the Distort submenu, squeezes a selection by a user-defined percentage. A negative value causes the image to bulge. The Polar Coordinates filter creates a specialty effect, a sort of radial smearing.

Ripple creates a wavy effect, like a reflection on windblown water. Shear is a combination of Skew and Distort from the Image menu's Effects submenu. It causes a bending of an image according to the curve you specify. Spherize is another specialty effect, giving an image the appearance of being reflected from a spherical surface. Twirl bends an image in a manner resembling a starlight mint. Wave is an elaboration of Ripple, in which the user is given many options

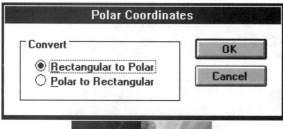

Figure 10-33

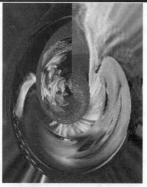

A popular amusement from the 19th Century was viewing of images drawn with anamorphic distortion using a cylindrical mirror. Image wraps around curved mirrored surface placed in center.

Figure 10-34

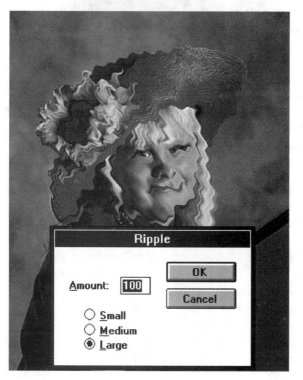

Ripple is one of myriad effects of this type, creating a distortion similar to that imparted by water on a reflection. Effect is variable.

Figure 10-35

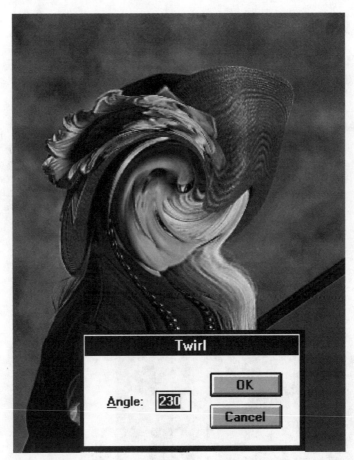

Twirl sends an image spinning down the drain.

with which to control the effect. Zig Zag creates another kind of wave distortion, an effect that can look like a image on a pond into which a pebble has been thrown.

The presence of the Noise filter seems contrary to common sense, but it can be used to add graininess to an image for photorealism. Despeckle is a more familiar concept, which removes noise from an image. The Median Noise effect is another method of noise reduction, in which clusters of pixels are averaged together to produce a median brightness level which is then applied to the central pixel of the cluster to decrease contrast.

Figure 10-36

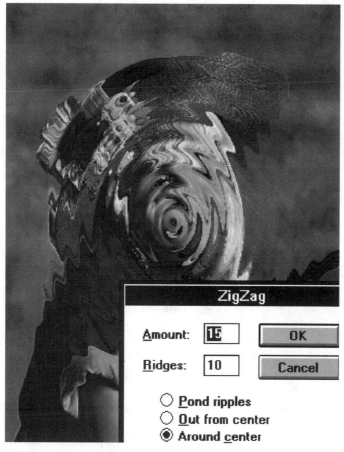

Zig-Zag is yet another wave effect, this one resembling the effect produced by dripping water into a puddle.

The various Sharpen filters all increase contrast between pixels to differing degrees. The Sharpen Edges and the Unsharp Mask concentrate on finding edges and creating light and dark contrast lines in those areas rather than generally heightening contrast throughout the image.

Stylize provides 15 submenu choices. Most of them deal with creating pseudo-three-dimensional effects (Emboss, Find Edges, Trace Edges, and Extrude) or with effects that break the image into fragments by clumping pixels together (Crystallize, Facet, Fragment, Tile, Mosaic,

Pointillize, and Solarize). These filters have many options, too many to discuss in detail.

Photoshop Plugins

Adobe Photoshop has had such an impact on image editing that it has created a whole new subspecies of software, the plugin. Plugins are small program modules that can be seamlessly integrated into another program to add additional functions. The main program and the plugin enjoy a symbiotic relationship, each supplying the other with something to produce a new, enhanced single entity.

The ability to add these modules is dependent on the construction of the main program. Object-oriented programming has made more of these programs possible, and the field of plugin programming has expanded as more host programs have become available. Aldus (now merged into Adobe) has taken the lead in defining the parameters of plugins.

On the Macintosh, Aldus has developed a series of plugins called Gallery Effects. They are typical of the tools that are now becoming available in the Windows environment in such packages as Kai's Power Tools. With a combination of these effects, virtually any real-world image or unreal darkroom effect can be recreated on the computer.

The simulation of surfaces is interesting. By applying a surface to an image, you can obtain a result that appears to be the photograph of an original painting, mosaic, drawing, etching, or woodcut.

Kai's Power Tools from HSC

Kai's Power Tools go far beyond the norm of the plug-in filter. Their interface is different, for one thing. Judging by the look alone, you know that there is something happening here besides simply sharpening the focus.

The user interface for KPT is rather more organic than you would ordinarily expect in a set of plug-in tools. The impression is by

design; Kai Krause wanted to make something that would be conducive to creativity; something that would be "almost a game."

If you are the kind of person who does not laugh at puns and who wants software to be "businesslike," then you will have problems acclimating to KPT. You may find that many of the effects are useless on first acquaintance, and they might be at the time. Later, with a different image on the screen, you might feel differently. You might find that an effect is to be added to an image, not simply used wholesale, but blended into the original. Some effects, such as Stereo 3D Noise, you might never find useful or even amusing.

Try out the obvious effects first. Take the Page Curl; this effect simulates transferring the image to a transparency and then curling back one corner of the page. You can control which corner is curled, and in which direction. This has obvious uses in advertising or in electronic book design.

One of the most fascinating features of KPT is the Texture Explorer. Selecting the Texture Explorer brings up a panel unlike any other in Windows, or elsewhere for that matter. It has a peculiar green color, and there is strange resemblance to the dashboard of a 1949 Ford or some other unlikely control cluster. Starting on the left side and sweeping right is a tree along the trunk of which green knobs or marbles have been inset. On the right side is a display of panes, one large pane surrounded by smaller panes. In the central pane is a

Figure 10-37

Kei's PowerTools Page Curl effect.

pattern, a fractal design generated by the software, and the surrounding smaller panes contain variations on that central theme, similar but not quite the same. When you move the mouse cursor over the tree and it touches one of the marbles, the marble turns red, and the images in each of the small panes changes. The farther up the tree that you move, marble to marble, the more that the images in the panes diverge from the original pattern in the central pane.

Figure 10-38

KPT's Texture Explorer is a fractal generator with an idiosyncratic interface. Its pea green controls and fade-away text are part of a counter revolution in intuitive interface design.

If you happen to see a pattern that takes your fancy, you can click on the pane that contains the pattern and transfer it to the central pane, where it becomes the source of new variations. Thereafter, as you move the cursor up and down the tree, or you click on the rainbow-colored marble near the center of the Texture Explorer, new patterns are generated based on the substituted central pattern.

This is a set of tools that cannot really be described. In this one case, you must simply try them on for fit.

Aldus PhotoStyler

Aldus PhotoStyler and Adobe Photoshop have been playing leapfrog with one another in power and features for years. Photoshop has the "look and feel" of traditional darkroom tools and techniques done down to the ground. If something can be done in the darkroom, it can be done in Photoshop.

PhotoStyler takes a slightly different approach. Instead of simply mimicking the darkroom technique, it forges ahead and introduces things that could only be done in a computer. PhotoStyler not only does things that can be done in the darkroom, it expands the toolset of the photographer with new electronic techniques of image editing that are easier to use than even the "natural" and familiar tools.

PhotoStyler's toolbox is arranged in a manner that also is slightly different from the norm. Whereas other programs will array their tools in clusters under "fly-out" icons, PhotoStyler bundles them into groups that are activated by master icons. The icons in the body of the toolbox change according to the master icon button currently depressed.

The Selection Tool Group is characterized by the Selection Group Icon, the first in the toolbox. Its constituents are the Rectangular Selection tool or marquee, the Freehand Selection tool or lasso, the Elliptical Selection tool, the Straight Line Selection tool, the Magic Wand, Selection Move/Scale Tool, and the Grabber or Hand. Some of these tools don't act quite as you might expect them to do. The Line selection tool is unique to PhotoStyler: it selects a vertical or horizontal line of pixels. Why you would need this tool is not entirely clear; perhaps to select a fragment of a border?

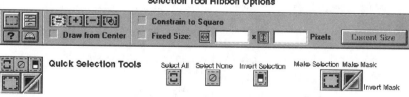

Figure 10-39

The Selection tools have Ribbon options to add to or subtract from the selection or otherwise modify it.

Using the selection buttons in the ribbon at the top of the window, you can add to and subtract from an active selection. You can also deselect and invert selections with smaller buttons at the bottom of the toolbox. Generally, you have total control. This is the basis of masking, the foundation of many image editing tasks.

The primary use of a selection is usually to copy or cut the contents in order to paste into another image. PhotoStyler completely voids that basic function by putting drag-and-drop to work: you can select a portion of an image in one window and drag the selection into another image's window, a great benefit to efficiency.

Figure 10-40

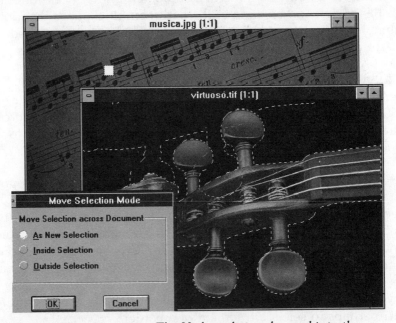

Drag-and-Drop in action. The Violin is being dragged into the underlying image in another window. The white cursor indicates that the selection has entered the destination. The Dialogue shows only if there is already a selection active in the destination.

The conversion of a selection into a frisket is quite simple. You click on one of the diagonally formed buttons in the area just above the color swatches. The left button turns the selection into a red mask, and the right button turns the selection into a white mask. When the mask is active, painting in the masked area reduces the mask by the amount of the painted area. Returning to the normal selection mode by clicking on the adjacent Selection button then permits you to paint or otherwise edit the area inside the selection.

Selections or masks can be used in creating composites. The Merge Command permits you to combine a pasted image with a target graphic. Merging is done after an image has been pasted into a graphic window. You can control how the merged graphics, both pasted and target, will react when the Merge command is used. Merge controls are found in a dialogue panel. You can choose how the pixels of the pasted image are added to the target by choosing options from the Use Floating Image drop-down menu. Always use all of the pasted image's pixels, painting over the target graphic. If Darker . . . prefers the pixels of the floating selection where they are darker than the pixels underlying them. If Lighter . . . prefers the selection where its pixels are lighter than those underlying. Hue Only . . . changes only

Figure 10-41

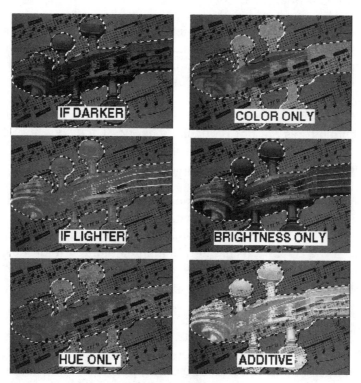

The results of different merge variations.

the Hue but not the brightness or saturation of underlying areas. Color Only . . . alters the hue and saturation but does not change the brightness of underlying pixels. Brightness Only . . . alters the brightness of underlying pixels to match those of the selection. Additive . . . mixes the underlying pixels with the selection's pixels. Subtractive . . . removes the selection's pixel values from the values of the underlying pixels.

Not content with creating composites through the Merge command, PhotoStyler's programmers have added other means by which you can combine images. These means are activated by the Compute command in the Image menu. You have 10 Compute options: Add, Subtract, Multiply, Blend, Extract, Composite, Difference, Lighter, Darker, and Shift. Extract and Shift do not combine images; the former takes the color value from a solid color or gray and combines it with the colors in the source, and the latter uniformly adds or deletes a color value from an image's pixels to lighten or darken the source.

Image editing tools are activated by the Iris iconic master tool button, immediately below the Selection master button. The tool palette is then altered to show the image editing tools: the Clone tool, the Dodge/Burn tool, the Soften tool, the Sharpen tool, and the Lighten and Darken tools.

These editing tools are not particularly exotic. The Clone tool lifts a portion of an image and duplicates it at another location. As in Fractal Design Painter, you can clone an image to another image window.

The Dodge and Burn tool lightens or darkens the selected part of an image. Dodging is accomplished with the left mouse button, and Burning with the right button. Defaults are programmed into the tools for each of the operations (lighten highlights, lighten midtones, lighten shadows, darken highlights, etc.) as well as for increasing and decreasing exposure, and increasing and decreasing contrast.

The Soften tool (the Water Droplet) is used to reduce the contrast or to blur by averaging adjacent pixels. The size and shape of the droplet can be set in the tool ribbon, as well as can the spacing of the droplet's track and the degree of blurring permitted. Additionally, you can choose to have the tool operate on all pixels or only on those

pixels that are lighter than or darker than the settings. The Sharpen tool, the chisel, increases contrast between adjacent pixels. Its controls are the same as for the Water Droplet.

The Lighten tool uniformly increases the brightness and decreases the saturation of pixels. The Darken tool decreases the brightness and increases the saturation of pixels. Both tools can be adjusted for the degree of effect and the softness of their edges.

The effects of the Retouching tools are neither cumulative nor relative. The action of a tool is determined by the tool settings, and is accomplished in one pass.

Not to be forgotten are the Image menu sub-commands. Brightness and Contrast, Tonal Correction, Focus (Sharpness), Color Balance, Hue and Saturation, and numerous other adjustments can be found under the Tune command and applied to whole images or to selections. There are some helpful displays included, particularly the Histogram, which shows the distribution of pixels at each level of brightness. The distribution can help in setting the White and Black points of an image to broaden the grays.

The Painting tools are actuated by the Paintbrush master button. The painting tools include the Paintbrush, Airbrush, Pencil, Eraser, Gradient Fill, Bucket Fill, Smudge, and Line.

The Paintbrush is the basic tool of the set. The size and shape can be changed. Custom shapes designed by the user can be saved and reused. The opacity and the reaction of the paint with underlying colors can be controlled. The Paintbrush can have a soft or feathered edge, with the degree of feathering set by the user.

Figure 10-42

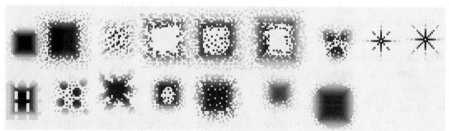

The preset custom brushes available for the painting tools.

The Airbrush paints with a spray of dispersed pixels. The flow rate and area of coverage are regulated by user-selected settings. The paint is more dense in the center of the stroke than at the edges.

The Pencil draws or paints with a solid line, but is otherwise similar to the Paintbrush. The Eraser paints with the background color. You can also specify that the Eraser paints with a white or black color, or, if the image has been saved, that it replaces the most recent stroke of a painting tool with the pixels stored in the saved version.

The Graduated Fill tool creates and applies fountain fills to selected areas. The starting and ending colors are the Foreground and Background colors, which can be changed from the Floating Palette of the Color Picker. You can also choose to use Custom Colors from the Floating Palette. These colors form a range and can be changed as desired. The same color painting reactions that occur between the underlying paint and the Paintbrush also apply to the Graduated Fill tool.

The Paint Bucket applies solid color fill and pattern fills. Patterns can be user-created or loaded from a library. You can control the extent of the fill by using selections. You can further restrict the extent of the fill by setting a numerical Similarity limit, which designates a range of color variance into which the paint may flow from the area where the mouse click occurs. Opacity controls and paint reactions with underlying paints are the same as for the Paintbrush.

The Smudge tool blends or smears colors into one another. The degree of smearing can be set, as well as the type of paint that will be affected. The size and shape of the Smudge tool can be changed as desired.

The Line tool is a constrained paintbrush. It draws or paints just as does the Paintbrush, except that it makes only straight lines. Lines can be drawn connected, so that each new line segment begins at the end of the most recently drawn segment. All of the options for the Paintbrush apply to the Line tool.

Most of the Painting and Image Editing (Retouching) tools can be used only on 24- or 32-bit RGB and CYMK images. Among the Retouch tools, only the Clone tool can be used when an 8-bit image

is open and active, and of the Painting tools, the Eraser, the Line, and the Bucket Fill tools can be used. To use any other tools requires that you convert the image to RGB first.

Each of the Painting and Retouching tools can be tried on the image in a Practice Pad or Scratch Pad, which is a duplicate of a portion of the active image. Any changes that are made to the Scratch Pad image can be applied to the original, or they can be discarded if unsatisfactory.

PhotoStyler's user interface can be customized to some extent. Instead of switching from one array of tools to another by clicking on the master tool button for each tool set, you can assemble custom or personal toolsets that contain tools from each of the separate tool varieties. These personal toolsets can be arranged in any order, and can be saved and recalled as needed.

Another shortcut or interface aid for the user is the Image Navigator, which allows rapid movement around within the active image. With it you can change the level of magnification, scroll the image, and fit the image to the display. If an image window has been reduced to an icon, the Navigator can be used to Restore it.

Figure 10-43

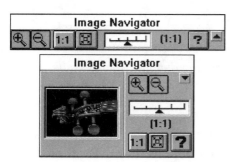

The Image Navigator can be used in one of two forms to move about in the active window.

In the lower middle of the Tool Palette are four tools that are always available, regardless of the type of Tool variety in use above. These are the Text tool, the Cropping Tool, the Eyedropper, and the Magnifying Glass.

The Text tool permits the entry of text into an image. Text can be entered as mask, as a floating selection, or as bitmaps directly on the image. Text attributes can be changed while the text remains

selected. Text fonts and font attributes are set in the ribbon at the top of the PhotoStyler window. Bold, Outline, Italic, Underline, and Strike Through styles can be set by clicking on the relevant buttons. Both PostScript and TrueType are supported.

The Cropping tool has the obvious function of trimming an image of extraneous area, but it also has the function of Resampling at the same time. If an area is already selected when the Cropping tool is activated, that selection will define the cropping border. You can also specify a new image size and a resolution if Resampling is enabled.

Figure 10-44

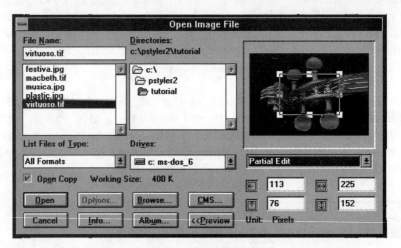

PhotoStyler has a flexible file opening dialogue that permits browsing and partial image editing.

The Eyedropper can select colors from the active image. If you simply click on a pixel, that pixel's color is lifted. You can, however, use a selection tool in the Eyedropper's tool ribbon to sample an area of the image, and the program will return an average of the colors within the selection as the new color.

PhotoStyler's default color-matching system is the Kodak Precision Color System, but the Windows, DIC, FOCOLTONE, Munsell, Pantone, TOYOpc, and Trumatch systems are also supported. PhotoStyler reads and writes .BMP, .DCS (Quark XPress), .EPS, .GIF, .JPG, .MAC, .PCD, .PCT (PICT), .PCX, .PSD, .RLE, .SCT (Scitex), .TIF(F), and .TGA formats.

Bundled with PhotoStyler is a version of Image Pals Album, the catalogue program. With Album, you can view thumbnails of images and group them into folders. Images can be loaded into PhotoStyler simply by dragging the thumbnails into the PhotoStyler window.

Effects in PhotoStyler are numerous, covering all of the usual photographic wizardry and discovering a few new spells into the bargain. There are six types of blur provided in the Effects menu under the Soften command: Blur, Gaussian Blur, Average, Maximum, Median, and Minimum. There are differences in the method of blurring and in the results in their more extreme manifestations, but the differences between the types tend to become less distinct as the effects are reduced. Blur is a lessening of contrast between adjacent pixels.

The Sharpen command has five subcommands: Sharpen, Edge Enhancement, Unsharp mask, Find edge, and Trace Contour. Each of these tends to detect and augment areas of greatest contrast in brightness or color.

The Noise command has two entries: Despeckle and Add Noise. Despeckle is used to remove stray pixels within areas of relatively even color values. It blurs over individual pixels that might have been introduced by dust or other imperfections on a scanned image. Add Noise is used chiefly to introduce random dots to areas that have heavily edited, resulting in unnaturally smooth tonal transitions.

The Special Effect menu command has 10 subcommands: Emboss, Diffuse, Monochrome, Mirror, Mosaic, Point Acceleration, Scratching, Solarization, and Vignette. Emboss creates a bas relief effect, combining edge detection and contour emphasis. Diffuse randomizes pixels within a user-specified cell. Monochrome converts to . . . what else, monochrome.

Motion Blur simulates the directional blurring that results from movement during exposure, either by the subject or the camera. Mirror has the effect of repeating an image as if seen through a faceted lens. The effect can be vertical or horizontal and resembles more than anything else the effect of a rolling (vertical) or slipping (horizontal) television image. Mosaic clumps pixels together and blends them into square or rectangular tiles.

Figure 10-45

Diffuse makes an image look as if it were being viewed through frosted glass.

Figure 10-46

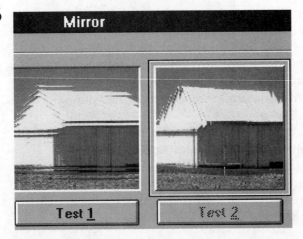

The Mirror effect is not the familiar symmetrical reversal found in other programs but a vertical or horizontal reduplication, similar to that of double vision.

Point Acceleration produces an effect similar to that achieved by zooming a camera lens in or out during exposure of a frame. Scratching simulates the effect of smearing the entire surface of a picture in a single direction; with it, some impressionistic effects can be created. Solarization is selective inversion of color values based on a threshold value supplied by the user. Vignette applies an effect that

Figure 10-47

Mosiac clumps pixels together in squares, averaging them to make a block pattern.

isolates a region in the image by shading back from the area to the edges of the image, similar to the superimposition of a matte.

The 2D Spatial effects include the Ripple and the Whirlpool. The Ripple reproduces the radiating distortions caused by a pebble which has been dropped into water. You can set the frequency of the wavelets and the amplitude. Whirlpool gives an image a swirling appearance, as though it were painted on the surface of water that is draining out of a sink. The degree and the direction of the spiral can be controlled by the user.

3D Spatial effects are Cylinder, Pinch, Punch, and Sphere. Cylinder simulates the wrapping of an image around a Cylinder. Pinch gives the image of a pincushion or puckered look, as if the center were drawing in the edges. Punch applies the opposite effect, making the image look as the center were being pushed outward from the back toward the viewer. Sphere gives an image the appearance of having been photographed with a fisheye lens.

There is also a Custom 3D effect available, with which the user can experiment to warp the image in new ways. You draw in a box a new

Figure 10-48

PhotoStyler catches the wave action with its own Ripple. The frequency (number) and amplitude (height) are individually adjustable. Concentric waves produce effects like Photoshop's Zig-Zag.

Figure 10-49

A Custom 3D Effect can be drawn by the user. This one is similar to the concentric wave.

mapping curve, which is reflected into the negative axis. The effects are elliptical, as though an image were being seen through a fresnel lens. You can apply mathematical variations to the drawn profile. Custom effects can be saved and reused.

Lastly, there is a User Defined command that permits you to make your own visual effects filters. The dialogue presents you with a grid that represents the possible pixel cell. Into the boxes of the grid you enter numbers to be applied to the pixels in the cell. These numbers weight the pixels artificially. Experimentation or knowledge of mathematical filtering can produce some useful or interesting effects.

Figure 10-50

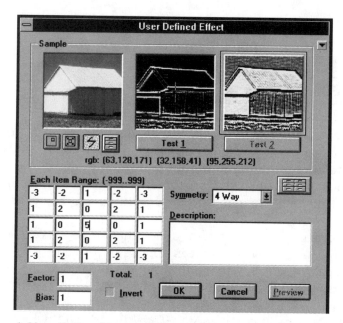

A User Defined special effect filter allows you to experiment with the principles of image manipulation.

A feature that is unique to PhotoStyler is the Sketch Overlay, a transparent layer that can be drawn and written on. The overlay is a grayscale image that can be used to make annotations on a copy of the original image without actually altering the original. Changes to an image can be roughed in as a guide to composition. This can be useful when a composite image is to be created.

Figure 10-51

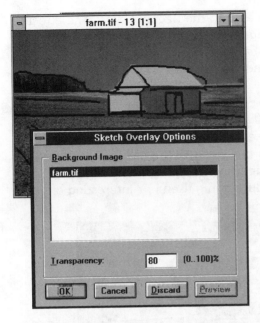

The Sketch Overlay is like tracing paper, allowing the creation of new images without changing the original.

Remember, PhotoStyler does not neglect the simple effects. You can Rotate an image or a portion of an image. Particularly helpful are the Rotate Level commands, which will align any edge that you select within an image to either the horizontal or vertical edges of the window. There are commands to Flip, Shift, Resize, Skew, and Distort.

PhotoStyler has a Multi-Transform option that displays a copy of the active graphic on which you can apply transformations, to judge the result before actually altering the original. You can apply the transformations to the original before leaving the Multi-Transform panel.

One hint of things to come is Auto Tonal Adjustment, which takes a stab at making color corrections without any directions from the user. No doubt we will see more of this type of unassisted activity in programs now being written. As more professional photographers and designers add their own experience to software through comments and suggestions, programs will be able to diagnose and automatically correct problems without the user's help.

Choosing between PhotoStyler and Photoshop may be one of the more difficult choices that you have to make. The decision is basically a

toss-up. Photoshop has the advantage in working with text, in the use of channels for masks, and in the number of file formats supported. PhotoStyler has the advantage of more numerous and more innovative tools and in program design; its use of drag-and-drop is first rate.

Both programs have excellent user interfaces; the choice may come down to one of taste. If you cannot decide, you might want to take a second look at Fractal Design Painter, which can do almost anything to an image that you can imagine.

CorelPHOTO-PAINT

CorelPHOTO-PAINT is a well-thought-out program that quite frankly admits that painting and photo editing programs are really one and the same. It resembles Photoshop in many of its tools, but lacks Photoshop's comprehensive options. It is sufficiently powerful that you might not need to buy another program for image enhancement.

PHOTO-PAINT uses roll-ups, those handy little palettes that you can tuck into themselves. Not all of the program's features are found in roll-ups, but there are enough of them to give the program a cleaner-than-normal interface.

The Fills roll-up governs the use of patterns, fountains, solid colors, and textures by the fill tool. Patterns can be made from any bitmap. Fountains can be linear, radial, or rectangular. Textures are practically unlimited in number. Some textures are extremely complex fractal patterns with multiple colors, while others are limited to two colors.

The Canvas roll-up is similar to the Texture fill of the fills roll-up. You can apply a canvas pattern to an image with a variable level of transparency. Canvas patterns are not impervious to overpainting. You can create your own canvas patterns, but they must be square and can be no larger than 128 pixels on a side.

The Color roll-up allows you to set the colors of outline, background, and fill in the three principal color models, RGB, CYMK, and HSB. There is no support for color matching systems, although a calibration command is available.

Figure 10-52

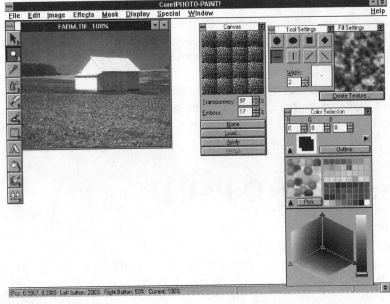

CorelPHOTO-PAINT uses roll-ups. It has a generous toolset.

Figure 10-53

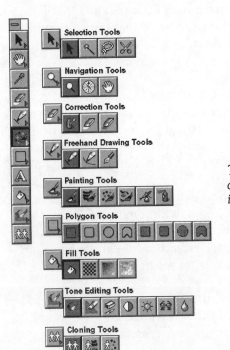

The flexible toolbox is by default a floating palette with fly-out iconic menus.

The Toolbox is not a roll-up, but it can be reconfigured in a number of ways. Flyouts that show the complete toolset for any particular class of tools can be converted so that all of the tools are displayed in rows and columns.

There are four selection tools: a rectangular pointer, a magic wand that selects by color, a freehand lasso, and a pair of scissors that cut in straight line segments. Selections can be used as masks. Masking is done at an elementary level, and does not rival the effects achieved with Photoshop. Masks are used to exclude areas from change by a tool: only the area within the selection will be altered.

The painting tools are extensive. You can choose from painting effects that emulate Pointillism or Impressionism. There is an Artist Brush (presumably the Pointillists and Impressionists were artists, as well) that has various characteristics of a brush applying oil paint. Brush size and shape can be customized in the Tool Settings roll-up. There is a spray can, but there is also an airbrush. The spray can cannot be configured for anything except size and shape of the paint spatter distribution, while the airbrush can be configured in a variety of ways.

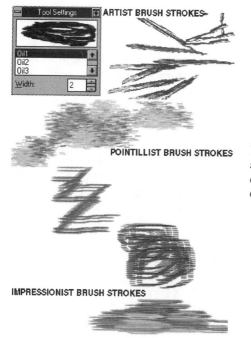

Figure 10-54

The Brush strokes that are supplied have some naturalistic qualities such as skips and clumping.

There are several brushes or tools that make possible the smearing and blending of paints. These work well, although it is difficult to see the difference in effect between the Water Droplet and the FreeHand Smear.

Tools for traditional photo retouching exist in several forms, also. There are the common adjustments to contrast and brightness, set with percentage gauges. There are also FreeHand Sharpen, Contrast, and Brighten tools that can be applied like brushes to spots or small areas. There are Cloning tools that reproduce one area of an image elsewhere in the same image.

There are controls to apply the standard filters: Sharpen, Unsharp Mask, Enhance Detail, Adaptive Unsharp Mask, Smooth, Soften, Diffuse, Blend, etc. There are controls for Gamma and Hue/Saturation correction, as well as commands to flip, rotate, distort, to change resolution, and to resample. You can also convert between color depths and split or combine channels. Combining channels is useful to create color images from grayscale scans using filters.

There are some special effects provided, such as embossing, adding or removing noise, despeckling, solarizing, etc. These are common effects available in most image and painting programs.

PHOTO-PAINT provides some prepress controls, but these are not extensive. It reads and writes the most common image formats, .PCX, .BMP, .GIF, .JPG, .PCD, .TGA, and .TIF, not a wide selection but one that covers about 90% of the sources.

PHOTO-PAINT is an adequate photographic editor and an excellent paint program. If you are more interested in painting than in image retouching, then it can be the program that fills the need. For heavy-duty, industrial strength photographic work, however, you would be wise to purchase a more capable program.

Micrografx PhotoMagic

PhotoMagic is very similar to PHOTO-PAINT in its capabilities, but its emphasis is reversed, more on the photo than on the paint. PhotoMagic is a capable image editor, and its painting tools are adequate.

Figure 10-55

PhotoMagic has a clean, simple user interface.

The image editing features of PhotoMagic comprehend the usual and the unusual. Some of the usual functions of the photo editor are implemented in unusual and sometimes inexplicable ways. The Contrast and Brightness control, for instance, is cross-hair that can be moved about in a small box. The intersection of the cross-hair can be shifted up and down and left and right, or any combination of the four directions. The control is obvious, but the size of the control surface places a severe limitation on the fineness of control that can be achieved; adjustment is in 10-percent increments.

Other effects are more precisely delivered. Color reduction or conversion is adjustable with a slider that provides increments of approximately three units, meaning that you can reduce a True Color image to 256 colors, 253 colors, 249 colors, 246 colors, etc. Dithering of colors can be precisely controlled. You can choose whether round dots will be used and if they shall be at a 45-degree angle, or whether horizontal or vertical lines will be used to produce the dither. While you may not have any idea what these effects will actually produce, you do have some input into the process.

Figure 10-56

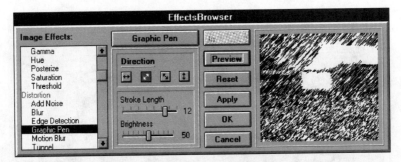

The Graphic pen effect is particularly striking.

There are a lot of special effects that can be applied besides the common solarize and blur. Many of the effects are seen in other programs only as add-in or plug-in tools. You can wrap images around a simulated sphere or cylinder, create a pincushion or barrel distortion, or add textures with embossing or engraving and other effects. More immediately useful effects include Stretch Detail, a form of sharpening that works very subtly and effectively, sharpening without inducing undue graininess. And there are transformations that can be applied, such as skewing, mirroring, flipping, and resizing.

Resizing permits you to use SmartSizing. This is a method of changing scale with the least possible loss of detail. When an image is reduced in size, pixels must be eliminated. SmartSizing applies an algorithm to the process that improves the result. When reducing an image, the color values of pixels that are eliminated are averaged or factored into the values of remaining pixels, and the final image is an entirely new version of the original. When an image is enlarged, the new pixels that are created are made by sampling the adjacent pixels to reach transitional values that enhance detail rather than diminish it.

PhotoMagic is a middle-of-the-pack type of program. It can probably satisfy most users, but it will not be of much use to those who need a lot of control over the tools of photo editing and painting.

File formats

T HERE are two basic types of computer graphic formats, the bitmap and the vector. Bitmaps are composed of individual, unrelated points on the drawing surface, and exist as absolute coordinates on the drawing page. In its simplest format, a bitmapped pixel can either be on or off. While compression is built into most bitmap formats, bitmap files are typically large.

Vector drawings consist of mathematical relationships between points in an absolute coordinate system. Vector drawings can be described in plain language and stored as text. All elements of a vector drawing are objects, and objects have two basic qualities, outline and fill. The outline defines certain properties of the object, most important of which is whether the object is open or closed. A line is open, because it has unconnected points or ends. A circle is closed, because its outline has no unconnected points.

Pixels, as such, do not exist in vector drawings. Many vector programs permit the importation of bitmapped drawings, but the bitmaps are considered single objects, and the pixels of those objects, with few exceptions, cannot be individually edited. Given this fact, it would be reasonable to assume that there should be two universal file formats, one for bitmaps and the other for vectors. However, where logic proposes, commerce disposes.

Every drawing program must have a means of storing and retrieving its files, and every programmer probably has entertained an idea of how that format ought to work. There are two objectives in a file format; the first and most important is to preserve the contents of the working file, and the second is to use as little storage space as possible. These two objectives are really mutually exclusive. File compression entails the removal of information, while file fidelity compels the preservation of data. The resolution of this conflict has

become a third objective of file format design, and has contributed to the present confusion.

Acting alone, programmers would tend to adopt standards in the interest of efficiency, and file formats would tend toward unity. The tendency of companies, however, is to protect their proprietorships by expansion. If a file format can be promulgated as both efficient and proprietary, the products that use it can become dominant. Self-interest has, thus, brought us a wealth of formats with which to disseminate information, and little understanding as those formats prevent the full exchange of those ideas. Formats, like languages, both preserve and destroy comprehension.

Bitmap

If all computer bitmaps were black-and-white, then there would probably be but one format, that of MacPaint. It balances the demands of fidelity and economy. MacPaint was actually a refinement of Lisa Paint, the precursor of Bill Atkinson's definitive painting program. He gave the Lisa the essential Toolbox ROM routines that later he rewrote and reformed for the Macintosh.

The MacPaint format is based on the idea that in a black-and-white image in which the background emulates a sheet of white paper, a pixel is either on (black) or off (white). With that simple rule, you can describe any image as digital ones and zeroes. Because an image will contain large areas of a single color, you can compress the file size by using a shorthand notation that contains the color to be used (zero or one) and the number of consecutive pixels that will have that color. Those two numbers can be written and read to recreate the original image. The arrangement, in its simplest form, is two bytes long.

The MacPaint format is for a fixed-size page, 8 inches wide by 10 inches long. The page is the same resolution as the Mac's original 9-inch black-and-white monitor, 72 dpi. A page is, therefore, 576 pixels wide. The page is further divided into scan lines, or rasters, by the progress of the cathode ray, creating a page that, if viewed in its entirety, would be 720 lines long (10 × 72). Thus, there are 414,720 pixels in every MacPaint document.

Because a pixel can be represented digitally in a one-to-one correspondence by one digital bit, a byte (composed of eight bits) can represent 8 pixels. A hexadecimal byte of FF (11111111 binary) would be eight black pixels. If that correspondence were maintained for the entire document, every MacPaint file would be 51,840 bytes in length. This does not take into account the innate compression that Atkinson programmed into the Macintosh ROM.

So effective is the MacPaint format, it was transported bodily by programmers into other paint programs for their own monochrome image file formats. The monochrome form of the file format .IFF, used by Electronic Arts in Deluxe Paint for the Amiga, is identical to that of MacPaint except for its header.

This manner of file compression is sometimes called Run Length Encoded, or RLE. There is a separate file format that uses the .RLE extension. Also, it is little known that the Macintosh and MacPaint were both color-capable from the beginning. The Mac had a system palette of seven colors, and MacPaint could display and use that palette. Of course, this was of no consequence to anyone; the Macintosh 128, 512, and Plus Macs had no color display. The first Macintosh to use color, the Mac II, had full-color display capability, and the original color potential was untapped. A third-party product was created eventually that used this capability on compact black-and-white Macs that possessed a SCSI port. It added an external color display that could use the basic colors of the original ROM routines.

Not all bitmaps are black-and-white, of course, and so complications arise. Color destroys the simplicity of the MacPaint format; you must have a way of indicating that a particular pixel is to have a particular color, and sometimes brightness as well. And, of course, repetitive pixel alternation is less likely with the addition of color. Color creates other problems; the number of colors can be as few as eight or as many as 16 million. Moving from computer to computer, you are likely to find that the colors used do not always have exact counterparts.

Creating a color look-up table (CLUT) or custom palette works fine if the image remains on one machine, but the table may have to be entirely recalculated if the image is moved to another type of computer. Embedding the CLUT in the header of the image file

simplifies the file and its translation and reduces the amount of data that can be potentially used in an image, thereby limiting the file size. A pixel can be assigned a number corresponding to a location in the palette, and its color is then unmistakable. When true color is used, however, it is not possible to use a CLUT, and each pixel must have the color information of its components attached.

 # Raster/bitmaps

The following is an associative listing of formats with their parent programs. Bitmapped formats are almost innumerable. The most commonly met are:

BMP This is the basic bitmap extension native to Windows and OS/2. The format is common to PC Paintbrush and Paintbrush, the Windows applet was developed by ZSoft. This format is identical to .DIB. Both are capable of storing color information up to 24 bits.

Figure 11-1

```
                          256COLOR.BMP
   Blck: 0 Part A

   0000: 424D D613 0000 0000 0000 3604 0000 2800    BM.......6...(.
   0010: 0000 5000 0000 3200 0000 0100 0800 0000    ..P...2.........
   0020: 0000 A00F 0000 0000 0000 0000 0000 0001    ................
   0030: 0000 0001 0000 0000 0000 0000 FF00 00FF    ................
   0040: 0000 FF00 0000 00FF FF00 FFFF 0000 FF00    ................
   0050: FF00 FFFF FF00 0408 0000 0000 7100 6D08    .............q.m.
   0060: 1000 9134 7D00 6124 4400 0055 0000 AE34    ...4}.a$D..U...4
   0070: A500 652C 3000 0000 8D00 0000 5900 752C    ..e,0.......Y.u,
   0080: 6D00 A534 7D00 5510 5500 7124 6900 5928    m..4}.U.U.a$i.Y(
   0090: 5000 7D30 7500 8924 4400 7128 6100 7128    P.}0u..$D.q(a.q(
   00A0: 6900 5924 4800 5524 4C00 DE38 B600 5024    i.Y$H.U$L..8..P$
   00B0: 4800 9540 8100 0099 0000 7D38 7100 AA10    H..@......}8q...
   00C0: 0400 AE34 9D00 6D2C 5500 DA48 CE00 7528    ...4..m,U..H..u(
   00D0: 7D00 3408 9100 6138 3000 A530 9900 8530    }.4...a80..0...0
   00E0: 7100 912C 8500 9144 7D00 812C 6D00 3459    q..,...D}..,m.4Y
   00F0: 1800 6D24 5D00 00BA 0000 5534 4800 793C    ..m$].....U4H.y<
```

Windows BMP sample.

PCX PC Exchange, the native ZSoft PC Paintbrush format. Common in Windows and Windows programs. The format has continued to evolve. It can store up to 24-bit color (Version 5). Uses the RGB color model exclusively. Earlier versions (2 and 3) stored up to 16 colors. Version 3 stored color palettes separately.

RLE Run Length Encoded, a compressed Windows format. If RLE compression is used with either the .BMP or .DIB formats, then those file formats become identical to the RLE. RLE cannot compress monochrome or 16-million-color files. Formerly the term was applied to an ASCII format for graphics.

GIF Graphics Interchange Format, a versatile, compressed format developed by CompuServe, with interlaced and noninterlaced forms. The format has evolved through several generations and is capable of holding several images in one file.

MAC Macintosh MacPaint format, black-and-white, 72 dots-per-inch. Also .PNT.

PCT More correctly PICT, a versatile and sometimes thorny Macintosh format that was primarily developed as the native MacDraw format, hence, a vector format. It is, however, a compound format, capable of storing color and grayscale bitmaps. Comes in PICT1 and PICT2 varieties.

TIF More properly TIFF, Tagged Image Format File, a general bitmap format that was jointly developed by Aldus and other companies for universal use in storing of monochrome, grayscale, and color images. It can be compressed or not compressed, and it comes in various "flavors" as companies have introduced variants to include their own enhancements. Not all variants can be read by all programs. Three types of compression are used, PackBits and Huffman for monochrome, and LZW for color or grayscale. Additionally, there are Group 3 and Group 4 fax formats, which are also compressed monochrome.

JPG JPEG, Joint Photographic Experts Group format, developed by committee to address the need for a standardized compression scheme for 24/32-bit color. Capable of variable degrees of compression inverse to quality (lossy), it has been adopted by most image editing programs. Also .JFF, .JIF, .JTF.

IFF Interchange File Format, another versatile format found exclusively on the Amiga. Promulgated by Electronic Arts in Deluxe Paint, it is capable of various resolutions and color depths.

HAM Hold And Modify, another Amiga only format. Designed to display all of the 4096 colors of basic Amiga palette at one time. Also called LBM.

CUT Dr. Halo format. A venerable file format from Media Cybernetics (Halo Desktop Imager) that predates Windows. Uses separate palette files for color data.

TGA TrueVision Targa file format. Workstation format based on Targa and Vista graphics hardware. Can store between 8- and 32-bit color information in compressed or not compressed forms.

MSP Microsoft Paint file format. Microsoft Paint, a MacPaint clone for Windows, was the predecessor of PC Paintbrush. Monochrome only.

IMG GEM file format. Similar to MacPaint, but from Digital Research. Commonly, you will find only monochrome .IMG files, although the format is capable of storing 8-bit color (256-color palette) information. Used in Atari computers and some IBM PC programs in the GEM iconic interface. A survival from another graphical user interface. Supported by Ventura Publisher.

CGM Computer Graphics Metafile. Similar to Windows Metafile and PageMaker Metafile. Primarily a vector format with raster potential.

DIB Device Independent Bitmap, another Windows native format. Identical to .BMP. When used with RLE compression, identical to RLE.

CLP Windows Clipboard format. Compound format that contains draw objects, text, color data, and other Device Dependent Bitmap data. May not always translate to computers using different hardware.

PIC An extension used in common by two dissimilar and incompatible formats, Lotus .PIC and PC Paint .PIC or Pictor .PIC.

Less common raster formats include those found on the Atari ST and Apple II computers.

PI1 Low resolution, 320 × 200, 256 color, Atari Degas format.

PI2 Medium resolution, 640 × 200, 16 color, Degas format.

PI3 High resolution, 640 × 400, monochrome, Degas format.

SPC Spectrum 512 Atari format. Similar in concept to HAM, allowing simultaneous display of 512 colors.

HRS Apple II Hi-Res format.

SRS Apple II Super Hi-Res format.

There are also formats found on the Unix based computers.

RAS or .SUN, Sun raster. Type 1 files are capable of storing 24/32 bit color information.

CAL A Government sponsored monochromatic format used by U.S. military and military contractors. Similar to ED5.

PCD Photo Compact Disc, the Kodak format for storing photographs as digital images on CD-ROM media. Image sizes are limited to 128 × 192, 256 × 285, 512 × 768, 1024 × 1536, and 2048 × 3072 pixels.

ED5 U.S. Navy sponsored format.

 # Vectors

A vector is a quantity with two attributes. Velocity is a vector, describing speed and direction. In drawing, a vector is a description of angle and distance. Because the direction can be in any dimension, vectors can be used to create representations of three-dimensional objects. Vector formats depend on a coordinate system that may be peculiar to the device or the program that creates the system. Some systems place the origin of the coordinate system in the upper-left-hand corner of the page, while others place it in the lower-left corner.

Vector formats are either text or mathematical descriptions of the points, lines, arcs, and angles that make up the objects in a drawing. In theory, these formats should produce smaller file sizes than

Figure 11-2

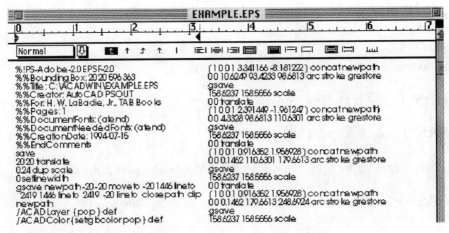

EPSF/AI PostScript file sample.

bitmaps for drawings that produce the same printed output. This is not always the case, however, as paint formats are typically compressed, and the number of points in a drawing is an important factor in the size of the file. You can, for instance, describe a circle with three points, or you can place an infinite number of points around the circumference; both objects will be circles, but one will produce a file of minimum size, while the other will produce a "disk full" error. Additional complications arise when a 2D format is used to describe 3D objects. Because many programs cannot display 3D objects, information is inevitably lost in translation.

The vector formats that you will meet with commonly are:

.AI Adobe Illustrator native format, a text file of PostScript commands and vectors based on the PostScript page coordinate system. PostScript files can contain fonts, halftones, fountains, color separations, and other page description data. See also EPS.

.ASC ASCII text, also .TXT.

.DXF AutoCAD Drawing Interchange Format, native to Autodesk products. An ASCII file containing descriptions of blocks, groups, and entities. Because .DXF files can contain descriptions of three-dimensional objects, they may not always translate properly into two-dimensional formats.

AutoCAD's proprietary format, .DWG, is almost never met; its specifications are subject to change in each release of AutoCAD.

.WMF Windows Metafile Format. A compound format supporting vectors, bitmaps, TrueType, and other Windows data. Also used by the Clipboard.

.CGM Computer Graphics Metafile. A complex compound file format that can contain RGB color, text strings, bitmaps, and drawing primitives. The format can vary, depending on the creating program and the data contained.

.DRW Micrografx Draw and Designer. Another compound file format that contains bitmaps, 24-bit color data, Bezier curve descriptions, drawing primitives, and 3D objects. Also .GRF and .PIC.

.EPS Encapsulated PostScript, a file format specifically for graphics. It can include a bitmap preview of the graphic. Depending on the computer and program of origin, the preview may be in TIFF or PICT format. When there is no preview or the software into which the graphic is placed cannot display the preview, convention has replaced the preview with a box containing two intersecting diagonals, and, optionally, text describing the date of creation and creator of the graphic.

.GEM Graphical Environment Manager Metafile, a compound file format from Digital Research.

.PGL Hewlett-Packard Plotter Graphics Language, a standard plotter description language, frequently incorporated into HP laser printers.

.IGES Initial Graphics Exchange Specification, a neutral format for drawing exchange, used by AutoCAD and other programs.

.PCT Macintosh PICT1 or PICT2 (color) format, created with MacDraw or other Macintosh drawing program. Can contain bitmaps. PICT2 supports 24/32 bit color.

Less frequently met formats are:

.GCA IBM GOCA metafile.

.MET OS/2 Presentation Manager metafile format.

Image conversion, capture, and cataloguing conversion

FILE formats have certain things in common, such as the general structure. Usually, the file will be divided into two parts: the header, containing information about the file such as file length, color depth, custom patterns, colors used, and file format version; and the actual file data that comprises the image. One can usually ignore the header and still recover the image data by trial and error. It is the arrangement of that data that can cause all the trouble.

Converting files between similar types, that is bitmaps to bitmaps or vectors to vectors, can be done with satisfactory results in most cases. There are always singular features, however, that one program will support but another program does not, and that will cause incomplete translation. These errors can be minimized by saving the original file in a common rather than proprietary format, but you may lose some of the special features that the parent program preserves in its native format. And, of course, you may not have the program that originally created the subject file.

Converting files between dissimilar types, such as bitmap to vector, can be very tricky, if not impossible. Conversion of vectors to bitmaps is not as difficult, although there is sure to be information loss. Because vector files are not resolution-specific, they can be displayed and printed in any resolution available. Bitmaps are highly resolution-dependent, and conversion of a vector drawing to a bitmap format will lock the target file into a particular resolution, perhaps one not at all flattering to the image. Some effects, such as drop-outs, may not translate from vector to bitmap. In general, it is best to translate within a file type than between them. Where this cannot be done, an intermediate step may help.

For instance, if you want to translate a bitmap into a particular vector format, you will probably have to first trace the bitmap with one program and then translate the resultant vector format into the desired target format using a second program. Some drawing programs can import bitmaps and place them in drawing, but the bitmaps cannot be edited, except to scale, crop, or rotate them. Tracing the bitmaps and importing the traced objects eliminates that restriction. Other drawing programs, such as Canvas, permit you to edit bitmaps with painting tools. In such programs you may not wish to trace a bitmap, but merely use it as-is.

The one general rule of file translation can be stated succinctly: there is no universal translator. Its corollary is this: simple formats translate better than complex formats.

Translation programming

Most drawing, painting, and image editing programs can open/import and save/export in several file formats. Those programs that support external filters or plug-in modules to handle file formats grow more compatible as new filters are added. However, there are still times when the software you have to use does not support the file format that you need to use. In those cases, you must turn to a conversion program. There are many on the market, but I will mention only a few.

Tracing programs

Programs that trace bitmaps and produce vector-format drawings are now quite numerous. Often that feature is built into a program or is added as an external tool. Deneba's Canvas and CorelDRAW both have internal tracing tools that are more than adequate for most tasks.

The object of the tracing program is to produce an outline that has the greatest possible fidelity to the original bitmap mass with the fewest possible points. The general rule is that the fewer the points, the less detail, and the more detail, the more points. You will usually be told that you should use the highest dots-per-inch bitmap available for the trace, since it will produce the greatest detail. However, as you must use what you have, the best advice is to tailor the tracing parameters to the bitmap's peculiarities. You are given two options in most tracing programs: one, to make the trace loose or tight, and two, to make curves or straight lines. The manner of setting these parameters differs from program to program. Some will be adjusted by numbers of pixels: the higher the number of pixels, the closer the fit. Some will be adjusted by percentages or by dragging a slider. Most will have a preview or example to illustrate how changing the parameters will affect the traced outline.

A loose trace will skip features below the level of perception that you have set; it will not see features with a prominence less than the number of pixels allowed. This will tend to make a smoother outline, but it will sacrifice details. A tighter trace will follow the bitmap's outline closely, producing greater detail but many points. Such a trace will be harder to edit and to print.

Using more curves in a trace will tend to make the outline smoother, but you will lose details. If you favor lines in the final trace, then there will be a greater number of joints or angles, some of which may be inappropriate, requiring editing.

You may also be offered the option to trace outlines or centerlines. An outline trace will tend to produce more objects than a centerline trace. If two areas are separated by a line, the program will trace the two areas separately in outline mode, and there will be a gap between the two areas where the line had been. When opened in a drawing program, each of the adjacent areas will have its own outline, creating a double-line effect, with a blank or open area between that cannot be filled. The centerline trace will eliminate such double-lining by making a single line through the center of the bitmap line. This type of trace when opened in a drawing program will consist of lines rather than objects. The type of trace ordered will depend on the type of bitmap. Some programs will permit you to assign a weight or percentage

preference to the outline or centerline, which will mix the two types of tracing in the same output file. This will allow the program to make areas into objects and to make lines into centerlines.

Almost every tracing tool or program will work best with black-and-white or high-contrast images. If you must trace a color or grayscale image, adjust the contrast or convert it to monochrome before running the trace function. This will increase the accuracy of the trace and reduce the number of spurious objects created.

Lastly, it should be noted that every autotrace tool or program will not produce perfectly clean or satisfactory results in every instance. Indeed, it is almost a certainty that every tracing will need at least some editing. The most common problem is the high number of nodes, which must be reduced to make the objects manageable and to keep the outlines smooth. You will undoubtedly have to do some experimentation to get the correct balance of nodes and detail.

As an alternative to autotracing, you might want to place the bitmap in a layer of a drawing program and manually trace it. If you have a digitizing tablet, creating an object from a printed version of the bitmap might be easier in the end than editing a complex tracing.

CorelTRACE

CorelTRACE is a separate tracing program in the CorelDRAW package. It offers more options to control the trace than does the built-in tracing tool in CorelDRAW itself. Certainly, if you own or plan to purchase CorelDRAW, then you will have no need for another tracing program.

CorelTRACE accepts input files in TIFF, .PCX, .BMP, .DIB, .GIF, .JPG (JPEG), .PCD (Photo CD), and .TGA formats. It converts all files to .BMP if they are not already in that format. You can also scan an image directly into CorelTRACE. The screen is divided to show the input file at left and the resultant output at right. It offers options to trace Outlines, Centerlines, Silhouettes, Woodcut, and to prepare scanned text for OCR (Optical Character Recognition) or for Form creation.

Outline traces can be adjusted for the Curve Precision (looseness or tightness to bitmap edges), Line Precision (affects the straightening of

Figure 12-1

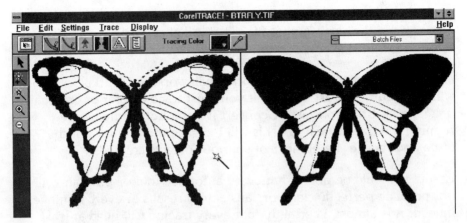

CorelTRACE's window design is simple: input on left, with tools to control program's functions, and output on the right.

Figure 12-2

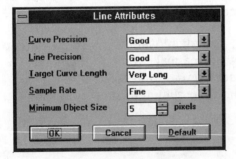

Parameters for outline tracing can be sufficiently refined to make the best possible trace from most subjects.

curves based on this value), Target Curve length (determines the length of curves; shorter curves make more detail), Sample Rate (a function of the source image's resolution in dpi, which determines the number of nodes; coarse setting yields fewer points), and Minimum Object size (determined by number of pixels in the object; small objects are filtered out as setting increases).

Centerline traces can be adjusted for the Max Line width (the highest number of pixels in a line that will still be traced as a centerline), Uniform Line Width (sets a specific line weight to all traced lines), and Horizontal and Vertical Line recognition.

Woodcut tracings are modified by the program to emulate the look of a woodcut. Lines are "etched" across the trace at a user-specified angle. The trace can be adjusted for Continuous Cut (when selected

makes woodcut lines without breaks; when not selected, lines will fade or break in lighter areas), Tapered Ends (narrowing of line), Sample Width (affects number of lines in output: the fewer pixels the more lines generated), and Angle of Cut. Woodcut traces typically create large numbers of objects and nodes. You would probably be better off simply modifying the original bitmap to emulate a woodcut.

Silhouette traces fill the outline (no internal detail preserved) with the user-specified color.

The OCR method of tracing creates editable characters from scanned text. The characters can then be modified as drawing objects. You can adjust the trace for Spelling (incorrectly spelled words eliminated), Source (different source types are automatically compensated for by the program), Normal (standard fonts at 300 dpi), Fax (fax source) and Dot Matrix (dot matrix printer source).

The Forms trace will trace text and lines to duplicate a scanned form. The program can be further adjusted to compensate for and to eliminate dithered patterns in the source file from the output. You can also select areas within the source image to be traced. You can also create batch lists for automatic tracing of more than one image.

When a bitmap has been traced, you can view the statistics for the trace by selecting Trace Info. . . from the Display menu. The numbers of objects and of nodes contained in the output image are given. This can allow you to decide whether the trace is satisfactory, or if new settings or another method of tracing is required. You cannot edit the output file within CorelTRACE. Output files can be saved only as CorelDRAW Encapsulated PostScript.

Adobe Streamline

Adobe Streamline is probably the most versatile of all standalone tracing programs. It has all of the expected controls, but it allows you to mix and match various control parameters with great precision. You can adjust the degree to which extraneous bits will be recognized (Noise level), which affects the level of roughness of the outline produced, the creation of separate objects when Centerline tracing is enabled,

Horizontal and Vertical line recognition (useful in paintings composed mostly of straight lines), the use of White lines, and even if the image is to be reversed. Tightness tolerance can be set with a slider in a range of 1 to 5 in tenth-of-a-point increments, with 1 being very tight.

Figure 12-3

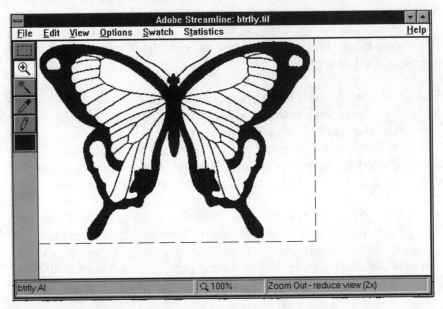

Adobe Streamline is versatile and easy to understand, two qualities that still make it attractive despite the competition.

You can select a mixture of curved and straight lines, with the program favoring one or the other. The balance between straight and curved is set with another slider with a range of 1 to 5. Or you can specify that all lines be either straight or curved.

Figure 12-4

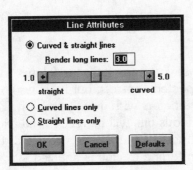

Preference for straight or curved lines can be adjusted on a scale from 1 to 5.

Color usage can also be customized, with levels of gradation determined by bit depths. You can choose to have as few as 2 colors (black and white) or 4, 8, 16, 64, or 256 colors. You can choose to have the color gradations smooth, less smooth, or sharp. If you choose to have distinct areas of color remain distinct by converting the selection edges, then the gradations options will be turned off. Centerline tracing is disabled when more than 2 colors are specified. But you can perform different types of tracing on different areas, combining the results of successive traces to make the final image. After converting an image, you can apply colors to both strokes and fills selectively.

The converted image can be further edited. Paths can be edited, and nodes can be deleted to make the image file smaller. Paths can be selected by line weight or by color, so that changes can be made globally. Selected paths can also be smoothed. A preview of the image can be displayed to provide a check of changes.

Figure 12-5

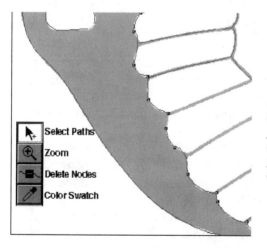

Elementary editing of traced image can be done while still in Streamline. Reduction of nodes and smoothing are primary functions available. Pre-trace editing of bitmaps is also possible with pencil, line, and eraser tools.

Input can come from TIFF or .PCX files for high-resolution images (300 dpi) and TIFF, .PCX, or .PNT (MacPaint) for low-resolution images (72 dpi). Output files can be saved to .DRW (Micrografx), .PLT (Hewlett-Packard plotter), .CGM, .DXF, and .WMF.

Text can be traced, but the recommended text font size is 36 points or greater.

In general, the program will work effectively when the default settings are used, an indication of the intelligence behind the programming. Left to its own devices, the program will produce a trace that is well-balanced between complexity and smoothness. Generally, without any user prompting, it will produce fewer nodes than either built-in tracing tools or CorelTRACE from the same bitmap. But there are plenty of ways that the user can adjust performance to suit individual needs and to fine-tune the output. Settings can be saved and used again for similar images. There is also an option to save a template from a bitmap.

The speed with which Streamline makes a trace appears to be largely processor dependent, but even a complex bitmap can be traced with a fair rapidity on quite ordinary equipment. Streamline is still worth a look, even in this age of tracing program proliferation.

Conversion, capture, and catalogue utilities

Most good painting and image editors will save or convert between many file formats. Still, an all-purpose utility program can be useful when you don't want to load up the heavy-duty programs like Photoshop merely to translate images from one format to another.

Capturing from a graphic display in Windows is a fairly elementary process: the capability is built into Windows itself. Print Screen will capture to memory (the Windows Clipboard) the whole Windows screen, and Alt+Print Screen will capture to memory the active Window. Having captured to memory, you must either save the Clipboard in the Clipboard Viewer or Paste the image from the Clipboard into a graphics program and save the image. While capturing screens, the utility program can edit the capture before saving it.

HiJaak Pro

HiJaak Pro is one of a group of multipurpose graphic utilities. It can capture graphic screens in Windows and in DOS, convert graphic files

from one format into another, edit graphic images (bitmaps), and manage or catalogue graphics.

The basic capture obviously is not very flexible, but it can be sufficient if you capture infrequently. However, if you need to make frequent captures or you want to be more selective in the portion of the screen that you capture, then a capture utility that expands on the capabilities of Windows capture is desirable.

Figure 12-6

HiJaak Pro is a straightforward image conversion and editing utility.

Virtually all capture utilities offer the same features and options. HiJaak Pro falls into this common definition. You can capture the Whole Screen, a Window or Object (a panel or dialogue box), or a Region or Area of the screen.

In HiJaak Pro, the Whole Screen capture and the Window/Object capture are more or less automatic. The Window/Object capture requires only that you click the mouse in the Window or Object that you want to capture. The Whole Screen capture requires no feedback. Each is activated by the user-defined key sequence that is set within

HiJaak Pro itself. You can select among a number of feedback options, choose to hide or display the HiJaak Pro application in its minimized form, and select the capture initiator (a key sequence).

The Window/Object capture uses a rectangular marquee to highlight the area that HiJaak Pro will capture. As you move the mouse from object to object (perhaps a text entry box or a checkbox and its text tag within a dialogue box), the marquee jumps from one object to the next. When the marquee is surrounding the window or window object that you want to capture, you click the left mouse button, and the capture proceeds. The computer can issue some feedback (a beep) to indicate that the capture is proceeding. If you have not elected to hide HiJaak Pro, its minimized icon will pop up and become a progress indicator, showing a percentage and filling with a solid color from left to right.

The Area capture requires that the user select with a cross-hair cursor a rectangular region of the screen. The area can contain overlapping features like windows and dialogue boxes.

Captures can be made to include or exclude a border of an object, can include or exclude the cursor, and to prompt or not to prompt for additional options. Cursor capture works only with full screen capture.

The capture can be sent to memory, to a HiJaak window, or to a file. The file type can be any of those supported by HiJaak. Many of the file types have options that can affect file size and compatibility. TIFF files, for instance, can be saved in any of the eligible classes and with or without the compression form applicable to a particular class.

Inset also includes a DOS capture capability in HiJaak. You might recall that Inset is the name of the DOS capture program that was part of the WordStar for DOS package for many years.

Frankly, while the number of options for capture is an attraction, the fact is that a simple, standalone capture utility like those supplied with CorelDRAW or Halo Desktop Imager will do most of the same things with less expenditure of memory.

The file conversion capability of HiJaak Pro is the program's real strength. The large number of supported file formats makes it

almost a certainty that you will be able to convert what you have to what you need.

HiJaak Pro supports the following bitmap formats: .ATT, .BMP, .CAL, .CLP, .CPR, .CUT, .DBX, .DIB, .ED5, .EPS, .GED, .GIF, .ICA, .ICO, .IFF, .IGF (INSET), .IMG, .JPG, .KFX, .MAC, .MSP, .PCD, .PCX, PCL4, PCT1, PCT2, .RLE, .RAS, .SBP, .TGA, .TIF, and .WPG. HiJaak Pro supports the following vector formats: AI, .CGM, .CLP, .DRW, .EPS, .DXF, .GCA, .GEM, .MCS, .MET, .IGF, PCT1, PCT2, .PIC, .PIX, .PGL, .P10, .WMF, and .WPG. HiJaak Pro also supports facsimile formats, making it possible to convert graphics directly into fax files that can be sent by fax modem.

You can perform some basic image manipulation in HiJaak. There are controls to change contrast, brightness, and gamma. You can reduce the number of colors in an image, effectively changing the file format. You can substitute colors in an image, replacing all occurrences of a particular color with another color selected from a palette. There are also options to resize, crop, and change the resolution of images.

HiJaak pro also functions as a printing utility, allowing you to print files in various page positions and from the File Manager. Drag-and-drop is supported for viewing and printing. HiJaak also can work

Figure 12-7

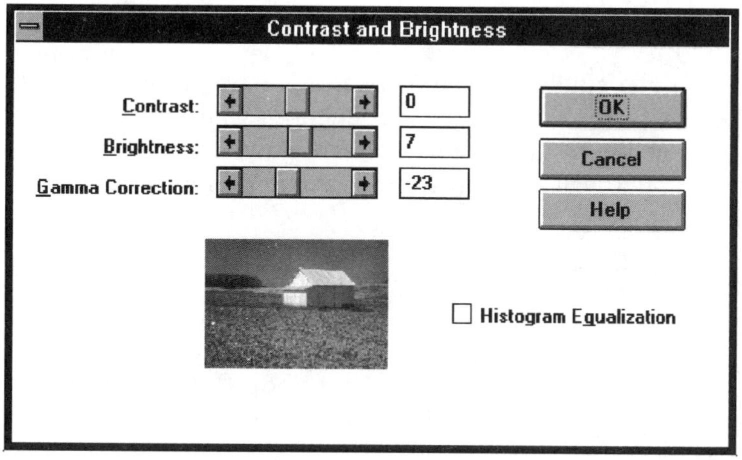

Simple editing, such as Contrast and Brightness can be done within HiJaak.

Figure 12-8

Cropping is done with scissors.

with certain programs (FreeHand, PageMaker, Word, Ami Pro, Persuasion, and PowerPoint) that support the Aldus plug-in standard for import filters. When HiJaak is installed, or later, you can specify that import filters for those programs be installed. Once installed, those programs will be able to open files in any of the graphics formats supported by HiJaak.

Supplied with HiJaak is HiJaak Browser, a program that permits you to create thumbnail images of your graphic files and to group the thumbnails in folders. You can then view the thumbnails and open the attendant file from the Browser.

As a utility, you could hardly ask for more. The program is well-behaved and performs many more functions than those named above. But it is its ability to handle and convert between most graphic file formats that you will find most important and impressive.

 # Paint Shop Pro

This is a shareware program, which means that you can use it for a span of time before paying for it. Paint Shop Pro is more like Halo Desktop Imager than it is like HiJaak Pro.

PSP offers screen capture like HDI and HiJaak, but with limited options. You can activate the capture with the right mouse button,

Figure 12-9

Paint Shop Pro can count colors to help in deciding how a palette could be constructed during color reduction.

instead of a key sequence, an option that is handy. You can capture the full screen, a window, an area, or a client like a dialogue box. The destination is PSP.

The program offers the same kind of image processing tools that are found in HiJaak: tools to change contrast and brightness, gamma, RGB values, to invert the colors, and to convert to grayscale. You can also count the number of distinct colors in an image and reduce the color bit depth. As with HiJaak and Halo Desktop Imager, you can resize and resample, plus you can rotate, mirror, and flip an image or a portion.

Like HDI, and unlike HiJaak, Paint Shop Pro provides some serious editing tools for images. There are filters for enhancing image detail, sharpening, softening, blurring, edge detection and enhancement, and embossing. You can select whether to apply the filters to all or to individual color channels, or to gray values. There are also user-defined filters that can be applied to an image.

You can alter the way that a filter treats the pixels in the image by changing the value that determines the weight given to each pixel's brightness or color, for instance, relative to one another when the filter's calculations are made. You can assign a bias and a division factor to further alter the filter's effect. The Enhance Detail filter is

Figure 12-10

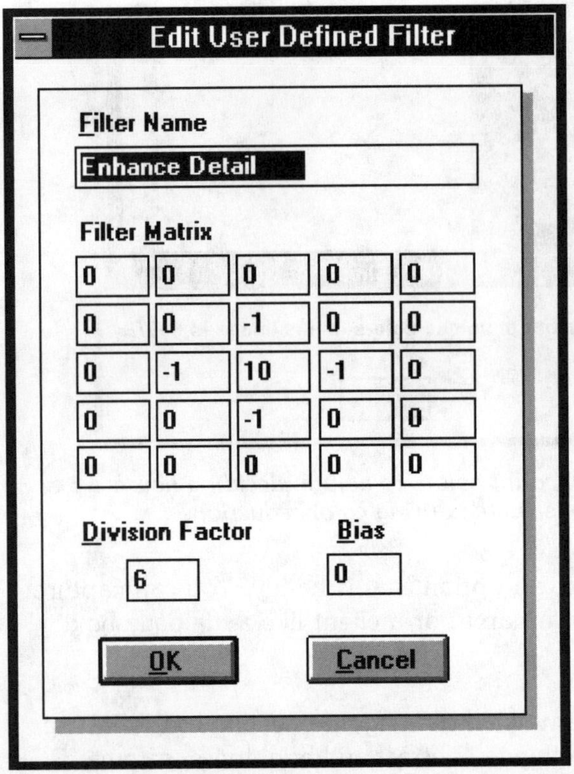

Edit User Defined Filter

Filter Name

Enhance Detail

Filter Matrix

0	0	0	0	0
0	0	-1	0	0
0	-1	10	-1	0
0	0	-1	0	0
0	0	0	0	0

Division Factor   Bias

6   0

OK   Cancel

User-defined filters offer the greatest possible control over visual effects.

entered as an exemplar on which you can experiment. You can create new filters from scratch. If you have some familiarity with the nature of image processing, you can achieve very finely calculated custom effects. This level of sophistication is unusual in a utility.

PSP supports a fair number of file formats, all of them bitmapped: .BMP, .DIB, .RLE, .GIF, .IMG, .JAS, .MAC, .MSP, .PCX, .PIC, .RAS, .TGA, TIFF, and .WPG. Conversion is possible between and among them all, although some are capable of greater color bit depth than others, and loss of image data will result in converting from greater to lesser bit depths. Naturally, converting from a low bit depth to a greater does not add information, but it does add channels in which new information can be added. (JAS, by the way, is a format similar to JPEG, in that it offers variable compression rates with proportionate loss of data as compression increases.)

ColorLab

ColorLab is an elementary image utility. It works with a few formats: .BMP, .CPI, .TGA, .TIF, .GIF, .PCX, .DVA, and .WMF. .CPI is a proprietary format that offers, like .JAS, significant compression.

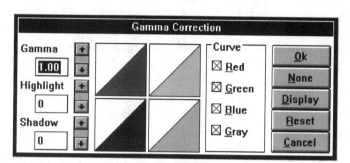

Figure 12-11

ColorLab provides excellent color correction controls.

There are controls to adjust brightness and contrast, color, color balance, and gamma. The color balance tool offers a meter that reads the RGB values of an area, allowing you to pick up a metered value and then adjust. Color palette use can be changed with the OPR sub-menu selections. Dithering can be controlled by choosing the method applied: None, ordered, Floyd-Steinberg, Burkes, and Linear. You can also flip, rotate, scale, and merge images. The merge image function is useful for scanning into the application. The program offers the usual capture options.

 # Adobe Acrobat

Adobe Acrobat is a special-case program suite composed of Acrobat Exchange, Acrobat Distiller, PDF Writer, and Acrobat Exchange Reader. It is, in the broadest sense, a conversion utility. Its purpose is to make available to everyone material that previously only some could see. Acrobat will take any computer file and make it into a file that any computer user who has access to a Windows PC or Macintosh will be able to read. Thus, it makes no difference if the image that you need was originally in True Color TIFF format, but

you can use only 256-color .BMP. Acrobat takes everything and converts it into condensed PostScript format, the Portable Document Format (.PDF), readable by the Acrobat Reader or Acrobat Exchange. Any computer user with either of those programs (the Reader is free) can view, copy, or print the material in the .PDF file.

The Acrobat suite of programs operates simply. You use your normal programs, word processors, paint programs, drawing programs, spreadsheets, databases, image editors, and prepare your documents as you normally would. When it comes time to distribute the documents in electronic form, either for comment or as part of a larger project, you print the files to disk using either the PDF Writer or the Distiller. The resulting file will look exactly as the paper version would have, but you will be able to send it by e-mail or on disk to others. Those persons can then use the Reader or Exchange program to view the document.

The PDF Writer is a replacement for the normal printer driver. It processes the file as though it were being printed to a PostScript device, making up the pages complete with fonts and illustrations, and then condensing the output into a PostScript shorthand that reduces the file size by a factor of 1:10. The file can then be passed on to others.

The Distiller works differently. Its purpose is to pick up where the .PDF Writer falters. Some files will not print correctly with the .PDF Writer due to their complexity or to other peculiarities. For those files to be converted into .PDF files, you must first print them to disk using a standard PostScript printer driver, like the Windows PostScript driver or a similar one. This creates the normal PostScript text file that would usually be sent to the desktop printer or on disk to a service to be printed. This file is then fed into the Distiller, which writes a .PDF file from it.

The Acrobat Exchange is used to view the file created either by the Distiller or PDF Writer. You can view the document as it originally looked on the parent computer, whether you have the original fonts on your computer or not. You can magnify the pages for a close view, you can view the pages in thumbnail, you can copy from the pages, and you can print them to your printer. You can also do some other things.

If the document was circulated as part of a project, you can annotate it, adding comments to the pages like electronic Post-It notes. You can

Figure 12-12

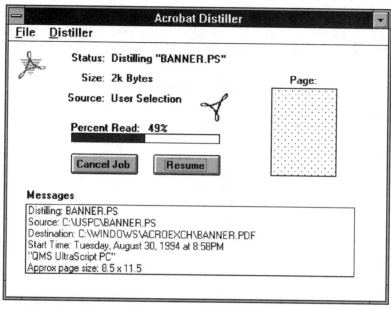

Adobe Acrobat Distiller turns standard PostScript files into .PDF compressed PostScript that can be viewed, annotated, and printed from any computer.

cross-reference items in an hypertext relationship, then pass the document on to others or back to its author. Naturally, the use of Acrobat as a conversion utility is limited by your software. If you cannot view a graphic or print it, you cannot put the graphic into a .PDF file. But it does relieve you of the need to have the same software as others in order to share with them a particular graphic in a particular format.

Parenthetically, Acrobat is based on the fact that PostScript is device-independent. You can, therefore, accomplish the same end as that achieved by Acrobat by simply transferring PostScript files from computer to computer and using a PostScript interpreter to view and print them. Freedom of Press, for instance, allows the transference of PostScript files and the viewing and printing of them on any computer and on virtually any printer. All that it lacks are the compression and annotation features.

Ventura Publisher files can be made into hypertext documents with Acrobat. Ventura footnotes and cross-references can be made into hypertext links in the Acrobat document.

Figure 12-13

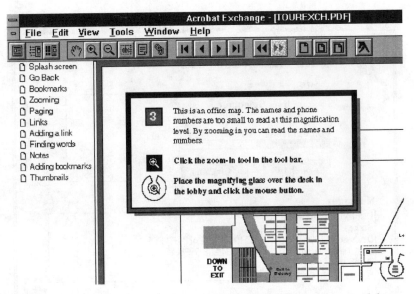

Acrobat Exchange reads and manipulates .PDF files generated from any standard PostScript printer driver or from Adobe's .PDF driver.

Multimedia presentation

THE field that was once occupied by presentation software has been usurped by upstart multimedia software. Presentations are now a subset of multimedia, and the old programs are no longer more than vestigial appendages. So diminished has become the role of presentation software, that it now comes bundled as part of packages that offer "graphic solutions," whole suites of interactive programs that allow you to create drawings, paintings, edit images, make animations, chart spreadsheets in graphs, and create slide shows. Even some drawing programs have swallowed the presentation engine whole and double as presentation programs.

 ## Presentation software

At one time, this category was extremely important to the business user. Now, it has become an endangered species as the lure of multimedia has been replaced by the proven advantages that multimedia has over simple presentations. For the same amount of money that you would spend on a top presentation program, you can buy into multimedia and the future of presentations. Why buy Harvard Graphics, Cricket Presents, or Aldus Persuasion when these programs are hopelessly outmoded?

 ## Presentations as a side order

Canvas is one example of this merging of functions. Primarily a drawing and 2D drafting program, Canvas has incorporated into itself the ability to make and exhibit slide shows. IntelliDraw has

taken this type of function a few steps farther with the addition of simulated animations and flip books. IntelliDraw is as much a presentation program, if not more of one, than most of the dedicated (and extremely overpriced) ones. Micrografx Designer also has all of the standard presentation software functions. It provides transitional effects, standalone portability of presentations, and automatic playback, or manual playback controlled from a panel resembling that of the Microsoft Windows Media Player. Corel includes a slide show presentation program, CorelSHOW, with the CorelDRAW package.

CorelSHOW does everything that the traditional presentation program does, and, because it comes as part of the DRAW package, you pay for it when you buy CorelDRAW. CorelSHOW can use drawings, animations, text, and videos imported from other applications. It will allow you to assemble the presentation to be replayed on the computer or on another computer. There is a standalone runtime module provided for computers on which CorelSHOW is not installed. You can also print the slides on acetates for the good old overhead projector. Should you be pressed to do so, CorelSHOW can be used as a page layout program, producing multipage brochures or publications with imported materials. (Ventura Publisher is included with the CorelDRAW 5 package.)

CorelSHOW uses the familiar slide metaphor. A library of backgrounds supplies that element. Transitions such as Close/Open Curtain, Wipes, Blinds, and Fades are built-in, with some offering variations of speed or combinations of effects. A Timer can be placed in the bottom of the display to keep track of projected elapsed running time as you build the presentation. The slides can be programmed to change at planned intervals or can be changed manually. Most of the program's actual slide elements are derivative; that is, they are imported from other sources. CorelSHOW is a means to organize your data and display it.

The program is OLE-aware, and there are iconic buttons that connect it to other members of the Corel package, specifically CorelDRAW, CorelMOVE, CorelCHART, and Corel PHOTOPAINT, allowing you to place objects from those programs into CorelSHOW slides. Animations from CorelMOVE, Autodesk Animator Pro (.FLI, .FLC), and Apple QuickTime (.MOV) are supported.

You can also paste objects from the clipboard, forming links in that manner. The slides can be shown in thumbnail display, and their order can be changed by dragging the miniature slides to different positions.

If you own any of the above programs, there is no need to purchase any of the usual presentation programs.

 # Full-time multimedia

Multimedia is the current buzzword. Basically, it is the marriage of the common computer with video recording and playback. Ideally, the recording and playback occur through the computer itself, but the computer can also be a control and editing device for external video sources and destinations. It puts at the user's fingertips technology that represents a total revolution in the management and delivery of information.

 # HSC InterActive

HSC InterActive is really CorelDRAW or Micrografx Designer viewed from a different perspective. Whereas those two software bundles look at multimedia as an add-on to their drawing programs, HSC looks at InterActive as the apotheosis of drawing. InterActive is a bundle of programs that are designed to work interactively in creating multimedia presentations.

HSC InterActive is a jellyfish, to describe it metaphorically. It is not a software bundle but a kind of colony of programs that assists one another symbiotically. Each program exists in its own right, as do the organisms of which the jellyfish is composed, but each is joined in a single purpose that exists outside itself. InterActive is the name of the whole organism.

The interface of InterActive might seem to some more than a little cute, but I suspect that whimsicality is not much in fashion nowadays. HSC is nothing if not whimsical. For instance, the package is emblazoned with a sticker that proclaims that it contains a free

Figure 13-1

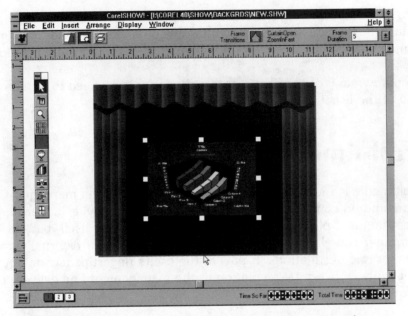

CorelSHOW is a traditional presentation program, using the slide show format.

interactive game. On opening the package and dumping out the contents, as though it were breakfast cereal, in the bottom of the box you find a folded paper stapled to a plastic bag filled with Jacks. The paper is the operating manual and technical glossary of the game, explaining such terms as Onesies, Twosies, etc.

Of course, having a sense of humor and being attentive to superfluous details does not mean that the actual program is worthwhile. If the interface of the program seems too cute at times, it is well to recall that there is no dictum that requires a serious product to be stuffy.

InterActive can be used either as a simple slide show or presentation program, or as the front-end connection to the multimedia phenomenon. If you view it as the multimedia equivalent of an object-oriented SQL, then you might be inclined to respect it more. InterActive provides a visual programming environment within which you can create multimedia works. Think of your time within it as time spent in a hired recording studio; you bring to it the prepared elements, the sheet music, the musicians, and the instruments from

which the end work will be assembled, and it provides the environment and tools with which to assemble them into the finished work.

The tools of InterActive are object code represented by icons. The icons are actually self-contained packages of computer instructions that perform particular functions when run. Each object or package of code will become a routine or subroutine within the new application that you build from them. The name of the routine is the name of the icon. Within the routines are defined and undefined variables that cause the routine to produce particular results. By altering variables, you alter the action of the application.

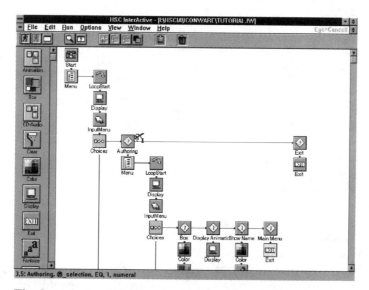

Figure 13-2

The InterActive interface is completely icon-driven.

Your work can remain an animation or slide show, or it can expand to include excerpts replayed from video sources, or .AVI and .WAV files. The format from which you assemble your work is immaterial. The program lets you build a work in whatever material you like. The building blocks are iconographic commands, and the end structure is a program that has the appearance of a simple map. Icons can be cut and pasted within an application, or they can be deleted. You can load previously saved applications into the currently active application by inserting a file, and you can save selected portions of an application to a file.

The program's icons contain the commands that, when executed sequentially, become the application you will build. You drag an icon from the toolset and drop it into a decision node, represented by a previously placed icon, in the nascent application. The newly deposited icon takes up its proper place in the order of things, ready to execute the embedded commands it contains. Execution of the application can be checked at any time from within InterActive. If the order of things is not correct, then you simply drag an icon out of position and drop it somewhere more appropriate.

Figure 13-3

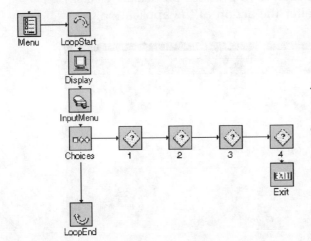

After being dropped into the program flowline, the icon resumes its appearance and is ready to execute its object code.

As a programming environment, InterActive has some concepts that are familiar to programmers: there are loops, nested loops, if branching based on equal, not equal, less than and greater than evaluations, and system variables. There are three system values that you can use to control program flow by evaluating input, @_Selection, @_Usertime, and @_Timeout.

Some icons have very simple functions. The Box icon draws a rectangle on the screen at the desired location. The drawing action is called dynamic, because the box is drawn directly to the display surface as a primitive, rather than loaded from a file. The Write icon places text on the display surface. Text is written to the screen in the font and type size last used. Type faces and styles must be established before the Write icon is used if you wish to have the text displayed in a particular typeface or size. The Font Size icon and Font Type icon control those parameters.

Many icons (Composites, the green icons) contain branching subcommands, and when these icons are dropped into the application there is a kind of spontaneous efflorescence, as icons spread and grow out from one another in a snaky network of possibilities. The branches and subcommand icons of a Composite icon can be collapsed into the Composite, just as in an outlining program subsections within an outline can be collapsed, to simplify viewing of the program structure.

Each of the icons can be individually edited; double-clicking on an icon produces a dialogue containing the essential, hidden structure of the commands that it contains. You can add sources for things such as pictures or animations to be invoked, enter or alter commands, or rewrite the command entirely (to drive a device, for instance, that has no preprogrammed icon). There is no prebuilt command to drive a VCR, but you can obtain a list from HSC of the necessary commands and use them to create your own custom VCR command icon by modifying the Laserdisc icon. There are MCI icons to play CD-Audio, control an audio board, or to use MIDI devices.

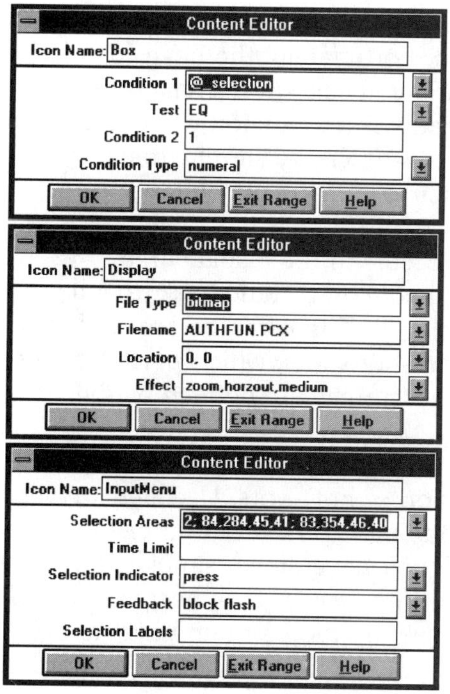

Figure 13-4

The internal program code of an icon is accessed through its Content Editor.

You can add your own Composite icons to the Icon Library, thereby making available routines that you think will be needed often to ensure a consistent performance from application to application. Icons can be renamed, and their default colors can be changed.

Icons alone are just strings of commands; until you have given them some materials to act on, most are empty and inert. The process of giving the icons materials with which to work is called adding content. The dialogue box that is attached to each icon, and that is displayed when the icon is double-clicked, is the Content Editor.

This is presentation programming carried to the next level, to paraphrase the Sega commercial. Of course, with so much assumed by the programmers, you are bound to run into instances in which the ability to change the internal arrangement of a command is necessary.

For instance, the command to center an element on the screen is designed relative to an assumed screen size. If you use a screen resolution other than the pre-set, then the command will not work according to its assumptions. You must calculate before time on such variances from the "standard" that has been programmed into the icons and make changes as needed. Fortunately, the need for such changes also has been assumed, and you can easily change the location of center, or the location at which an action will occur or an object will appear, to broaden the reference, by simply dragging objects around the screen while their command dialogues are open.

The activity within an application occurs in the display area. Generally speaking, the display will contain a static background against which the actions will be played. There can be areas of the background that are control areas or hot spots, which permit the user to interact with the application. These areas are defined by the properties in the Menu icons.

Menu icons contain the configuration of hot spots. Usually you will have prepared a background or slide in a paint program or the included Graphics Editor on which you have drawn simulated buttons or control icons. When loaded into InterActive, they become part of the display area. The buttons or icons on the painting have no actual functions, because they are simply painted on the slide or background

of the slide. You create hot spots in those areas by using the Content Editor of the various menu selections. The Content Editor can invoke a Template Editor, within which you designate the areas that are to be used as hot spots. After loading into the Editor the graphics file that will serve as the background for the menu, and which serves as the template for the hot spots, selections are made by dragging the mouse across the painted surface where the icons or buttons are located. Or you can simply type in the screen coordinates.

Once an area has been designated as a hot spot, you can give the area certain properties that will define how it reacts to the mouse. You can, for instance, make the hot spot become inverted in color when the mouse pointer passes within it. When the mouse is clicked within the area of the hot spot, you can have the area flash (alternate between inverse and normal) a set number of times to indicate that a choice of action has been made.

You can select only a rectangular area to be a hot spot, but, because the actual appearance of a button is determined by the bitmap used for the template, any image can represent a hot spot. You must use the special effects sparingly with irregular shapes lest you highlight areas not within the shape of the button.

Applications can be run either in their entirety or in segments as small as one icon. You can disable portions of an application for debugging purposes to isolate program bugs.

InterActive provides a separate Graphics Editor that can be accessed from within the program. The Graphics Editor is a paint program with which you can create backgrounds or modify templates. It has all of the typical tools of painting programs, such as brushes, spray paints, filled and empty primitives (rectangles, ellipses), irregular polygons, lines, and a couple of unique tools that will automatically draw buttons. The button tools make only rectangles and rounded rectangles, but the buttons have three-dimensional shading and optional shadows added as they are drawn, saving you the time that would otherwise be consumed in applying the effects manually. The Graphics Editor will load a file on startup if one has already been selected in a content editor as a backdrop for a display or template. It can save only in the .WMF format.

Figure 13-5

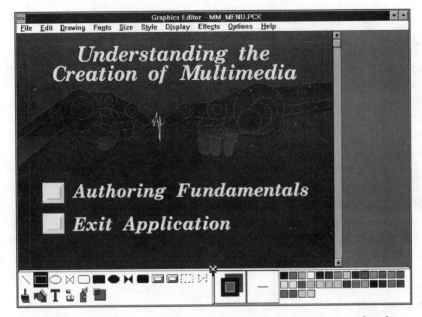

The InterActive Graphics Editor is a linked paint program. It edits bitmaps with the familiar tools and some specialized primitives, such as button tools.

Figure 13-6

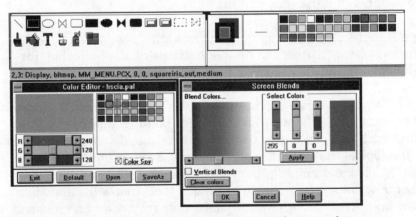

The toolbox of the Graphic Editor (top) is simple to read.

InterActive provides for other variations with the accessory programs that make up the suite. The necessity of resizing a prepared bitmapped graphic, say a specimen from a clip-art disk, often arises. Resizing or scaling a graphic is a process that invariably leads to unpredictable

results as bits are lost or expanded to fill the new size. This stricture applies particularly to captured or scanned images, the resolution of which may not always match the current or target screen resolution. Against this possibility, InterActive provides the RezSolution program that will intelligently resample and dither a scaled graphic.

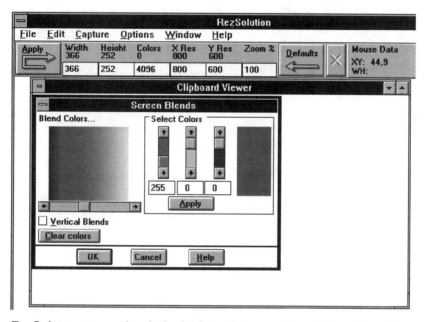

Figure 13-7

RezSolution is another linked editor that permits resizing of graphics with interpolation to reduce the lose of detail and improve anti-aliasing.

RezSolution is a very limited utility, designed to augment InterActive. It works only with the file formats that are supported by InterActive, .PCX, .BMP, and .RLE (Run Length Encoded), and it is limited to 256 colors. If you need to use an image that is in another format, e.g., TIFF, then you must load the image into another program and save it in a compatible format, or copy it to the Clipboard and transfer it to RezSolution in that manner. RezSolution displays automatically any image already on the Clipboard. When running in 15-, 16-, or 24-bit color, RezSolution cannot save images to files. It can convert files from one format to another, convert to different color depths, and change resolutions. RezSolution is also a screen capture utility, allowing you to capture screens, windows, or areas.

IconAnimation is a third program, designed to serve as a source of animation files for InterActive. It shares with InterActive its icon driven programming interface. IconAnimation uses the iconic interface to assemble animation scripts that describe the actions that will be depicted in the animation. The icons here also have content editors attached, in which you enter the variables that establish the objects and determine their disposition in the animation. You can selectively preview the animation as you proceed.

Figure 13-8

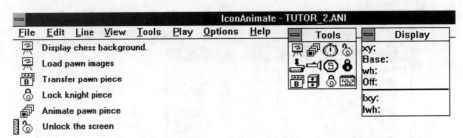

IconAnimate, the third major linked editor, is an animation program that can move objects around the screen. It uses the same icon-driven interface as InterActive, and has a similar toolset (first palette, center right).

Given its scope, IconAnimation is a major program in itself. With it you can create two-dimensional animations. It depends on imported graphics, but it supplies the environment that establishes the stage and the commands that control the actors.

Actors are graphic entities that move across the backdrop. An actor can be made to follow a path within the scene, and you can determine a path with as few as two points. If, for instance, you want an actor to move from the left edge to the right edge of the display, you can click on the left edge and then on the right edge of the screen to set the path. You can control the amount of time that it takes the actor to traverse the screen. Slower motion is smoother, while faster motion is less smooth.

An actor is moved as a whole. The movements within the actor must be drawn in the old-fashioned way, one step at a time. Therefore, while the program will move the actor from place to place about the screen, if you want the actor's arms or other appendages to move, you will have to make those movements by changing the actor from frame to frame.

Figure 13-9

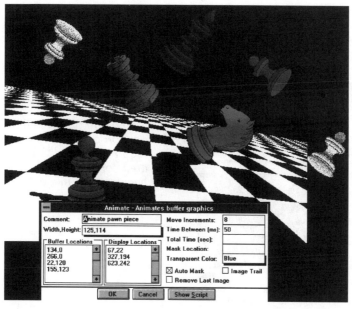

To move the pawn from the upper left to the lower right requires clicking on starting and ending locations, specifying number of frames (Move Increments) and speed (Time Between multiplied by Increments).

It is possible to make actors pass behind other actors in order to simulate perspective by locking the features that will be in front of the moving actor. Locking parameters are entered into the Content Editor of a Lock icon. The area to be locked can be rectangular, ellipsoid, or polygonal. To save you the trouble of having to precisely edit the outline of an actor so that background objects are not obscured by openings within the area occupied by an actor, such as the area between limbs, you can make the background color of the actor's image file transparent.

Each of the steps in the script can have comments attached to them in their respective Content Editors. The comments are displayed to the right of the icons in the script. The entire program can be annotated with a note added with a Notepad icon.

As applications can be included in InterActive, so can animations be concatenated or interleaved by adding a Filing Cabinet icon to the

Figure 13-10

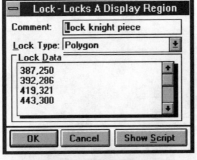

Moving an object behind a portion of the background requires locking the screen area containing the background image.

current script. This icon loads another animation file and executes its script from within the first or parent animation's script.

The completed animations can then be used in InterActive, summoned from a Display icon, for instance. Other types of animations can also be used. An animation icon is supplied that will play Autodesk Animator Pro .FLI or .FLC files.

InterActive has three other utility editors for making quick changes or additions to an icon's content. Each uses the mouse for input, and each returns values to the Content Editor that generated it. The Location Editor is used to get the coordinates of a point on the screen and to transfer them to a Content Editor for placing items on the display surface. The Area Editor provides a means to select an area on a screen and returns the coordinates of its upper left and lower light corners to the parent Content Editor of the Box icon. Color Editor gives you control over color selection, color palettes, and color mixing. There are sliders to change or create colors and a color spy to pick up color from an area on the screen.

InterActive can be customized to some degree, apart from the changes already discussed above, by altering its .INI file. You can, for

instance, change the zoom levels that are available. You might want a 400% magnification added, or a 20% reduction. You can also add applications that can be launched from within InterActive. You can specify default colors for icons or palettes.

HSC InterActive is not easy to master, but it puts some powerful tools in the hands of the user. Although there are some editing limitations, they can be worked around by preparing the materials for the presentation in more capable image-editing or painting programs and then saving those materials in formats compatible with InterActive.

Adobe Premiere

Adobe Premiere is like Photoshop; it's an analogue of the real-world video editing studio, just as Photoshop is the equivalent of a darkroom. You will find that the tools of Premiere are very much like the tools to be found in the studio. The nomenclature is the same, and the procedures are very much the same as those that would be employed by a video director.

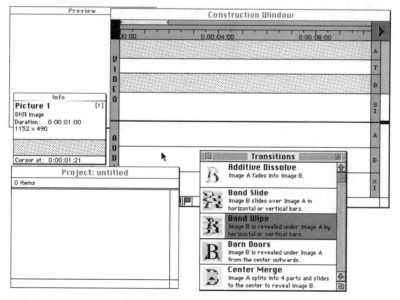

Figure 13-11

Adobe Premiere is the computer equivalent of the video editing room, with the digital tools of the trade.

Premiere doesn't interleave its functions with those of Photoshop. Photoshop is not an adjunct of Premiere, but it can be a source from which Premiere assembles a finished "movie," as can PhotoStyler or Fractal Design Painter; Premiere will work with them all. Premiere looks like the video editor's toolbox. It has the electronic equivalents of storyboard, movieola, timing charts, and electronic transitions.

In general, videotape editing requires an input source, a videotape machine, an editing machine that can mark frames for inclusion or exclusion, and a videotape machine output destination. For QuickTime or Video for Windows, you need only Premiere to act as all three components of the editing suite. Premiere will take existing movie files or will capture video as its source, will edit the video, including or deleting frames, add special effects and transitions, and then assemble and save the completed movie.

Adobe Premiere opens with a dialogue requesting that you select a format size and speed for the project that you are undertaking to

Figure 13-12

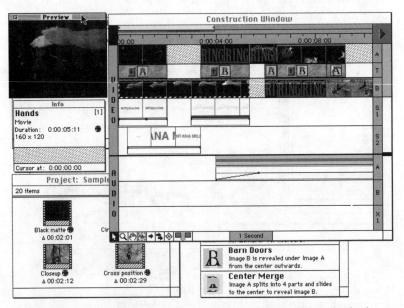

The five basic windows presented by Premiere within which the activity of editing clips into a finished movie occurs, clockwise from top left, Preview, Construction, Transitions (partially hidden), Project, and Info.

create. There are 13 preset formats: CD-ROM Authoring, CD-ROM Mastering, Offline Videotape—NTSC, Offline Videotape—PAL, Online Videotape—NTSC, Online Videotape—PAL, Presentation— 160 × 120, Presentation—240 × 180, Presentation—320 × 240, Re-Mix Audio, Timebase—24fps-Film, Timebase—25fps-PAL, and Timebase—30fps-NTSC. You can modify any of the preset formats. You can attach comments to a format to provide a description of its uses and parameters. New formats can be saved and loaded into other projects. Loading a format into an open project will impose the format on the project, altering its parameters. When loading a format while a project is open, a description of the current project's parameters will be displayed.

After selecting a format, Premiere continues, opening five windows in the workspace: Project Window, Construction Window, Info Window, Transitions Window, and Preview Window.

The Project window is the temporary storage area for video sequences and single frame still images that will be used in the creation of the movie. These are the digital equivalents of the stock film footage or videotape from which motion picture or videotape programs are made. You can import the following file formats: .AVI, QuickTime, FilmStrip, PICS, PICT, Adobe Ilustrator, Adobe Photoshop, Backdrop, Title, and sound formats .WAV, .SND, Audio Interchange, and SoundEdit.

Clips in the Project window are displayed in thumbnail form, with information concerning the clip's duration, file type (audio or image), attached comments, and labels. The Project window can be reconfigured to display clips in other forms. You can display clips in name format, in which case they will be in alphabetical order. You can also alphabetize them according to their labels. Duration is in the standard SMPTE (Society of Motion Picture and Television Engineers) format, showing hours, minutes, seconds, and frames (HR:MN:SC:FR) separated by colons.

You can search for clips by name, by labels, or by comments. Management of clips can be simplified by using the Remove Unused command, which deletes clips that have not been used in the Construction window. The Project window can be used to arrange

clips, as if on a pasteboard, in order before they are transferred to the Construction window.

The Construction window is where the movie is assembled. It displays the clips in the sequence that they will have when the movie is played. As in a professional editing studio, you have multiple tracks in which to place clips, and there is a timeline at the top against which the running time of clips and the entire movie can be measured. The default number of tracks is seven. Tracks A and B are video tracks, while track T is used for video transitions effects. Track S1 is the superimposition track, used for overlaying still images and movie frames. There are three audio tracks: A, B, and X1. A maximum of 99 audio and 99 video tracks can be placed in the Construction window. The minimum number of tracks is three each for both audio and video. When the number of tracks exceeds the space available in the window, you must use the scroll bars to work with tracks not in the display area.

Clips are added to the Construction window by dragging them from the Project window and dropping them into a track. Clips can be

Figure 13-13

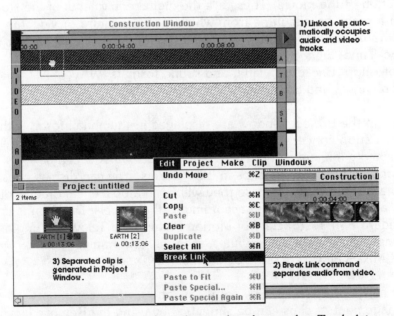

The Grabber Hand over the video track indicates that Track A is receiving the video portion of the clip. The darkened audio Track A indicates that the audio portion of the clip has been placed.

placed only in tracks corresponding to their type, video clips in video tracks and audio clips in audio tracks. Multiple clips can be dragged from the Project window into the Construction window at one time. They will be positioned in the destination track in the same order that they had in the Project window.

Clips that contain both the audio and video tracks are said to be linked. When a linked clip is moved into the Construction window, the audio and video tracks are placed separately in appropriate track types of corresponding numbers. Thus, if a linked clip has been dropped in video track A, the video portion of the clip will be placed in track A and its linked audio clip will be placed in audio track A. Linked clips can be separated.

As with the Project window, you can customize the Construction window's mode of display, suppressing tracks, or using clip names rather than thumbnails. You can also change the unit of time that is used in the timeline; the default units are one-second increments. This also affects the mode of track display, because one thumbnail is placed in a track for each unit of time consumed by a clip.

Clips can be arranged in the tracks in any order. Clips can be abutting or overlapping. When a clip is being moved, the clip is bracketed by alignment guides that extend across the tracks to facilitate positioning of the clip. The cursor always generates a guideline in the timeline as you move it about in the Construction window. If you desire to have clips arranged end to end, you can use the Snap to Edges option to constrain clips. You can insert place markers in the timeline to indicate locations for clips, and the Snap to Edges constraint will cause the cursor to snap to the markers when a dragged clip approaches.

The Preview window is used to view portions of a movie before the movie has been compiled. This permits editing changes to be made interactively. The portion to be previewed can be selected by positioning the work area bar, which is a yellow bar that slides above the timeline. The length of the bar, and thus the length of the portion to be previewed, can be changed by dragging the red arrows on the ends of the yellow bar. Once a portion has been designated, it can be previewed by using the Preview command.

Figure 13-14

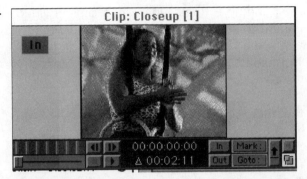

Clip: Closeup [1]

The Clip Window is used to pre-edit clips before dropping them into the Construction Window.

Alternately, you can preview a portion of the movie by dragging the Selection cursor along the timeline. The speed of the drag determines the speed of play of the preview. By moving the cursor backwards, you can make the preview play in reverse.

Other methods of previewing include the preview movie and the preview snapshot. Each method uses its own window rather than the Preview window. During snapshot previewing, an indicator scrolls over the timeline as the preview plays, corresponding to the frame currently being displayed. The indicator can be used to place markers in the timeline.

The Info window displays the location of the cursor in terms of the timeline while it is in the Construction window. If a clip has been selected, the Info window displays the name, the type, the duration, the size, the starting and ending points, and other information concerning the clip.

Premiere can use libraries of clips that have been prepared in advance. You can add clips to a library by dragging and dropping them from the Project window or the Clip window.

The Clip window is used to view clips, and to set start and end frames for the clip. It can be used to change the duration of still images, or to place markers within a clip. The Clip window can be opened by double-clicking on a clip in the Project or Construction windows, by issuing the Open Clip command from the Clip menu, or by Opening a clip from the File menu. The Clip window controls are the familiar ones of the Media player.

Figure 13-15

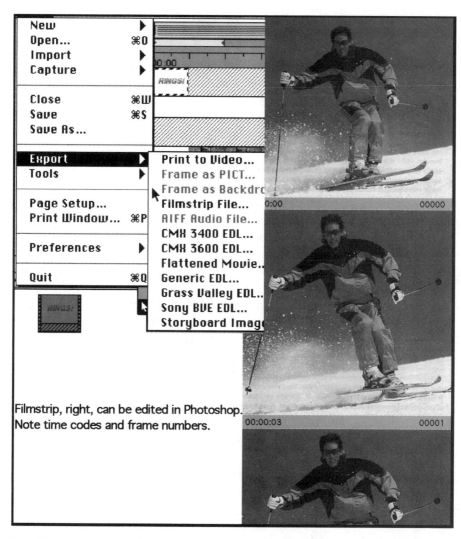

Filmstrip, right, can be edited in Photoshop.
Note time codes and frame numbers.

The Flimstrip export function creates a format that can be edited in Photoshop.

Clips can be trimmed in the Clip window. Trimming is accomplished by setting the in and out points. To set a point, advance the clip to the desired frame and click on the appropriate button in the Clip window controls. Setting in and out points does not affect the source clip only the way that the program processes the clip. The duration of a clip cannot be extended beyond its full duration, unless you slow the

speed of the clip, that is, the number of frames per second. Changes to a clip are reflected in the Project and Construction windows.

As mentioned above, you can create virtual clips by selecting a portion of a movie across all tracks with the Marquee tool. Virtual clips can be manipulated in the same manner as ordinary clips, and they can be included in other virtual clips. Premiere permits up to 64 levels of nesting of virtual clips.

You can edit Premiere clips in Adobe Photoshop by exporting them as FilmStrips. FilmStrips consist of frames that are opened in Photoshop as a column of frames. The individual frames can be edited, as can the channels of each frame. You can paint as you would in any image in Photoshop.

Premiere can be used to create full-frame video for recording directly to videotape. With the proper board, such as the Rocgen Pro, you can edit videotape on-line or off-line. Editing off-line requires that you be able to create an Edit Decision List (EDL). Premiere can create EDLs. The information for an EDL is derived from the clips and transitions in the Construction window. You can export the EDL in CMX 3400, CMX 3600, Sony BVE, and Grass Valley formats.

The Transition window contains the 60 or so transitions that can be placed between clips in Premiere. Among the transitions are Additive Dissolve, Barn Doors, Checkerboard, Cross Dissolve, Iris Round, Pinwheel, Slide, and Zoom. Transition settings can be adjusted to your liking. You can change the start and end points, borders, direction from track to track, orientation, and other parameters peculiar to a transition.

For editing frames and clips, Premiere has filters similar to those available in Photoshop for enhancing images. There are specialized filters that permit you to focus on an area within an oversize image, or to flip images horizontally or vertically. There are audio filters to apply special audio effects such as echo.

Superimpositions, called matte effects in motion pictures and key effects in video, permit the overlaying of one image on another by making the background of the top image invisible. In video production

Figure 13-16

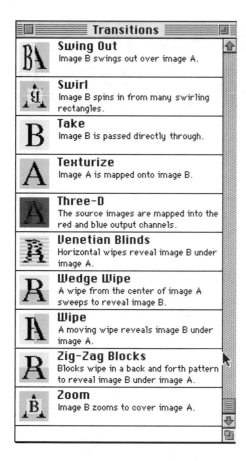

Some of the more than 60 transitions that can be used in a Premiere movie.

this is done with blue-screen chromakey, in which the actors are videotaped against a blue backdrop. The background on which the actors will be seen in the finished effect is created separately. In film, the traditional way of shooting this effect is to make a matte painting of the background and to have the film effects lay in the actors by placing the negative of the actors over the one of the still background, and making a new master negative that combines the two source negatives.

Many television programs shot on film still use this technique, although digital editing techniques are quickly replacing the traditional means. The film *Forrest Gump* uses the digital superimposition technique to make it appear that the title character is actually in the same time and place as three former Presidents of the United States.

Figure 13-17

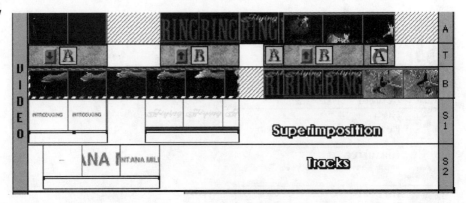

The Superimposition tracks are used for overlaying images, such as titles, on the contents of the main tracks.

It was a matter of precision timing to synchronize the actions of the actor with those of the President. The real person who had appeared in the original news film was digitally erased, allowing the image of the actor to be superimposed.

Premiere uses this technique with the S tracks in the Construction window. The clips that are to be the background are placed in tracks A or B, and the clips that are to be played against those background clips are placed in the S tracks. Superimpositions are constructed after all of the clips in tracks A, B, and T have been processed by Premiere. Additionally, clips in higher-numbered S tracks are superimposed over clips in lower-numbered S tracks.

When all of the clips, transitions, titles, and superimpositions have been arranged in the Construction window, you compile the actual movie with the Make Movie command. You can make changes to the Project Output Settings at this time. If you are going to print the movie to videotape, you can select options for Aspect Ratio and NTSC or PAL compatibility, or you can use the EDL for later on-line editing.

Adobe Premiere is an extremely powerful video and multimedia tool. Its ability to create digital movies with sophisticated special effects is nothing short of amazing. Its techniques are nearly the same as those used by professional special effects artists working with millions of dollars worth of equipment.

 # AuthorWare Star

AuthorWare Star, from Macromedia, is a more straitlaced clone of HSC
InterActive. It employs the same basic interface and methods to create
interactive multimedia presentations. Like InterActive, AuthorWare Star
is an iconic, object-oriented programming language and environment.

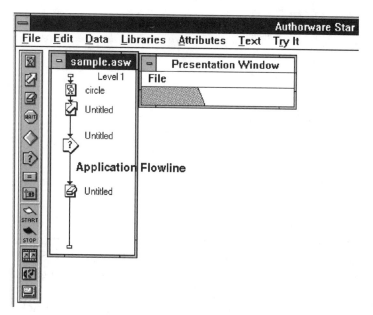

Figure 13-18

*AuthorWare Star from Macromedia is very similar to HSC
InterActive, using the same sort of icon-driven
programming methods.*

Star opens to a workspace window and a palette containing the iconic
building blocks from which you can build multimedia applications.
Each application is constructed in its own window on the workspace.

The icons, as in InterActive, are actually programming modules
(containers for program code that can be placed on a flowline).
Program flow normally proceeds top-to-bottom along the flowline
and left-to-right in program branches. The Icons supplied are Display,
Animation, Erase, Wait, Decision, Interaction, Calculation, Map,
Start and Stop flags, Movie, Sound, and Video.

Figure 13-19

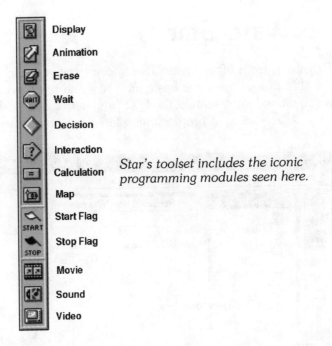

Star's toolset includes the iconic programming modules seen here.

The Display icon permits showing of text or graphics. The content of the display can be either imported or drawn directly within the Presentation window with the drawing tools provided by Star. The drawing tools are simple primitives: lines, constrained lines, ellipses, rectangles, rounded rectangles, irregular polygons, and text. There are no painting tools. Imported graphics can be in BMP (including .RLE and other variants), .EPS, MacPaint, PICT, Metafile, Paintbrush (.PCX), and TIFF formats.

You can manipulate various attributes of the graphics, both drawn and imported, from menu selections. Graphics can be stacked in order, and the order changed by sending back and bringing forward. Graphics can be shown in Opaque, Matted, Transparent, Inverse, and Erase modes. These modes perform Boolean operations between graphics in the same display.

Text is entered from the keyboard or can be pasted. Typefaces, sizes, and styles are selected from the standard Windows menu items. Justification is limited to Right, Left, and Centered. Text can be entered in single lines or in a scrolling text box with wrapping.

The Animation icon is used to move objects, displays, and movies around the screen. Motion can be to a Fixed Destination, along a Fixed Path, along a Scaled Path, on a Linear Scale, or a Scaled X-Y path. A Fixed Destination is determined by dragging the display to a position. The speed at which the mouse drags the display is used by Star to calculate the duration of the motion, or you can enter a rate or duration numerically or in the form of a variable or expression. Duration is in seconds. Speed is a calculated value, distance multiplied by time, with distance measured in 72-pixel (approximately 1-inch) increments and time in seconds. Thus, if 4 is entered in the Rate field and the distance is 3 inches (216 pixels), then the object will be moved 1 inch every 4 seconds, and will be moved the entire 3 inches in 12 seconds.

It is possible to control the overlapping of multiple animated objects. Normal overlapping is last to first, with the more recently initiated animations being placed over the earlier animations. This order can be changed by assigning a Layer value to each animated object, with the highest value being foremost in the display and lower values being layered inversely. Movies played Direct to Screen always have the highest priority.

Fixed Path animations occur along a straight line selected by dragging a triangular marker from the origin to the destination. The path is indicated by a line, and it can be changed in length or direction as desired. The Concurrency option for Perpetual animation is governed by a TRUE/FALSE state of a variable or expression. When the variable or expression evaluates as True, the animation is begun. When the animation has concluded, if the state of the variable remains True, then the animation begins again. When the variable or expression evaluates to False, the animation ceases.

The Scaled Path option permits a calculated value for the next position of the animation to be used. Depending on a variable or expression, the application will position the animation based on the scale values, which can be fixed numerical or a variable. Looping controls the position of the animation if the value of a variable falls outside of the specified scaled range.

The Linear Scaled Path is similar to the Scaled, except that the animation jumps directly to the point calculated. This type of

animation can go to points beyond the specified end points. Scaled X-Y animations can move anywhere in the display area based on calculated values for screen coordinates.

The Erase icon removes all text and graphics in a display. Erasure can be accomplished with a special effect. Effects supported include Mosaic, Pattern, Spiral, Remove Up, Remove Down, Remove to Right, Remove to Left, Iris In, Iris Out, Venetian Blind, Vertical Blind, Barn Door Open, and Barn Door Close.

The Wait icon halts application execution for a specified time span or until a keystroke or mouse click is detected. If a time span is used, there is the option to display an alarm clock with numerical countdown of time remaining before execution resumes. A Continue button can be displayed, in which case execution pauses until the button is clicked on.

The Decision icon controls branching within the application. Branching is controlled by the evaluation of a branching setting and a repeat setting. Branching is evaluated according to user definition. Branching can be Sequential, Random With or Without Replacement, or Calculated. Sequential branching selects the first optional icon path for execution during first encounter, the second icon path during second encounter, and so on. Random branching will select an icon path randomly for execution. If With Replacement is selected, then the application will branch at random each time through the decision loop, and paths that have already been executed may be executed again. Without Replacement restricts the execution of a random selection to branches that have not already been executed until all branches have been exhausted. Decision icons are basically automatic switches.

Interaction in an application can be supplied by the Interaction icon. The interactive features are very rich and can be used with very little or no additional modification. Interaction combines display and branching programming, allowing you to place information on the screen and then have the application branch to one of several possible program issues based on the response to the displayed information.

Interaction icons have several optional parameters to control display and branching processes. You can have the application Pause before

Figure 13-20

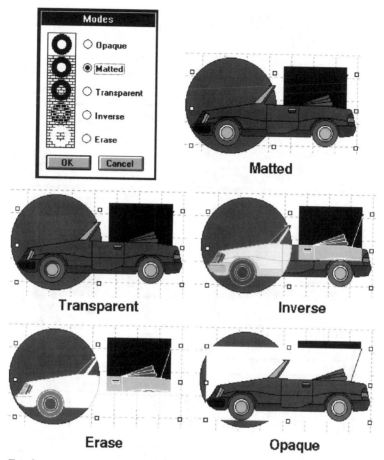

Matted

Transparent

Inverse

Erase

Opaque

Boolean or logical modes can be used to govern the interaction of layered graphics.

Exiting, allowing the user to view the display contents. A Continue button can be enabled. Erasure can be On Exiting, After Each Entry, or None. Erasure effects are the same as for the Erase icon. Text Entry can be required of the end user.

Icons used to elicit the response to an Interaction icon are attached to the Interaction, and have their own settings. Response icons have these forms: Pushbutton, Click/Touch, Clickable Object, Move Object, Pull Down Menus, Conditional, Text, Key Press, Tries Limit, and Time Limit. Types of response icons can be mixed in the same interaction.

Figure 13-21

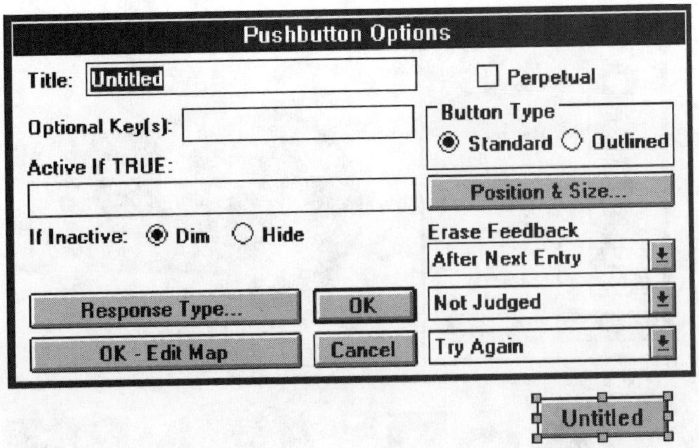

Pushbutton Options

Title: Untitled   ☐ Perpetual

Optional Key(s):   Button Type
                                    ◉ Standard ○ Outlined
Active If TRUE:
                                    [Position & Size...]

If Inactive: ◉ Dim   ○ Hide   Erase Feedback
                                    After Next Entry ▼

[Response Type...] [OK]   Not Judged ▼
[OK - Edit Map] [Cancel]   Try Again ▼

[Untitled]

*Pushbuttons have options for their appearance and their
behavior (Feedback) when clicked on with the mouse.*

Figure 13-22

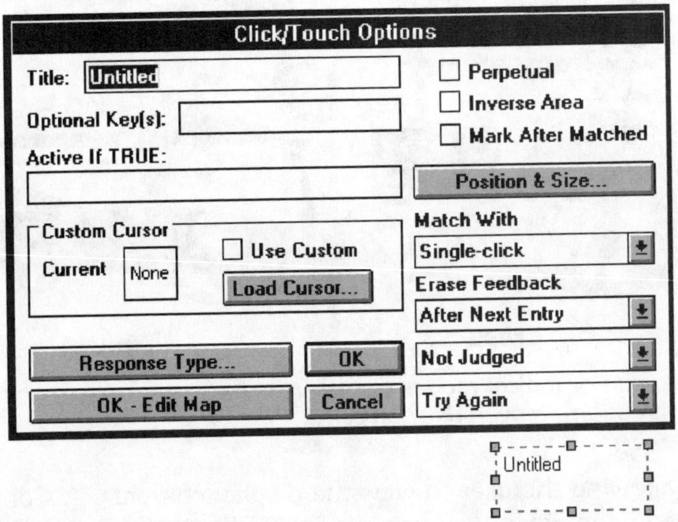

Click/Touch Options

Title: Untitled   ☐ Perpetual
                                    ☐ Inverse Area
Optional Key(s):   ☐ Mark After Matched

Active If TRUE:
                                    [Position & Size...]

Custom Cursor   Match With
                ☐ Use Custom   Single-click ▼
Current   None   Erase Feedback
                [Load Cursor...] After Next Entry ▼

[Response Type...] [OK]   Not Judged ▼
[OK - Edit Map] [Cancel]   Try Again ▼

Untitled

*Click/Touch areas afford interaction when the mouse
enters or is clicked in an area, a method allowing greater
freedom in interface design than the pushbutton.*

The Pushbutton icon presents the user with a button to click. The
name, position, and size can be changed.

The Click/Touch response icon creates a hotspot in which the user
clicks or moves the cursor. Size and position can be changed.

The Clickable Object response icon converts a displayed object into a clickable object to process response.

The Movable Object response requires that the user drag an object to a location on the screen to indicate a response.

The Pull Down Menu groups response options in a menu from which the user makes a selection.

Conditional response icons evaluate responses from other icons according to variables or expression you specify and then act.

Text responses require the user to input text, a number of parameters of which can be set. The most basic of these are font, size, and style.

Keypress responses evaluate keyboard entry. Keys used need not be keys currently available on your keyboard. Programmed key names are provided and will be recognized by the application.

Time Limit and Tries Limit evaluate the performance of the user or continue execution after unattended operation.

The Calculation icon permits entry of a calculation in the flowline of the application. The program recognizes arithmetic and logical expressions, including exponentiation, and relational expressions such as greater than >, less than <, and greater than or equal to >=.

A Map icon contains a group of other icons and has its own flowline. Icons can be grouped or ungrouped by the author of the application.

Stop and Start flag icons are debugging control icons that permit execution of portions of a flowline in an application under development.

The Movie icon permits the playing of movies in an application. Movies can be compiled into the application or loaded from an external source. Movie types supported are: Macromedia Director, AVI, QuickTime, Autodesk Animator, Macintosh Movie Editor (earlier Mac version of AuthorWare Star), and PICS (Mac AuthorWare Pro).

You can specify the starting and ending frames, display location, play rate, whether to skip frames, the color palette to use (movie or

display), and if audio included with the movie is to be played. Externally loaded movies can be on any logical device.

The Sound icon plays audio clips if a sound board is being used.

The Video icon allows the playing of video from an external source in an application. Laserdiscs are the only external sources currently supported.

This is a versatile and powerful multimedia programming tool. In many respects it is more powerful than HSC InterActive, although it does have its limitations. Star cannot be extended, as can InterActive, which permits the programming kernel within its icons to be modified by the user. There is a more powerful version of Star, AuthorWare Star Pro, which does have greater capabilities.

 # CorelMOVE

CorelMove is a simple two-dimensional cel animation program. It permits the creation of cartoon animations that can be saved in its own format or exported to an AVI file format.

CorelMOVE takes a traditional approach to creating animations. You prepare the actors, props, and sounds in other programs and assemble them in CorelMOVE. It offers the tools of an animation camera. You can overlay actors and props on a background and manipulate them as you desire.

Actors can be edited cel by cel within the program, and the digital equivalent of onion skin paper can be used to view the current cel in relation to the previous or next cel. Animation paths can be drawn that will determine the movement of the actor within the area of the frame.

A few years ago, this program would have been worth hundreds of dollars in itself. It is easy to use and can produce very satisfying and professional results. That it is included with CorelDRAW is one more very good reason to buy that package of programs.

Figure 13-23

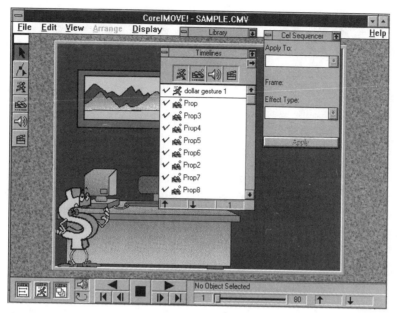

CorelMOVE is a fully operational cel animation program that uses traditional methods of creating two-dimensional animated motion pictures.

Desktop publishing

WHILE desktop video is just beginning to find its market, desktop publishing (DTP) is well into its third generation. DTP has become an industry within an industry. Once the private domain of the Macintosh, DTP has now established itself in Windows, and the huge market that Windows represents has led to the acceleration of the development of the software. Considering how large the Windows market is and is expected to become, and how much DTP has been simplified since its beginnings on the DOS machines, there is no better time to make the move to Windows DTP.

PageMaker

Desktop publishing began with PageMaker and an Apple LaserWriter. PageMaker still defines the field. It has been refined and expanded over the last 10 years, and the current Windows version has benefited from the history of its Macintosh revisions. PageMaker for Windows has the polished look of a program that knows what it is doing.

PageMaker opens to the same metaphorical pasteboard that is used by FreeHand. The pasteboard is the region on which all objects in the program reside. This includes the pages themselves and all other objects such as graphics and text blocks, whether they are on the page or not. Items on the page are printed, and items wholly on the pasteboard are not. The area of the pasteboard which is not covered by pages is a scratch work area, and you can store items on it that need to be fitted in when the composition has been corrected.

Unlike FreeHand, which fills the pasteboard with a sequence of pages, PageMaker places the active page (or the two active facing pages) in the center of the pasteboard, hiding other pages. The size of the pasteboard in PageMaker is variable. The dimensions change only by fractions of an inch at different resolutions.

Figure 14-1

The portrait of Aldus Manutius, trademark of Aldus Corporation, links the computer age to one of the heroes of the Renaissance, the Italian printer who rescued Classical Literature.

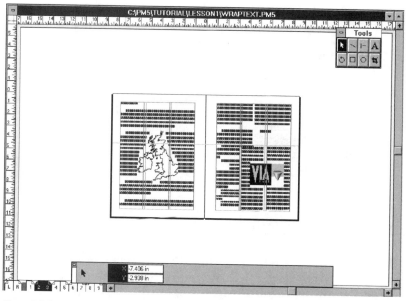

Figure 14-2

PageMaker uses the pasteboard metaphor for composition of its publications.

The toolbox in PageMaker is sparse. It contains the Pointer or selection tool, the Line tool, the Constrained Line tool, the Text tool, the Rotation tool, the Rectangle tool, the Ellipse tool, and the Cropping tool.

The Pointer is used to select and move or resize objects anywhere on the pasteboard. It can be changed temporarily to a Grabber hand for moving the publication's page around in the window or to a magnifying glass to zoom in on an area. Both are useful, and the Grabber is a necessity if you choose to turn off the scroll bars in order to have a larger view of the page. The Line tool draws straight lines, and Constrained Line tool draws lines at multiples of a 45° angle. The Rectangle and Ellipse are self-explanatory. The Cropping tool is used to cut a graphic by removing the areas outside its cropping frame.

Lines can be selected from the Line submenu in the Elements menu. You have a reasonable choice among solid, dashed, dotted, double, and triple lines. Fills are selected from the Elements menu, also.

Figure 14-3

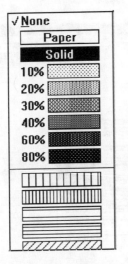

Patterns are not particularly inspiring, but they provide a basic selection.

Besides the Toolbox, there are other floating palettes that can be invoked and placed on the display area. They are the Control palette, the Styles palette, the Colors palette, and the Library palette.

The Control palette changes according to the nature of the object, if any, that is selected. It displays information about the location of the object and is an alternative to the use of the mouse to directly manipulate an object. With the Control palette you can Rotate, Crop, Scale, Skew, and Move objects by entering figures into the text entry boxes. It can be used with or without a mouse, as complete mobility can be had within the Control palette by way of the keyboard.

Figure 14-4

Bitmap selected

Vector selected

Text selected

No selection

The Control palette changes its aspect with the selection of different types of objects on the page.

The Control palette has nudge buttons that will move the selected object minute fractions of an inch (defaults are 0.01 and 0.1 with the modifier key). You can change the defaults of the nudge buttons, and you can change the units of measurement that are used in the publication within the palette.

There is a display called the Proxy, which represents the currently selected object. Along the edges, at the corners, and in the center of the Proxy are handles, which correspond to the handles on the selected object. Clicking on a handle, either on the Proxy or on the object itself, causes the handle on the Proxy to become selected; when selected, the handle becomes the reference point from which measurements are made concerning the object and around which transformations to the object are performed. Thus, selecting the handle at one corner causes rotation of the object to occur around that corner. These actions and annotations apply to text objects as well as to graphic objects.

The Styles palette stores styles that you apply to text with the Text tool. A style can be applied by simply clicking on its name within the list. New styles can be created and saved.

Figure 14-5

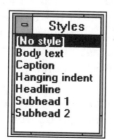

The Styles palette contains the named styles used in the current document.

The Colors palette stores the colors used in the document. The colors can be applied to selected objects' line and fill. You can create new colors; you can also add colors from the color matching systems supported by PageMaker, PANTONE, TRUMATCH, Toyo, DIC (Dainippon Ink & Chemicals), Macbeth Munsell and FOCOLTONE, or from libraries.

The Library palette is used to create and maintain libraries of text and graphics that are to be reused. Objects are displayed in the palette either as a text list or as thumbnails. An object can be added to a current publication by simply dragging the object from the library into the document.

Figure 14-6

The Library palette, an Addition, is used to store boilerplate and other commonly used elements, both text and graphics.

New documents are set up in the Page Setup dialogue. You can specify page size, orientation, starting page number, total number of pages, whether the document is to be printed on both sides of a sheet and with facing pages as in a book, the page margins, and the printer to be used as a basis for various internal calculations such as gray shades available and halftone screens. You can also select the type of page numbering system to be used, Arabic being the default, with upper- and lowercase Roman and upper- and lowercase alphabetic schemes offered for introductions or other matter outside the main body of text.

Documents are called publications, and a publication can have as many pages as you need. Multiple publications can be open at once.

PageMaker's documentation suggests that, if you are producing a book, it should be divided into several publications (one for each chapter, for instance). Consecutive pagination can be arranged for the publications, and different numbering schemes (Roman, alphabetic, etc.) can be applied to different publications within the book. A book is organized through a Book list.

The Book list is basically a list of the publications and their order within the book. It tells PageMaker how the book's publications are to be organized. You can change the order of the publications. It is a sensible arrangement, allowing you to keep the files at manageable sizes and making optimal use of the computer and the software.

The quickest way to set up a new document is to use a template. Templates are not new, of course, but they are treated in a slightly different manner in PageMaker than in most other programs. PageMaker's templates are shipped in a compressed form and need to be set up by running a script. Scripts are written in the PageMaker Script Language and tell the program to perform certain tasks. Sample scripts are included with the program. Some of the scripts have practical uses quite apart from their use as demonstrations: one script will format fractions and another sets up an envelope template.

The script that unpacks the templates is Open Template . . ., and it is found in the Aldus Additions item of the Utilities menu. Additions

Figure 14-7

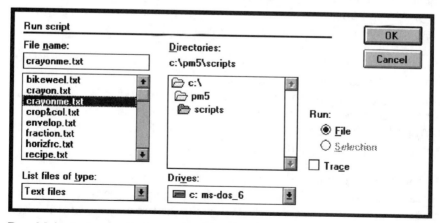

PageMaker can run Scripts, text files that utilize a command language to perform complex or repetitive tasks.

are plug-in modules that add external commands or tools to PageMaker. When you run the script to open the template, you are presented with a list of available templates. Choosing one, the template is shown in thumbnail and then installed when you click OK. Once a template has been decompressed and created by the script, you can save it as a template and thereafter open it with the Open command dialogue of the File menu. You can, of course, create your own templates and save them.

One wonders that Aldus did not simply add a plug-in that would compress templates automatically when saved and decompress and open them again when needed. Other Additions are planned.

Font substitutions are made in PageMaker documents according to the PANOSE substitution list in your Windows directory.

PageMaker opens in a reduced view, with the first page centered in the display. You can set the magnification to default on opening the program. There is no thumbnail view of all or of selected ranges of pages in a publication. It is impossible, then, to drag a graphic from page 3 to page 14, as you can in FreeHand.

PageMaker makes use of two master pages, one for left-hand and the other for the right-hand or facing page. Elements such as columns or guides established on the master pages become common for all subsequent corresponding left and right pages in the publication. Each page will be consistent. You can override the master page design elements by hiding the master page items on the chosen pages.

PageMaker continues to use the common method of separating text from the remainder of the publication by utilizing a Story editor, a primitive word processor that displays only the text in a continuous format. In some programs this form of editor is called the galley. Stripped of all the bells and whistles, text is given only basic character and paragraph formatting.

The idea behind this is that it will speed up text entry, searches, and corrections. You don't have to flip from page to page to find the place where you want to work. When the text is as you want it, then you can change the view back to the layout, where the text is displayed in the formatted document.

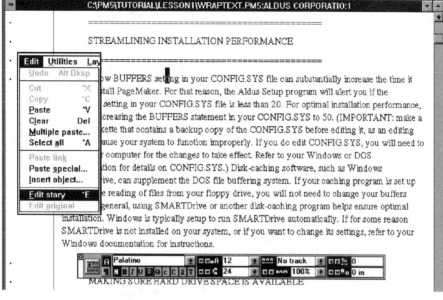

Figure 14-8

PageMaker continues to use a Story editor for text entry, despite that it offers only minimal visible formatting.

While in the Story editor, certain menus are changed. The Find, Change, and Spelling commands in the Utilities menu become active: they are grayed out and inactive in the Layout editor. The Additions become grayed out and inoperative while Story editor is being used. The Layout menu is completely removed and the Story menu replaces it.

As if the story editor were not enough, when you import text, there is the option in the Edit menu to Edit Original, which brings up your particular word processor. This seems like overkill, especially with the OLE and Link support built into PageMaker. There is a spelling checker, and the dictionary can be customized. A Dictionary Editor is provided.

There appear to be few limits to what you can do with text and graphics on a PageMaker page. Text and graphics can be placed where you please, with text wrap around irregularly shaped graphics being supported through manual adjustment. Normal text wrapping is to a rectangular area, but you can shape the area wrapped.

Inline graphics can only have a rectangular text wrap. Inline graphics are those that have been attached to a particular location in the text. They are contextually located, flowing with the text as the text is moved. Independent graphics, however, are static. The resolution of the bitmap can have a bearing on the quality of the displayed version of the image. The samples provided with the program are 155 dpi.

There are instances when an independent graphic and text will not interact correctly automatically. In those cases, it is necessary to make adjustments to the wrapping envelope, the text, or to both in order to obtain the desired text wrap. Sometimes, if you run the Addition "Balance Columns," the text will be correctly wrapped.

Graphics formats supported by PageMaker for placing are: .EPS, .CGM, .WMF, .TIF (TIFF), .ADI, .PLT, .PCX, .DXF, .PIC, PICT (Mac), .PNT (Mac), .MSP, .BMP, .GEM, .PCD, and Excel charts and spreadsheets. I was also able to place a GIF image. You can also import tables that have been created in the Table Editor, a separate application supplied with PageMaker.

Guides can be drawn out of the rulers to make snap points and lines for easier placement of text blocks and graphics. You can have a maximum of 40 guides per page, including any guides that were laid down on master pages as repeating elements. There is a lock guides command that prevents accidental movement of guides. Left and right pages can have different column layouts created automatically by choosing that option in the Column layout dialogue.

Text is entered both by typing and by importing through the Place command. Placing of text or graphics is as simple as choosing the item to be placed and pointing and clicking on the page. Text that has been imported can be set to flow automatically from column to column or page to page, called threading, or you can make the flow manually. There is a semiautomatic text flow option.

The manual text flow setting (Autoflow off) will fill the current text column only. The tab or window shade at the bottom of a full text block will indicate with a red triangle when there is more text, hidden beyond the bottom edge of the block. Clicking on the tab will change the cursor to the Loaded Text cursor, a page corner with a squiggly

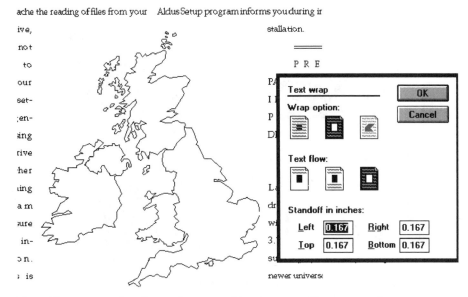

Figure 14-9

Text Wrap around independent graphics is normally rectangular.

arrow, signifying that you have picked up the hidden text and that you can deposit it into another text block. You do so by clicking on a page or by dragging a new text block on a page.

Automatic flowing of text will fill the current text block and will continue to fill all available blocks, and, having exhausted all available blocks, will create new ones. New pages will be added automatically. Text will wrap around any placed independent graphics.

Semiautomatic text flow fills the current block, and automatically loads the cursor with any extra text remaining. You can then create new text blocks into which the text will flow. The automatic reloading of the cursor will continue for as long as there is text that remains unplaced.

You are given full control over the text, including both kerning and tracking. There is also the option of adjusting the character spacing with precise amounts of space applied to text. Both kerning and tracking affect the space between letters. Kerning is usually a localized effect, within one or two words, but you can apply kerning pairs to whole sections of text if you desire to do so. Tracking can

Figure 14-10

Text Wrap can fail to work properly in some cases, requiring reformatting.

affect whole blocks of text, also. A page that is too light or too dark can be balanced by applying the appropriate kind of tracking.

Leading is adjustable in tenths-of-a-point increments if entered in the callout of the leading dialogue. The presets are limited to half-point differences at 11.5, 12.5, and 13.5 points.

You can set most type parameters, such as type family, size, style, character width, kerning, and tracking, individually or in a group on the Type Specs dialogue. You can also use the Control palette to set many of the same attributes.

Paragraph parameters can be similarly treated, either one at a time or in a group. Paragraph alignment has the usual options, familiar from

Figure 14-11

Text objects can be drawn out to span columns, as for a headline.

word processors, right and left aligned, centered, and justified. Widows and Orphans are provided for in PageMaker.

One of the big changes to PageMaker in its 5.0 version is the inclusion of Additions, plug-in modules that perform specialized tasks. They are invoked by the first item in the Utilities menu.

The Additions provide functions ranging from the creation of running headers and footers to building booklets from your publication. I have already mentioned the Balance columns . . . and Open template . . . additions. The main function of Balance columns . . . is to even out the lengths of columns to improve their appearance or to fill out evenly an allotted space. It is noteworthy that the Library palette is also an addition.

The included Additions are grouped by Aldus into three categories, those that manipulate text, those that assist in page layout, and those that help to print.

Figure 14-12

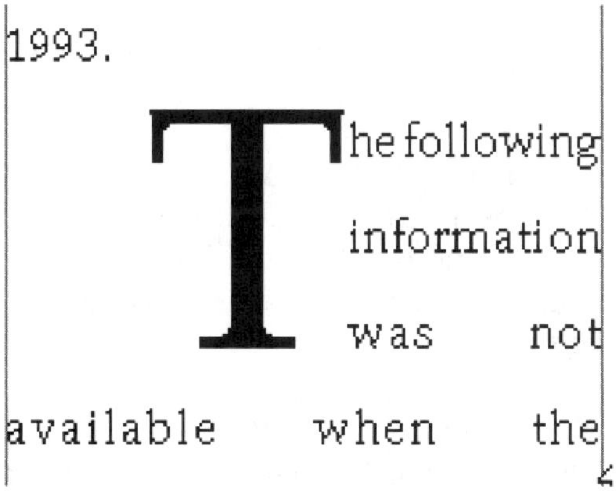

```
1993.

T he following
    information
    was      not
available  when  the
```

Drop Caps is a programmed Addition that makes the production of oversized initial characters easy.

The text additions are: Open story, Display story info, Traverse text blocks, Find overset text, Drop Cap, Bullets and numbering, Expert kerning, and Edit tracks. If you edit the tracking or kerning files kept by PageMaker and you plan to have your publications printed by a print shop, you must include those altered files with the publication files in order for the printed publication to match the displayed publication. The last text addition is Add continued line, which looks for connected text blocks at the ends and beginnings of pages and

Figure 14-13

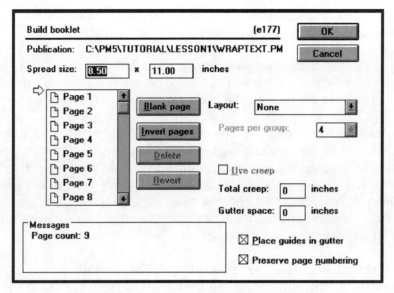

Another useful Addition is the Build Booklet plug-in, that converts a publication into common booklet formats.

adds phrases such as "continued on page . . ." and "continued from page . . ." as appropriate.

The Layout Additions are: Open template, PS Group it, which combines selected objects in an Encapsulated PostScript image, Library palette, Balance columns, Running headers and footers, and Sort pages, which displays thumbnails of pages and allows you to change their order by moving the thumbnails.

The printing Additions are: Create keyline, which places a border around objects or performs trapping of adjacent color objects, Create color library, which lets you convert the current color palette into a library, Display Pub info, which shows statistics of the current publication, and Build booklet, which automates the creation of booklets in various configurations, including 2-up saddle-stitch and 2-up perfect bound, with adjustments for creep.

Creep is the unevenness of the edges of the stacked and folded pages, due to the thickness of the pages, which causes inner pages to protrude beyond the outer pages at the open side of the booklet.

Trimming the sheets flush leaves the outer edge margins of the trimmed pages progressively more narrow. This Addition successively offsets inner pages on the sheets, producing even margins after trimming of the creep.

Two of the more tedious processes in book production are the creation of indices and tables of contents. PageMaker relieves you of some of the tedium by providing commands to add index and table of contents markers in the text, which it can later retrieve and use to compile an index and table of contents. Embedding the index markers is handled by a dialogue.

The index can have three levels of nesting, sufficient for most purposes. If your index requires greater nesting, you will have to make manual emendations. Tables of contents are usually based on the recurrence of styles; headings typed in certain styles are accumulated and turned into the table.

PageMaker comes with an extensive online help system and tutorial. The tutorial can be run independently of Help, and it will run PageMaker in the background to allow you to perform the lesson

Figure 14-14

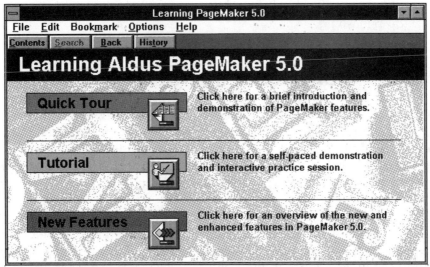

PageMaker ships with a tutorial that is linked to the program's various features.

activities. There is also a printed tutorial. The User's Manual is clear and thorough, and a separate Commercial Printing Guide is provided. There is a small manual that explains the Aldus Additions. Lastly, registered users can obtain a free copy of the Scripting manual by using a coupon enclosed with the program.

For those of you who do not save your files frequently, PageMaker is well behaved and recovers with grace from GPFs and other Windows disasters, with your work mostly intact on restarting the program.

What needs to be improved in PageMaker? Undo is very limited. Many actions cannot be undone at all, and those that can must be undone immediately. There could be an improvement in the display of certain types of graphics. The ability to drag graphics from one page to another would be a boon. More extensive image editing tools would also be appreciated. As it stands, you can alter the contrast and brightness of grayscale images, but no other effects can be applied. The interactive nature of OLE does make up for the lack of image editing to some extent, but more simple graphics tools would be useful.

PageMaker has earned its place, in the beginning by being there first, then by inertia, but it has continued to improve, and it has maintained its position by filling the needs of its users. It is the standard in desktop publishing.

Corel Ventura Publisher

Ventura Publisher has always enjoyed an excellent reputation for power and performance, and it has inspired loyalty in its users. Part of the Corel product line, we can expect Ventura Publisher to continue to improve and perhaps to expand its installed user base by attracting users who have never used a DTP product.

Ventura Publisher gets off to a bad start, however. Starting up, there are too many notices in dark-edged boxes posted on screen, telling you what is being initialized and what is loaded. They look like condolence cards. Further, the Ventura Publisher interface is rather more intimidating than that of PageMaker. There are iconic buttons

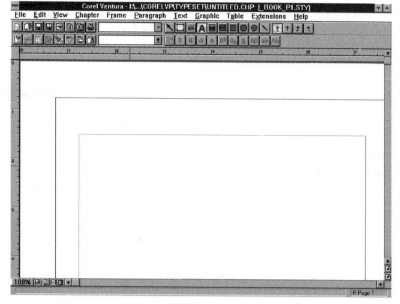

Figure 14-15

Corel Ventura Publisher's interface is extremely busy and rather intimidating.

running two deep along the top of the design window, and the page stares back starkly, as though it wants very much for you to do something, and do it now.

Perhaps that description is too melodramatic, but the Ventura interface is busier than the sedate interface of PageMaker, and that does generate a sensation of anxiety. The training manual hints at something of the sort, saying somewhat grimly, that ". . . although Corel Ventura Publisher may seem complex at first, the additional power and capabilities it has over other desktop publishing products makes it easier and faster to use in the long run." Without being too critical, in the long run we will all be dead. We want it to be better now, or at least to be apparently better.

Ventura Publisher's user interface can be customized. Having complained at the outset about the busy nature of the Button bar, I should mention that it need not be displayed, but can be suppressed. The program will revert to what the manual calls the "classic interface." The "classic interface" consists of floating palettes for

tools, files, and tags. Items are accessed only from menus in the "classic" format. The manual insists that the new interface is far superior to the old, but to accommodate old-fashioned users, the "classic" interface remains an option.

Figure 14-16

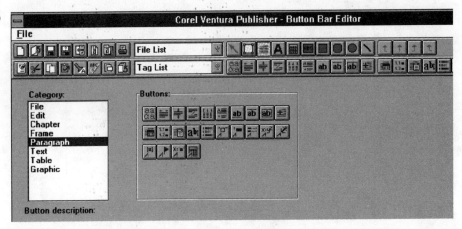

The included Button Editor allows customization of the tool bar's contents.

There is only so much that can be different in two programs that are aimed at the same buyers and have the same purposes. That is the case with Ventura and PageMaker: PageMaker uses templates, while Ventura uses style sheets; Ventura uses text tags, while PageMaker uses styles; PageMaker uses publications, and Ventura uses chapters. Both put text and graphics in blocks or boxes.

Ventura Publisher behaves differently than PageMaker. It is faster, for one thing. Things seem to take place instantaneously in Ventura, but in PageMaker you can wait quite a while for an action to be completed.

Ventura doesn't save a document as a whole, only as its parts. When you save a Ventura Publisher chapter, the chapter files contain only pointers to the text file containing the chapter's text, to the graphics files that contain its illustrations, and to the style sheet containing the chapter's formatting. If the text has been changed, then the text file is also updated and saved. Because the components of a chapter are stored separately, if you make changes to the components with other programs, the chapter will be changed when the chapter file is read by Ventura and the chapter reassembled. A change to the style sheet,

for instance, can cause all chapters that use that style sheet to be changed. This is very flexible if you want to alter the layout of a multiple chapter document. It is also a little dangerous, because you might inadvertently alter a style sheet while working on another, unrelated document.

Ventura works with frames to a greater extent than does PageMaker. Frames are the basic building blocks for the page. Unlike PageMaker, a frame in Ventura is necessary before text or graphics can be placed on the page. You can create frames on a template, or you can add frames to a blank sheet. Frames are associated in a mysterious fashion.

The most basic form of the frame is the page itself, which is called the base page frame. It is the area on the paper that is defined by the margins of the page. You can, if you wish, enter text or put graphics directly into the base page. In practice, pages will be defined by style sheets that have been provided with the program or ones that have been created by modification of the supplied style sheets and saved by the user. A completely new style sheet format can be created from scratch by loading and modifying the default style sheet.

A frame drawn on a blank page becomes associated with the page frame, and it has little potential for forming associations. Once other frames have been added, however, the picture changes. The basic procedure in Ventura is to place text first, to add frames for graphics, and then to apply the style sheet that carries the formatting instructions.

Usually text will be imported or typed into a style sheet or into a blank base page frame, after which you will draw frames to receive the graphics. A graphic frame is a frame that contains a graphic; the frame acquires characteristics that it did not possess when it was merely a frame without contents. A graphics frame has automatically acquired the potential for a caption. You need not make use of the caption, but the option is there, nonetheless.

The caption has properties also. It can have a Label, and Labels have Inserts. It can be placed anywhere around the frame, and it can be numbered automatically by Ventura. These properties are set in the Anchor/Caption dialogue.

Figure 14-17

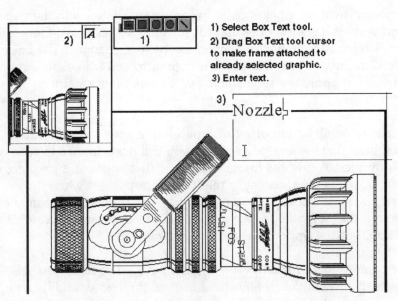

The basis of many important functions is the Anchors and Captions dialogue.

The number (also called a counter) is an Insert, and it can be a figure number, a chapter number, or a table number. Inserts appear in the first paragraph of text in a caption, which constitutes a Label. The remainder of caption, the descriptive paragraph, can be of any length. It is entered in the text frame in the layout, rather than in the dialogue.

A graphic frame is not the same size as the illustration that it contains. The graphic can be scaled independently of the frame, or the frame

Figure 14-18

1) Select Box Text tool.
2) Drag Box Text tool cursor to make frame attached to already selected graphic.
3) Enter text.

Creating a callout, a floating text block that is linked to a graphic block, requires three steps.

can be used to scale the graphic. The frame can be resized to be larger or smaller than the illustration, and the illustration can be moved about within the frame. If the frame is smaller than the image, then this movement has the effect of cropping the image. The original image file is unaffected by this cropping: only the cropping information is saved.

Another way to provide a text caption for a figure is to add a callout using the Block Text tool. This tool makes a moveable or floating text frame which can be associated with or anchored to a graphic. When the graphic frame is moved, the callout or Block Text will move with the graphic. It can be placed anywhere on the page.

Anchoring a frame to another frame or to its contents involves using the Anchor/Caption dialogue with the frame to be anchored. The frame can be given a name, and all frames associated with that frame will be affected by changes made in the dialogue. You can specify how the frame will react when the text into which it has been anchored is moved and where, relative to the text, the frame will be placed when it moves. You can choose whether the frame moves automatically or in response to a manually entered Re-anchor command.

In effect, an anchored graphic frame is the equivalent of the PageMaker inline graphic. Anchored graphics need not be within the text block to which they are anchored, and can, in fact, be anywhere on the page. Nor are you limited to simple rectangular text wrapping. By turning off text wrapping for the frame containing the graphic, and superimposing smaller, empty frames on the graphic, you can cause text to wrap around an irregularly shaped object, creating a text runaround.

Ventura Publisher has some fairly sophisticated control options over text. Besides all of the ordinary things like justification, leading, and tracking, you can make paragraph rules that overprint text to create a transparent gray overlay. With rules you can have white dropout characters on a black background. You can examine and change the typography for a paragraph, affecting the range of spacing permissible between characters, the amount of vertical justification, how underlines are placed, the point size and placement of subscripts and superscripts, where strike-throughs are placed across the characters, and whether a paragraph has a large first character and how many lines it will occupy.

Figure 14-19

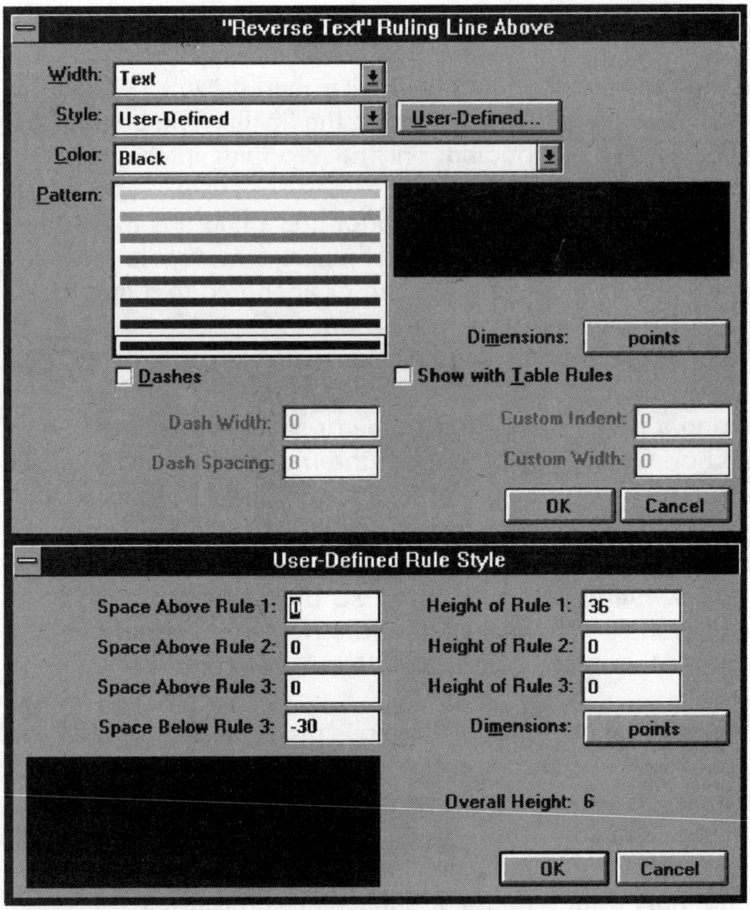

"Reverse Text" Ruling Line Above

Width: **Text**

Style: **User-Defined**   User-Defined...

Color: **Black**

Pattern:

Dimensions: **points**

☐ Dashes   ☐ Show with Table Rules

Dash Width: 0   Custom Indent: 0
Dash Spacing: 0   Custom Width: 0

OK   Cancel

User-Defined Rule Style

Space Above Rule 1: 0   Height of Rule 1: 36
Space Above Rule 2: 0   Height of Rule 2: 0
Space Above Rule 3: 0   Height of Rule 3: 0
Space Below Rule 3: -30   Dimensions: **points**

Overall Height: 6

OK   Cancel

Creating Dropout or Reverse lettering is performed with paragraph rules that cover the text.

Figure 14-20

The Adventure Begins

The resulting Dropout.

There is an option that allows you to set the conditions that will determine line breaks in a chapter or a paragraph. In essence, you can override the effect of a paragraph marker by using the Break dialogue to remove or alter the placement of the line break. Normally, a paragraph break comes at the end of a line and forces a carriage return and issues a line feed, which causes a new line to be begun.

Long documents are prepared in Ventura Publisher by compiling a publication. A publication is the same as a Book in PageMaker. You create a new publication with the Manage Publication dialogue invoked with the similarly command in the File menu. The Manage Publication dialogue is simply a list of chapters to assemble into a publication, with options to perform certain tasks associated with the creation and maintenance of a publication. You can add and remove chapters from the publication list, move chapters into correct order within the list, create Tables of Contents and Indices, and print.

Adding and removing chapters is as simple as clicking on the appropriate button and scrolling through the chapter lists. Selecting a chapter and clicking on the Open button will display all of the files referred to by that chapter. If a chapter is selected and you move the cursor into the list box, the cursor changes to a thick bar with which you can move the chapter up and down within the list by dragging or clicking, affecting the order in which Ventura Publisher will use the chapters when creating TOCs, Indices, numbering chapters, and when printing.

Figure 14-21

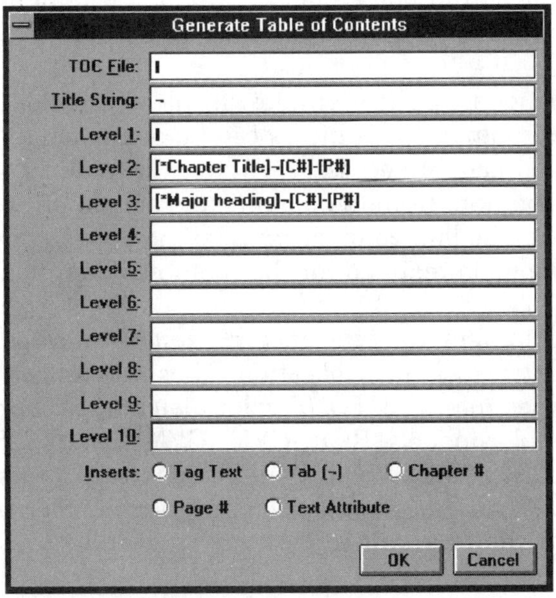

A Table of Contents can have ten levels of indenting.

The Copy All command must be used to duplicate chapter files, because, as you will remember, neither publications nor chapters contain any of the actual text or graphics used in the final document. Both publications and chapters are simply lists of files to be included, along with other information affecting formatting or order. Copying a publication or chapter with File Manager or DOS COPY will copy only the lists.

Creating a TOC from the chapters in the publication list entails Ventura Publisher reading all of the paragraph tags (styles) that have been used in the chapter files for chapter titles, chapter headings, and subheadings, etc., sorting the tags that will be used for the TOC into a list, and then finding the paragraphs that have had those tags applied to them in the chapters. You specify which tags are to be used to make the TOC list.

Creating an index, once all of the index markers have been put in the text of the chapters, is reasonably easy. It is the insertion of the index markers that is the back-breaking portion of the labor. Unfortunately, while Ventura Publisher provides tools to make the process fall into a routine, there has yet to be created a way to have the computer software simply go through a manuscript and pick out all the items and their page numbers that ought to be indexed.

Ventura Publisher supports footnotes. It will automatically number and renumber footnotes. Footnotes can be of any length and will spill over to the next page if necessary. A ruling line can be specified to separate the footnote from the main text. The amount of space used by footnotes can be limited by decreasing the above and below spacing for the main text and for the footnotes themselves.

Color support in Ventura is satisfactory. You can have 253 colors defined for any chapter or publication. These colors can be any in the 24-bit color spectrum. PANTONE color matching is supported, as are the common color models, RGB, CYM, CYMK, and HLS. Eight default colors are assigned and cannot be altered. Colors can be imported from other documents. The program handles separations, and knockouts can be specified.

Generally speaking, Ventura Publisher can do anything that PageMaker can do and can do it as well, if not always as easily or elegantly. There are some things that Ventura Publisher can do, such as the inclusion of equations and text runarounds of anchored graphics, that PageMaker cannot do at all. There is every reason to prefer Ventura Publisher as your DTP program.

There are other DTP programs available for Windows. At the top of the line you will find FrameMaker and QuarkXpress, either of which is the equal of PageMaker and Corel Ventura Publisher.

FrameMaker

FrameMaker is the kind of program that tries to make things simple by breaking them down into minutiae. You can control every aspect of the page's design, and every aspect has some sort of iconic button to give access to that control. Users who want or need a complex user interface will find FrameMaker to their liking. Good program design, however, usually begins by making things clear, and clarity generally means simplification rather than ramification.

The program is probably the most widely represented of any DTP program, with versions existing on Macintosh, Sun, HP, IBM mainframe, and Windows computers. If you need to maintain file compatibility and to preserve user skills across a number of computer platforms, then FrameMaker will fill those needs.

At this level of professional page makeup you will find that all of the products have large areas in which they appear to have almost identical features and commands. Certain things are essential. The use of templates, for instance, will vary little among programs. FrameMaker's templates are much like Ventura Publisher's. As in Ventura, you create frames for the reception of text, which then is automatically formatted according to the text tags that are attached to the frames.

For long documents, FrameMaker adopts the common idea of a publication, a composite that binds together smaller sections that are actually free-standing documents in themselves but which share a common layout. Page numbering, footnotes, indexing, etc., reach across all of the component documents.

Among its unique features, FrameMaker possesses drawing tools that surpass those of other DTP programs. Besides the usual boxes, rules, and circles, there are Bezier and polyline drawing tools, allowing the creation within FrameMaker of complex drawings that would usually have to be imported.

FrameMaker offers all of the necessary tools and commands to manage color, with RGB, HLS, and CYMK color models supported. Pantone color matching is also supported. Custom color lists are created automatically as needed if new colors are contained in imported EPS graphics. FrameMaker has prepress capabilities, being able to print color separations and halftones.

As in Ventura, footnotes and other material within a document can be linked in a HyperText manner. Ventura can create HyperText documents in Acrobat format, but Ventura can create its own electronic publications that can be distributed and viewed with a runtime module.

QuarkXPress

QuarkXPress is the other of the professional page design programs. It is unique in that it has not one but two intercaps in its name. It is the one that has earned the most fanatical following among those who need absolute control over page elements such as leading and pair kerning. The program offers unequalled precision in page layout. In addition, QuarkXPress accepts plug-in modules, called XTensions, the inspiration for PageMaker's Additions, no doubt, that augment the program's native features.

XPress organizes its tools in floating palettes, much in the manner of FreeHand or CorelDRAW. The palettes consolidate related functions or tools, placing color management in a Color Palette and document management in the Layout Palette. Color matching in most of the major systems is provided, and custom colors belonging to imported EPS graphics are automatically added to the palette. The palette permits the creation of color fountains, a feature usually found in drawing or painting programs.

XPress documents can contain up to 2,000 pages. Unlike the other programs discussed above, it does not create a long publication from smaller documents, preserving the unity of a work. It does not compile indices or tables of contents, however, which can be a drawback. And, although there is a Macintosh version which permits group editing of a document through a Quark Publishing System, the Windows version does not support that option.

Making a choice between DTP programs is not easy. The Big Three, PageMaker, Corel Ventura Publisher, and FrameMaker, are about equal in the basics, and each has substantial power to compose a pleasant and effective page. Because Ventura is now bundled with CorelDRAW 5.0, that decision may have become moot for users looking for a drawing program at the same time. As a standalone product, PageMaker will continue to be first choice for those wishing to stay in the software mainstream. FrameMaker is probably the best choice for users who must work with others across diverse networks of dissimilar computers. This is one category in which a wrong choice is hard to make.

Putting it all together

BY now, you will have read my opinions of the Windows graphics software and hardware types that constitute the resources from which a graphic workstation in the Windows environment can be assembled. Some areas are better represented than others. Some areas of graphic workstation usage are not represented as well as they ought to be in Windows. This will change as more applications are ported to Windows. Some are probably being held back by the transitional state of Windows.

While it is certain that eventually Windows will be exclusively a 32-bit environment, users will continue to buy 16-bit technology and software. The costs of maintaining parallel development of 16-bit and 32-bit software will hold back many companies from optimizing their programs for the Windows NT or Chicago environment until the trend is overwhelmingly in the 32-bit direction. The problem is not really with 32- or 16-bit architecture, which really has little to do with the actual code, but in the way that the 32-bit Windows will be designed. The resources that 32-bit Windows will provide for the programs have to be stable before the applications that will exist in that environment can be fully fashioned.

Some programs that exist in DOS do not yet exist in Windows versions. Although they are important, I have excluded them. Running DOS programs in Windows is not and will never be satisfactory. Important programs will issue in Windows versions, but you may have to wait.

Entry level

At the entry level of Windows workstation, you will be running software primarily from the drawing and drafting categories, with some

occasional photographic image editing or painting. These latter may involve some image capture or simple multimedia capture and playback.

While the newer DX4 clock-tripled 80486 chips will have been on the market for some months, their prices will still be higher than for the older 486 DX2 chips. An entry-level machine with a DX2 50 MHz CPU is perfectly adequate for the work that you will be doing with drawing and drafting. Although the ISA bus computers will still be viable, there is really no reason to purchase a machine with a bus design that will soon become a liability. (It is possible to find ISA bus computers that will operate at a higher bus speed, 12 MHz, rather than the normal 8 MHz. Despite that most of the slots on a motherboard will be ISA type, a VESA Local Bus 80486 DX2 50 is indicated. The use of external hardware cache is really not necessary at this level, although a 64K cache is handy.

Photographic editing and painting work depend heavily on the graphics card, but the programs that you will choose here will not require the utmost acceleration to function well. The Hercules Dynamite Pro with 2 MB of RAM will do nicely. This card can handle 64K colors in the 1024×768 resolution when 2 MB DRAM are installed, and the speed is very good. Other cards that will provide satisfactory performance at this level include the Volante WarpVL with 2 MB of RAM.

Since you will be using a local bus motherboard, a local bus disk controller is indicated. This is a generic choice, but you may want to insist upon the latest implementation of the IDE to make possible the future installation of hard drives larger than 0.5 GB. Hardware caching is probably not necessary.

The larger the hard drive that you can install, the better. Windows applications, and Windows itself, occupy an unnaturally large amount of space, and they'll probably get bigger. You can survive with a 340-MB drive using DoubleSpace or some other compression software, but you will probably find that two 340 MB drives will be advisable. Maxtor and Seagate are the brands to look for, although Quantum drives are acceptable.

RAM is a persistent and increasingly annoying thorn in the side of efficient computing. You might as well simply expect to pay a

299

premium price for RAM into the foreseeable future. Eight megabytes is a good starting place for an entry-level computer. The problem with beginning at 8 MB is that you will probably purchase eight 1-MB SIMMs, and, when the time comes to expand RAM, you will have to sell or discard some or all of those SIMMs to make room for the denser RAM modules. If you can afford to do so, purchase four 4-MB SIMMs, making a total of 16 MB, at the beginning. You can then easily expand your computer's memory to 20 MB or to 32 MB without discarding SIMMs.

Software will consist of Windows for Workgroups, which provides the 32-bit file and disk addressing, either Deneba's multipurpose Canvas or Aldus IntelliDraw, Halo Desktop Imager, Adobe Acrobat, Adobe Type Manager 3.0 with master type fonts, and Virtus WalkThrough.

 # General purpose

For general graphic workstation work, which routinely is used for image editing and multimedia production, a faster DX2 or DX4 computer with local bus is needed. (It is worth noting that you can add a DX4 CPU to a standard 486 system by installing a voltage regulator that decreases the 5 volts normally sent to the CPU to the 3.3 volts used by the DX4 chips.) A 66 MHz clock-doubled 486 computer with VESA local bus is the minimum general-purpose computer.

You will be using Windows for Workgroups, and graphics software such as Photoshop, AutoCAD, Premiere, and Fractal Design Painter. You will want Adobe Type Manager 3.0 with master fonts, PageMaker, and Adobe Acrobat. Micrografx Designer, because of its three-dimensional capabilities, or trueSpace, with its rich animation and three-dimensional modelling, should also be in your software suite.

A video capture board will prove necessary for multimedia work. The Media Vision ProMovie Spectrum is a simple and easy-to-use board. A genlock board such as the Video Toaster or Rockgen Pro will be necessary for video output.

The use of a 32-bit disk controller is necessary, but it should be a SCSI controller. BusLogic makes an excellent family of SCSI

controllers. The EISA version is very quick and can handle two internal hard drives in addition to external devices. A large disk controller cache, at least 256K, is recommended.

You must have a CD-ROM drive. CorelSCSI is recommended to provide drivers and a SCSI manager. It supports a wide variety of SCSI CD-ROM drives. A double-speed CD-ROM will suffice; the triple-speed drives are only marginally faster and are not as yet supported by applications at their faster speeds. CD-ROM expedites installation for large programs such as Designer and CorelDRAW. Programs such as AutoCAD supply bonus CDs with hundreds of files to supplement the installed resources.

A faster SCSI hard drive will outperform IDE drives, both in throughput and seek time. A drive cache is not necessary, if the drive controller has its own cache. The drive should be at least 540 MB, although a gigabyte drive would be a wise choice; the programs that you will be running will benefit from the extra space. Hewlett-Packard makes excellent large drives.

A fast video board from Matrox or Number Nine Corporation is indicated, with at least 3 MB of DRAM or a mixture of VRAM and DRAM in a 2:1 ratio. The VESA Local Bus Number Nine boards are first-rate and slightly less expensive than the Matrox MGA equivalents. A TIGA board from Number Nine, which supports both VGA and TIGA applications simultaneously can be a solution if you will be using AutoCAD or another CAD program frequently. The Number Nine GXI boards can support two monitors, one for normal Windows output and the other for the TIGA applications such as CAD. The hardware panning and zooming is instantaneous and relieves the software of the much slower zooming and Window scrolling. National Design's Volante TIGA boards are also highly recommended.

A 17-inch monitor is recommended. I cannot suggest a better choice than the Panasonic C1795E, which is a flat square monitor with excellent specifications in all resolutions up to and including 1280 × 1024. Two-page monitors and grayscale full-page displays can be used for page layout or CADD work, but the 17-inch monitor in high-resolution mode is really the better choice. The Radius monitor system that pivots can be a compromise solution, permitting both

landscape and portrait monitor viewing with the same monitor. But you are forced to use the Radius boards.

 # High performance

The highest performance computer systems now available will be based on the 90 MHz Pentium or the DEC Alpha chips. The Intel 486 DX4 100 MHz chips are an alternative, but they are better-suited to the general purpose computer system. The 60 MHz and 66 MHz Pentiums are fairly viewed as dead-end products. There have been significant complaints about their overall performance, and there are specific bugs that have been verified in them and in their support chips.

It must be said that Pentium computers will be commonplace shortly, but not everyone really needs one. They are a necessity only for heavy-duty 3D rendering and modelling and animation tasks, in which basic brute-force computational speed is the determining factor in completing the job. A Pentium computer is also a necessity if you are going to run Windows NT or its successors. These operating systems cannot function well on anything less than a full Pentium PCI system with a couple of wide, fast SCSI drives of one gigabyte capacity each.

A PCI graphics adapter from Matrox is really the only choice in this category. The 4 MB version of the MGA board is recommended highly. Again, I recommend the Panasonic C1795E monitor. A larger monitor really makes sense only if it is going to be used for presentations.

You will be running Windows NT or Windows for Workgroups. Truly high-end jobs could demand more than one processor. Windows NT can support multiple processors in the same server, making the splitting of jobs between processors possible. If multiple processors are not used, then distributed processing on a network, in which each computer station performs one portion of the job can do almost as well as the multiple-processor solution.

Very little software exists that is optimized for 32-bit operating systems. AutoCAD for Windows NT exists in Beta form and will likely be available by the time Chicago is available. MicroStation has already been released in a 32-bit version for Windows NT. The release of

Adobe Photoshop for the PowerPC provides some encouragement to expect that a Windows 32-bit Photoshop will soon be available. At this time, I would basically recommend that the purchase of a Pentium system be delayed until the software that can use it efficiently has been delivered.

Processor upgrades

The chip that many people have been waiting for and which has been promised by Intel on many occasions is the P24T, the so-called Pentium Overdrive, designed to fill that oversized socket on the 486 motherboard. The chip is supposed to deliver a Pentium chip in a package that can be compatible with existing hardware and yet be only fractionally less powerful than the real Pentium chips. If the P24T ever arrives, it will probably be too little too late. The clock-tripled DX4 486s are almost as fast as the promised P24T, and the prices of the real Pentiums is assuredly going to fall rapidly as the PowerPC becomes increasingly a viable competitor for the high-end user's dollars. Squeezing a Pentium into a 16-bit system was a pretty stupid idea anyway, designed more for the marketing phrase "Pentium Ready" than for reality.

The DX4s, as mentioned above, can be dropped into a 486 motherboard with nothing more than small alteration, the addition of a voltage regulator that will reduce the 5 volts used by the older 486s to the 3.3 volts used by the DX4s. If you are considering a Pentium machine and are certain that you need more than the 486 DX2 66, then take a look at the DX4 100. It is only about half as fast as the 90 MHz Pentium, but that speed disadvantage is really illusory when you consider that the Pentium is really not going to be delivering its best speed until it is running real 32-bit software in a real 32-bit environment.

And what of the PowerPC? The Apple version has been received with great, almost unanimous praise. The PowerPC Macintosh is undoubtedly the best value in high-powered desktop computers, bringing a true RISC computer to the best-designed graphic interface. IBM, Apple's other partner in the PowerPC consortium (Motorola

being the chip's maker), has stumbled in bringing its own PC-compatible PowerPC to market. The PowerPC Macintosh makes a great leap over the current technology, including Pentium, but the IBM version seems to be on an ever-receding horizon. As a heretical last word, the PowerMac might be worth looking at; it already has a headstart in software over the Pentium and whatever IBM finally brings forth. It can even run Windows.

Index

G

H

I